THE ORIGINS OF THE FIRST WORLD WAR

ORIGINS OF MODERN WARS
General editor: *Harry Hearder*

Titles already published:

THE ORIGINS OF THE FIRST WORLD WAR
   James Joll
THE ORIGINS OF THE ARAB-ISRAELI WARS
   Ritchie Ovendale

THE ORIGINS OF
THE FIRST WORLD WAR

James Joll

LONGMAN
London and New York

Longman Group Limited
Longman House, Burnt Mill. Harlow
Essex CM20 2JE, England
Associated companies throughout the world

*Published in the United States of America
by Longman Inc., New York*
James Joll 1984

First published 1984

BRITISH LIBRARY CATALOGUING IN PUBLICATION DATA
Joll, James
    The origins of the First World War.
    — (Origins of modern wars)
    1. World War, 1914–1918 — Causes
    I. Title   II. Series
    940.3'11   D511
    ISBN 0-582-49016-2

LIBRARY OF CONGRESS CATALOGING IN PUBLICATION DATA
Joll, James.
    The origins of the First World War.
    (Origins of modern wars)
    Bibliography: p.
    Includes index.
    1. World War, 1914–1918 – Causes. I. Title.
II. Series.
D511. J735   1984   940.3'11   83-17589
ISBN 0-582-49016-2(p.b.k.)

Set in 10/11pt Linoterm Times
Printed in Hong Kong by
Commonwealth Printing Press Ltd.

CONTENTS

LIST OF MAPS

EDITOR'S FOREWORD

In spite of the considerable wealth of international history published in Europe and the USA over the last 100 years, there seems never to have been, in any language, a substantial series of volumes dealing with the causes of wars. Much of the diplomatic history is now also somewhat dated in tone and approach. It has tended to be centred a little too heavily on the flow of despatches between foreign ministries and embassies, often to the exclusion of the pressures of economic forces, public opinion, the preoccupations of domestic politics or the deeper motives of governments. Sometimes historians studying the origins of wars have seemed to regard their task as a polite intellectual exercise; they have failed to ask themselves what were the basic factors which unleashed this or that particular phase of homicide. Or – to put it another way – historians have perhaps been too defeatist. They have assumed that their extensive knowledge of the past can have no relevance for the present or the future.

The question of whether the study of history has utilitarian value is a vexed one, and cannot be considered properly in an editor's foreword. But this particular editor would like to assert that so far as the social sciences go (and history is one of them) we can learn only from the past, since the past is all we have. This does not mean, of course, that slick analogies between past and present situations are ever likely to be helpful; on the contrary, they will invariably be misleading. But certain general points – very often negative ones – can and must be learnt from history.

To juxtapose studies of the origins of wars since the French Revolution in a single series can hardly fail to increase our understanding of the causes of war or to illuminate international history. The editor is gratified to have secured so distinguished a list of contributors. From their work certain general points will almost certainly emerge. In the present volume James Joll touches upon points which have a wide application. He writes, for example: 'We often feel that the reasons the politicians themselves were giving are somehow inadequate to explain what was happening and we are tempted to look for some deeper and

vii

more general cause to explain the catastrophe.' It is a temptation which writers in the series, Professor Joll among them, will certainly not resist. And in the same context Joll quotes Luigi Albertini's reference to 'the disproportion between the intellectual and moral endowments [of the decision-makers of 1914] and the gravity of the problems which faced them, between their acts and the results thereof'. It is a thought which is no less spine-chilling in 1983 than it was in 1914.

There is then the question of miscalculations by governments – a question which will surely be present in all the volumes in the series. Professor Joll points out that the Austrians and their German allies believed that if they took a strong line against Serbia in July 1914 Russia would not intervene – a somewhat doom-laden miscalculation. An Australian historian, Geoffrey Blainey, in an interesting work, entitled *The Causes of War*, has pointed out that very many wars have occurred simply because governments believed that they could win the wars, perhaps quickly and easily, when better information, or more sober judgement, would have discouraged them. The sad fact is that at the outbreak of wars political leaders are more often inadequate than wicked. Joll quotes the terrible and damning statement by the German Chancellor, Bethmann Hollweg, on 30 July 1914: 'The great majority of the peoples are in themselves peaceful, but things are out of control . . . ', and Joll himself adds: 'events had moved faster than the imagination of politicians'.

International wars are usually preceded by arms races. One school of writers has blamed the growth of armaments for causing wars; another school has insisted that the arms race is only a symptom of underlying hostilities. The truth, as usual, probably lies somewhere between the two arguments. This series will probably give a variety of explanations of the role of armaments in causing wars, but some general points will emerge. Of 1914 Professor Joll says:

> The arms race itself contributed to the feeling that the war was inevitable: and although governments claimed that their preparation for a defensive war was a sign of their wish for peace and their will to deter aggression, deterrents in fact often provoke as much as they deter. While some governments were more ready than others to start or at least to risk a war in pursuit of their policies, no government felt able to exclude the possibility of war and therefore took action which made its outbreak more likely.

A message which may emerge from the series is that it cannot be said of any war that one particular nation – or one particular group in the case of civil wars – was the aggressor. But more measured judgements can still be made. It is difficult not to accept Joll's conclusion in his Chapter 4 that 'German and Austrian [military] plans involved the highest danger of general war'. On the other hand, the 'conspiracy theory' of history will probably not stand up to the kind of scrutiny which this series is going to provide. So far as 1914 goes, in Joll's words, 'A detailed examination of the political and strategic decisions taken in the crisis suggests that the motives of statesmen and generals were far less rational and well thought out than the view that they deliberately embarked on war as a way out of their insoluble domestic social and political problems would suggest.'

Given their uncertainty and inadequacy, the political leaders built up deterrents of one kind or another, sometimes independent ones – large armies or navies, sometimes partially collective ones – the close alliance system. And from 1871 to 1914 the deterrents were effective. But if the First World War teaches no other lesson, it can perhaps be said to have illustrated that deterrents cannot be depended upon to deter for ever.

HARRY HEARDER

PREFACE

The list of books and articles relating to the causes of the First World War is apparently endless, and it would take a lifetime to read them all. Even keeping up with the relevant new literature as it appears can keep one fully occupied. I have certainly not read all the books; and the only excuse for adding to them is that it is now perhaps worth trying to summarize, on an international and comparative basis, some of the arguments and explanations which historians have been discussing over the past twenty years.

I have started from the crisis of July–August 1914, and I have limited myself to those states which went to war then. I have, for example, said little about Italian policy except in so far as it contributed to the final crisis, and I have said nothing about the United States, whose policies do not seem to me to have been of international importance till after the war had started. The war began as a European war, though it did not end as such. While attempting to show why this particular war occurred at that particular moment, I have also tried to look at some of the general trends which made a war of some kind likely. The difficulty for the historian remains that of linking the general to the particular; and I have not solved it.

Before 1914 it was at least as usual to say England and English as Great Britain and British, and I have not tried to be consistent in this respect. Equally, I have sometimes written Austrian when it would have been more accurate to write Austro-Hungarian.

I should particularly like to thank those friends and colleagues to whose writings and conversation during the time I have been writing this book I am especially indebted: Volker Berghahn, Lancelot L. Farrar Jr, David French, Paul Kennedy, Dominic Lieven, Wolfgang J. Mommsen, Hartmut Pogge von Strandmann, David Schoenbaum and Zara Steiner. I should also like to take the opportunity of acknowledging how much I owe to Professor Fritz Fischer, even if I do not agree with all his conclusions, since it was he who reopened the whole

x

question of the origins of the First World War and suggested new directions in which to look for answers. I am very grateful to Mrs Susan Welsford for her skill and care in preparing the final typescript.

At various points in the book I have incorporated parts of earlier articles published in *Aspekte der Deutsch-Britischen Beziehungen im Laufe der Jahrhunderte*, edited by Paul Kluke and Peter Alter (publications of the German Historical Institute, London, Vol. 4, Stuttgart 1978), and *The Idea of Freedom: Essays in Honour of Isaiah Berlin* edited by Alan Ryan (Oxford 1979). I am grateful for permission to use this material.

JAMES JOLL
London, January 1983

KING MARK: 'Den unerforschlich tief
geheimnissvollen Grund,
wer macht der Welt ihn Kund?'

['Who will make known to the
world the inscrutably deep
secret cause?']

TRISTAN: 'O König, das
kann ich dir nicht sagen;
und was du frägst,
das kannst du nie erfahren.'

['That, King, I cannot tell
you; and what you ask, that
you will never learn.']

Richard Wagner, *Tristan und Isolde*, Act II

Chapter 1

INTRODUCTION

The outbreak of the First World War in 1914 still seems to mark the end of an era and the beginning of a new one, even though we can now see that many of the social, political, economic and cultural developments of the later twentieth century were only accelerated rather than produced by the war. The experiences of the war, and especially of the trench warfare on the western front, have entered deeply into the language and imagery of the countries of western Europe[1] and continue to haunt the imagination of writers and artists born years after the war ended. Its immediate consequences – the Russian revolution, the political and social upheavals of 1918–22 all over Europe, the redrawing of the maps with the emergence of new national states – have determined the course of history in the twentieth century. This alone would be enough to account for the continuing interest in the causes of the war, but there are several other dimensions and perspectives to our views of the crisis of 1914.

The immediate origins of the war are better documented than almost any other question in recent history. This is largely because from the start the argument about the responsibility for the outbreak of war had great political importance; and with the signing of the Treaty of Versailles in June 1919, the question of war guilt – *Die Kriegsschuldfrage* – became one of intense political and emotional significance. The first reaction in the victorious countries after the end of the war was to put the blame for its outbreak on the Germans. Article 231 of the Treaty of Versailles – the 'War Guilt' clause – stated that 'Germany accepts the responsibility of Germany and her allies for causing all the loss and damage to the Allied governments and their nationals imposed on them by the aggression of Germany and her allies.' Elsewhere in the Peace Treaty the moral blame was made even more explicit and was attached particularly to the person of the German Emperor: 'The Allied and Associated Powers publicly arraign William II of Hohenzollern, former German Emperor, for a supreme offence against international morality and the sanctity of treaties.' This individual indictment of the Kaiser was the result partly

1

of a blind instinct for revenge on the part of the public in Britain and France: 'Hang the Kaiser' had been a popular slogan in the British general election of November 1918. But the demand for a formal trial of William II was also the result of a more considered, though not necessarily more accurate, diagnosis of the role of the Emperor and the Prussian military caste in the origins of the war. Already in 1914 Sir Edward Grey, the British Foreign Secretary, was obsessed with the evils of 'Prussian militarism'[2] while in the armistice negotiations at the end of the war, President Wilson had stressed the necessity of getting rid of the Kaiser and doing away with what he called 'military masters and monarchical autocrats'.[3]

During the latter part of 1919 and early 1920 there were vigorous attempts by the British and French governments to bring the Kaiser to trial and to persuade the government of the Netherlands, where William II had taken refuge, to hand him over. The British and French were extremely angry with the Dutch – and in the despatches of the British minister at The Hague one can see the accumulated bitterness at four years of Dutch neutrality. Lloyd George was particularly virulent against the Dutch and their refusal to see the Kaiser's personal responsibility in the same light as he did. In the Supreme War Council he ranted against the Kaiser, and his phrases were embodied in the note sent to the Netherlands government demanding his surrender. The Kaiser was, Lloyd George maintained, personally responsible for 'the cynical violation of the neutrality of Belgium and Luxemburg, the barbarous hostage system, the mass deportation of populations, the carrying away of the young women of Lille, torn from their families and thrown defenceless into the most promiscuous environment'.[4] The rhetoric was in vain, as were the threats to break off diplomatic relations with the Netherlands and even to impose economic sanctions. The Dutch government maintained its dignified refusal either to surrender William II or, on the analogy of Napoleon, to banish him to Curaçao in the Dutch West Indies.

The attitude of the Netherlands government made the idea of trying the Kaiser and of pinning responsibility for the war on him personally impossible to realize. The search for responsibility became less immediate and moved to another level. By the middle of the 1920s the idea was gaining acceptance that the war was the result of a faulty system of international relations. It was, on this view, the existence of a system of alliances dividing Europe into two camps which had made war inevitable, while the 'old diplomacy' was blamed for making sinister secret international agreements which committed countries to war without the knowledge of their citizens. As the *Manchester Guardian* had put it in 1914: 'By some hidden contract England has been technically committed behind her back to the ruinous madness of a share in the violent gamble of a war between two militarist leagues on the Continent.'[5] This view had been strengthened by the policies of the

American administration after the United States had entered the war in April 1917. President Wilson was much influenced by the British radical tradition which throughout the nineteenth century had criticized secret diplomacy and called for a foreign policy based on morality rather than on expediency, on general ethical principles rather than on practical calculations about the balance of power. Thus, when in January 1918, he enunciated his famous Fourteen Points which were to serve as the basis for a just peace, he stressed the need for 'Open covenants of peace openly arrived at, after which there shall be no private international understandings of any kind, but diplomacy shall proceed always frankly and in the public view.' The foundation of the League of Nations as an integral part of the peace settlement of 1919 encouraged the belief that a new system of international relations was about to come into being in which diplomatic bargains and secret military agreements would be abolished and international relations be conducted by consensus before the eyes of the public and under their control.

The search for an explanation for the outbreak of the war in terms of the nature of the international system – a view summed up in the title of an influential book published in 1926, *The International Anarchy 1904 – 1914* by the Cambridge classicist G. Lowes Dickinson – was aided by the publication by most of the governments involved in the war of numerous volumes of documents from their diplomatic archives. The first attack on secret diplomacy in which the publication of documents was used to discredit opponents was launched before the end of the war when Trotsky, the first Foreign Minister of the Bolshevik regime, ordered the publication of the secret treaties entered into by the Tsarist government, greatly to the embarrassment of Russia's allies France and Britain. Then, after the German revolution of 1918, the republican government authorized the eminent socialist theoretician Karl Kautsky to prepare a volume of documents from the German archives on the events immediately preceding the outbreak of war. Subsequent German governments believed that one way to refute the allegations of Germany's war guilt was to show the detailed working of the old diplomacy and to demonstrate that the methods of all governments were much the same and that therefore no specific blame should be attached to the Germans. Accordingly, between 1922 and 1927 thirty-nine volumes of German diplomatic documents were published under the title *Die Grosse Politik der Europäischen Kabinette* (The High Policy of the European Cabinets). This German initiative which aimed at countering the allegations of Germany's war guilt meant that other countries felt obliged to follow the example and show that they too had nothing to hide. Consequently the *British Documents on the Origins of the War* appeared in eleven volumes between 1926 and 1938; the French *Documents Diplomatiques Français 1871–1914* began publication in 1930, though the last of the volumes did not appear until

1953. Eight volumes of Austro-Hungarian documents were published in 1930 by the government of the Austrian Republic, while the Italian documents were only published after the Second World War. Members of the Russian diplomatic service who remained abroad after the revolution published selections from their embassy archives, and the Soviet government printed a quantity of archive material in the 1920s and 1930s.[6]

This mass of published documentary material meant that, even though the government archives themselves in many cases remained closed until after the Second World War, historians had a great deal of evidence on which to base an examination of the diplomatic relations between the powers. The study of the diplomatic history of the nineteenth century and of the background to the First World War became one of the most prestigious branches of historical investigation. A number of distinguished historians developed the idea of the autonomy of diplomatic history as a branch of historical study and so seemed to confirm the view of the great nineteenth-century German historian Ranke that it is the foreign policies of states which determine their internal development and decide their destiny. It is due to this generation of historians and the students trained by them that we know more in greater detail about the history of the relations between states in the years before 1914 than in almost any other period. Many of these historians were still concerned with the allocation to the belligerent governments of responsibility in one form or another: Pierre Renouvin in France and Bernadotte Schmitt in the United States inclined to put the blame on Germany, another American, Sidney B. Fay, on Austria-Hungary, the German Alfred von Wegerer on Russia and Britain, to name only a few examples. The most monumental of these detailed studies, that by the Italian journalist and politician Luigi Albertini, only appeared after the Second World War had begun and it was some years before it achieved international recognition; and by then the focus of the discussion was changing.[7]

After the Second World War, for which the immediate responsibility was generally accepted to be that of Hitler and the National Socialist government of Germany, the discussion of the causes of the First World War tended to be linked to the discussion about the causes of the Second. How far did the Treaty of Versailles, and especially the War Guilt clause, contribute to the collapse of the Weimar Republic and the rise of Hitler? To what extent was there a continuity in foreign policy between the Kaiser's and Hitler's Germany? The notion of a continuity in German aims between 1914 and 1939 was familiar enough to Anglo-Saxon historians from their reactions to the Second World War, when for some of them, indeed, the tradition of Germany's inherent wickedness went back to Bismarck or Frederick the Great or even Luther.[8] For many conservative German historians, although they were ready to accept German responsibility for the Second World

War, it was extremely painful to face the fact that the notion of Germany's 'guilt' in the First World War was still flourishing outside Germany. This partly accounted for the violence of the controversy aroused in Germany by the publication of the Hamburg historian Fritz Fischer's work *Griff nach der Weltmacht* in 1961[9] which showed not only the extent of German annexationist aims in the First World War but also suggested that the German government deliberately went to war in 1914 in order to attain them. Worse still from the point of view of many of Fischer's German colleagues, he suggested that there might be some continuity between Germany's aims in the First World War and those in the Second.

However, the aspect of Fritz Fischer's work which was most important for the discussion of the causes of the First World War has been the suggestion, made almost incidentally in *Griff nach der Weltmacht* but developed in his next book *Krieg der Illusionen*, and carried further by several of his students and followers, that it was domestic political and social pressures which determined German foreign policy before 1914.[10] This assertion of the *Primat der Innenpolitik* in reaction against the Rankean *Primat der Aussenpolitik* has made historians look again at the domestic political situation in Europe before 1914. The spread of this view was helped by the fact that in the 1960s many American historians and political scientists were analysing contemporary American foreign policy, including the origins of the Cold War and of the war in Vietnam, in terms of economic interests and pressure groups, so that it seemed natural to apply similar models to Europe before 1914 and to believe that, in Arno J. Mayer's words, 'the decision for war and the design for warfare were forged in what was a crisis in the politics and policy of Europe's ruling and governing classes'.[11] These ideas came close to the Marxist explanation that wars are inherent in the nature of capitalism and that the internal contradictions of capitalist society had by the beginning of the twentieth century reached a point where war was inevitable.

Such explanations can take us very far away from the immediate situation in 1914 and involve us in a consideration of the entire economic and social development of Europe for several centuries. And ideally, no doubt, an account of the causes of the First World War would lead to a moment of profound Hegelian insight in which everything in the world would be related to everything else and all the connections and patterns would become clear. However, this book has a more modest aim and will attempt to look at some of the reasons which have been suggested why this particular war occurred at this particular time.

Our explanations form a pattern of concentric circles, starting with the immediate decisions taken by the political and military leaders in the crisis of July 1914, decisions in which their characters and personal idiosyncrasies necessarily played a part. But these decisions were themselves limited both by previous choices and by the constitutional and political framework within which they were taken. They were influenced by recent international crises and by the diplomatic alignments contracted over the previous forty years. They were the result of an intricate relationship between the military and civilian leaders and of long-term strategic plans and armament programmes. They were subject to domestic political pressures, both short- and long-term, and to the conflicting influences of different economic groups. They depended on general conceptions of each nation's vital interests and of its national mission. Moreover the decision to go to war had to be acceptable and comprehensible to the public and to the soldiers who were going to fight; the reasons for going to war had to be expressed in language which would meet with an emotional response. And that response depended on long national traditions and the constant repetition of national myths.

The aim of this book is to look at the decisions of July 1914 which determined the outbreak of this particular war at that particular time and then to consider some of the factors which inspired those decisions and, perhaps more important, limited the options available. When we read an account of the crisis of July 1914, we often feel that the reasons which the politicians themselves were giving are somehow inadequate to explain what was happening and we are tempted to look for some deeper and more general cause to explain the catastrophe. We are often struck, as the Italian historian Luigi Albertini was, when he considered the decision-makers of 1914, by, as he put it, 'the disproportion between their intellectual and moral endowments and the gravity of the problems which faced them, between their acts and the results thereof'.[12] This is perhaps unfair in so far as they did not and could not know what the results would be or realize that the war they decided to fight would not be the war which actually followed, and that it would turn out to be longer and more destructive than any of them had ever imagined. It is pointless to speculate whether they might have chosen differently if they had known what the consequences of their choice would be. Their decisions must be examined within the context of what was open to them in 1914. As Isaiah Berlin has written, 'What can and cannot be done by particular agents in specific circumstances is an empirical question, properly settled, like all such questions, by an appeal to experience.'[13] The difficulty is, however, that the evidence which we have about the factors determining what could or could not be done in the specific circumstances of July 1914 is vast, and it is not easy to decide which factor was dominant in any particular decision. All we can do is to look at the kinds of explanation which have been suggested and try to see how far they account for the decisions actually taken. Accordingly, this book discusses some (but by no means all) of the suggested 'causes' of the war and tries to see how much each contributed to the development of the crisis of 1914.

As we have seen, many people in the 1920s blamed the international system, the existence of rival alliances and the evil influence of the 'old diplomacy', and this indeed set the scene within which the crisis developed. Once it started, the freedom of action of the civilian ministers was limited, often more than they realized, by the strategic plans and decisions of the general staffs and the admiralties, and these in turn were linked to the vast arms programmes which were a feature of the period immediately preceding the war. While some have seen the cause of the war in the international system or the plans of the military and naval authorities, others have blamed financiers and industrialists and the whole economic structure of international capitalism. What were the economic pressures for peace and for war? Then again, should we accept the idea of the *Primat der Innenpolitik* and look for the causes of the war in the domestic social and political problems of the belligerent countries and the belief that war might provide a solution to them and avert the threat of revolution?

The war of 1914 has seemed to some the climax of an era of imperialism: and many have believed that it was imperial rivalries which led inevitably to war, so that we must also attempt to analyse what part these played in creating the situation in July 1914. Finally, we can try to see how far the mood of 1914 – the political, intellectual and moral beliefs of the age – helped to make war possible and provided a scale of values to which governments could appeal once they had decided on war. In what follows each chapter is devoted to a different type of explanation. The list is by no means exhaustive; but if we try to see how far each explanation fits what happened in July 1914, how far the different categories of historical phenomena relate to the decisions taken during the crisis, we may begin to form, not a complete picture of the causes of the First World War, but at least a sketch of the complex and multifarious factors which contributed to it.

REFERENCES AND NOTES

1.   See, for example, Paul Fussell, *The Great War and Modern Memory* (London 1975).
2.   See Michael Ekstein, 'Sir Edward Grey and Imperial Germany in 1914', *Journal of Contemporary History*, **6**, No. 3 (1971) pp. 121–31.
3.   *Foreign Relations of the United States, 1918* (Washington 1933) Supplement I, Vol I, p. 383.
4.   E. L. Woodward and Rohan Butler (eds) *Documents on British Foreign Policy 1919–1939*, 1st series, Vol. 2 (London 1948) p. 913.
5.   *Manchester Guardian*, 31 July 1914, quoted in Lawrence Martin, *Peace without Victory* (New Haven 1958) p. 47.
6.   For a discussion of these materials, see A. J. P. Taylor, *The Struggle for Mastery in Europe* (Oxford 1954) pp. 569–83.

7. See e.g. Pierre Renouvin, *Les Origines immédiates de la Guerre* (Paris 1927); Bernadotte E. Schmitt, *The Coming of the War 1914*, 2 vols (New York 1928); Sidney B. Fay, *The Origins of the World War*, 2 vols (New York 1928); Alfred von Wegerer, *Der Ausbruch des Weltkrieges*, 2 vols (Hamburg 1939); Luigi Albertini, *Le Origini della Guerra del 1914*, 3 vols (Milan 1942–43).

8. For example Rohan Butler, *The Roots of National Socialism* (London 1941).

9. Fritz Fischer, *Griff nach der Weltmacht* (Düsseldorf 1961), Eng. tr. *Germany's Aims in the First World War* (London 1972); *Krieg der Illusionen* (Düsseldorf 1969), Eng. tr. *War of Illusions* (London 1974). For the controversy over Fischer's views, see e.g. John Moses, *The Politics of Illusion: The Fischer Controversy in German Historiography* (London 1975); H. W. Koch (ed.) *The Origins of the First World War* (London 1972); Wolfgang Schieder (ed.) *Erster Weltkrieg: Ursachen, Entstehung und Kriegsziele* (Cologne 1969).

10. See the two volumes of essays celebrating Fischer's sixty-fifth and seventieth birthdays: Imanuel Geiss and Bernd Jürgen Wendt (eds) *Deutschland in der Weltpolitik des 19. und 20. Jahrhunderts* (Düsseldorf 1973); Dirk Stegmann and Peter-Christian Witt (eds) *Industrielle Gesellschaft und politisches System* (Bonn 1978), and especially the works of Hans-Ulrich Wehler, e.g. *Bismarck und der Imperialismus* (Cologne 1969); *Das deutsche Kaiserreich 1871–1918* (Göttingen 1973).

11. Arno J. Mayer, 'Internal crises and war since 1870' in Charles L. Bertrand (ed) *Revolutionary Situations in Europe* (Montreal 1977) p. 231. For a development of Mayer's view that the war was a last attempt by the old European aristocracy to preserve its position, see his *The Persistence of the Old Regime: Europe to the Great War* (New York 1981).

12. Luigi Albertini, *The Origins of the War of 1914*, Vol. III (Eng. tr. 1957) p. 178.

13. Isaiah Berlin, *Historical Inevitability* (London 1954) p. 33, fn. 1.

Chapter 2

THE JULY CRISIS 1914

On 28 June 1914 the Archduke Franz Ferdinand, heir to the throne of Austria-Hungary, was assassinated by a member of a group of Serb and Croat nationalists. He was on a visit to Sarajevo, the capital of the formerly Turkish province of Bosnia which had been administered by Austria-Hungary since 1878 and annexed to the Monarchy in 1908. The murder of prominent people – kings, presidents, leading politicians – had been for some three decades a familiar technique used by groups and individuals anxious to draw attention to what they believed to be national or social injustices, but no previous assassination within living memory had provoked a major international crisis, as the killing of the Archduke was to do. To understand why this was so, we must look at the development of the July crisis and at the crucial decisions which led from an isolated act of terrorism to the outbreak of a world war. In this chapter we will try to give a narrative of the decisions in terms of the way in which the participants themselves described and discussed them. Later in this book we shall examine some of the explanations at a deeper level which have attempted to go beyond the evidence in the diplomatic and political documents on which this account is based, but for the moment we will look at what the responsible political leaders said they were trying to achieve in their handling of the crisis and the reasons they themselves gave at the time to justify these decisions.

The governments directly involved at first were those of Austria-Hungary and Serbia, since it was immediately assumed by the Austrian authorities that the assassins had been operating from inside the kingdom of Serbia and with the connivance of the Serbian government and officials. Ever since 1903, when a new ruling dynasty had seized power in Serbia with the support of a group of intensely nationalist officers determined to expand Serbia's frontiers so as to include those Serbs still living under foreign rule, the Emperor Franz Joseph and his advisers had become increasingly worried by the attraction which Serbia could exercise over the Southern Slavs – Croats as well as Serbs – within the Monarchy.

The survival of the Habsburg Monarchy was believed to depend, if not on solving the problem of the subject nationalities which may well have been impossible, at least in keeping them in what one Austrian statesman had called 'a balanced state of mutual dissatisfaction'.[1] Any move by the Serbians to encourage separatist national feelings among the Southern Slavs inside the Monarchy was therefore seen as a direct threat to the existence of the Austro-Hungarian state. The assassination of Franz Ferdinand seemed to provide an excellent excuse for taking some sort of action against Serbia in order to remove this threat. During the days immediately after the murder, the Austro-Hungarian government was discussing what form this action should take. There was an additional argument for vigorous action against Serbia in that the Austro-Hungarians had been unable to prevent the Serbs from winning substantial territorial gains in the two Balkan wars of 1912–13, so that Serbia was by 1914 considerably larger than it had been two years before.

The solution proposed by the Chief of Staff, Franz Baron Conrad von Hötzendorf, was to call for immediate mobilization against Serbia so as to force the Serbian government to exercise more control over the terrorist groups and to recognize that any subversive action against Austria must be abandoned. There were two arguments against this course. One, soon abandoned, was that the threat of military action against Serbia might provoke other subject nationalities in the Monarchy, especially the Czechs, into attempting a revolution. The other, advanced by Stephen Tisza, the Hungarian Prime Minister, was that there were quite enough Serbs in Austria-Hungary already (and especially in the Hungarian half of the Monarchy), so that in no circumstances must action against Serbia involve the annexation of Serb territory and increase the number of Serbs directly under Austro-Hungarian rule.

The success of any action against Serbia with the intention of reducing her to the position of a satellite state depended on this being managed in such a way as to avoid provoking a major international crisis in which Russia might intervene in support of Serbia. From the start the Austro-Hungarian government was aware of this danger, but they hoped that Russian intervention could be prevented if Austria had a firm promise of German support – and in 1908 at the moment of the Austro-Hungarian annexation of Bosnia, Russia had given way when Germany made it clear that she was backing Austria – or else believed that the risk of war with Russia was one which had to be run even though it was a risk to meet which no effective military plans had been made.

Immediately after the Archduke's funeral, therefore, the Austro-Hungarian Foreign Minister, Count Berchtold, and Conrad, the Chief of the General Staff, had decided to ask for German support, and the head of Berchtold's private office was sent to Berlin with a personal letter from Franz Joseph to the Kaiser which was delivered on 5 July. After lunch in the royal palace at Potsdam, the Kaiser assured the Austrian envoy that Austria could count on full German support even if Russia were to be involved. On 7 July the Austro-Hungarian council of ministers met to consider the reply from Berlin and to decide on the next step. It was now that some of the reservations of Count Stephen Tisza, the Hungarian Premier, were expressed: but the decision of the meeting was to go ahead with some sort of measures against Serbia. Berchtold then set out to report to the Emperor, who was spending the summer as usual at the resort of Bad Ischl in the Salzkammergut. Over the next week there were further discussions, and Tisza's hesitations were finally overcome, so that on 14 July the Austro-Hungarian government were able to agree on a draft ultimatum to be sent to Serbia, the text of which was finally approved on 19 July. The note demanded that Serbia should agree to a number of Austrian conditions including the suppression of anti-Austrian propaganda in Serbia, the dissolution of the Serbian nationalist association Narodna Odbrana, the purging of officers and officials who were guilty of propaganda against Austria, the arrest of named officers suspected of aiding and abetting the conspirators who murdered the Archduke and the tightening up of controls on the Serbian-Austro-Hungarian border. It also demanded that representatives of the Austro-Hungarian government should participate in the enquiry which the Serbs were to carry out into the origins of the assassination plot, as well as in the suppression of subversive activities directed against the Austro-Hungarian state. This stiff list of demands was to be handed to the Serbian government on 23 July and they were to be obliged to reply within forty-eight hours. Throughout these days the German leaders repeated on several occasions their support for Austria-Hungary and pressed on the Austrians the advantages of rapid action. The Austrian ambassador in Berlin reported that government circles there believed that the moment was a favourable one even in the event of Russian intervention, since Russia was not yet fully prepared militarily and not nearly as strong as she was likely to be in a few years. At the same time Jagow, the German State Secretary for Foreign Affairs, while realizing Austria's internal weakness, thought that Germany must support her ally at all costs if Austria was to survive as a Great Power and an effective partner in the alliance. Jagow also hoped, as the Austrian leaders did, that vigorous action would make the Russians less rather than more likely to intervene. While the discussions about the precise terms of the ultimatum were going on in Vienna, the allies in Berlin were therefore repeatedly urging the need for action and leaving their own willingness to risk war in no doubt, and they even showed some anxiety at the delay in despatching the ultimatum.

So far, during the three weeks or so since the Archduke's murder, there was little popular awareness of any impending international crisis, and those Europeans who could afford it set off on their summer holidays as usual. Moreover, the Austro-Hungarian government and their German allies had two good reasons for delaying the despatch of the ultimatum to Serbia. First, this would give more time for the completion of the harvest before the disruption to agriculture which mobilization was bound to cause. Secondly, the despatch of the ultimatum on 23 July would ensure that it did not arrive in Belgrade during the visit to St Petersburg of the President of the French Republic, Raymond Poincaré, and his Prime Minister, René Viviani, which had been arranged some time before as part of a regular series of meetings between the French and their Russian allies and which was planned to take place between 20 and 23 July, since, as Berchtold put it to the German ambassador in Vienna 'under the influence of champagne . . . a fraternal relationship might be celebrated which would influence and possibly determine the attitude of both countries. It would be good if the toasts were over before the transmission of the ultimatum.'[2]

Sazonov, the Russian Foreign Minister, had gone to his country estate from 14 to 20 July for a short holiday before receiving the French visitors. But already before the arrival of Poincaré and Viviani on 20 July, the Russian government was beginning to suspect that the Austrians were preparing some sort of decisive action against Serbia and Sazonov was already thinking that Russia might have to take some precautionary military measures. They had broken the cipher used by the Austro-Hungarian Foreign Ministry and were presumably aware of the contents of the telegrams between Vienna and the embassy in St Petersburg. In any case, by 16 July the Italian ambassador to Russia was warning a senior official in the Russian Foreign Office that 'Austria was capable of taking an irrevocable step with regard to Serbia based on the belief that, although Russia would make a verbal protest, she would not adopt forcible measures for the protection of Serbia. . .'.[3] And on the same day the Russian ambassador in Vienna was reporting much the same thing. It was therefore in an atmosphere of some apprehension and uncertainty that Poincaré arrived in Russia on the afternoon of 20 July.

We know surprisingly little of the conversations between the leaders of the French and Russian governments. The French representatives had been briefed on a number of points by their foreign office, and especially on some questions affecting French business enterprises in Russia. The German ambassador reported that, although Poincaré was treated with great ceremony, there was little popular enthusiasm when he appeared in public, while a printers' strike reduced press comment on the visit. But both the Germans and the Austrians were worried that the nationalist and anti-German figures in St Petersburg, such as the Grand Duke Nicholas, whose Montenegrin wife had passionate pro-Serb feelings, reinforced by the French ambassador,

Maurice Paléologue, might be effectively influencing the decisions taken; and even if nothing concrete was in fact decided, the visit gave the impression of close and cordial co-operation between the two governments. Poincaré, Viviani and their party left by sea late in the evening of 23 July. Earlier that afternoon the Austro-Hungarian ultimatum had been presented in Belgrade to those Serbian ministers who were available at short notice to receive it.

Although rumours of a dramatic move by Austria-Hungary had been circulating for some days and had been repeated in St Petersburg during the French visit, and although by 22 July some action was generally believed to be imminent, the publication of the terms of the Austrian ultimatum and the shortness of its forty-eight-hour time limit came as a great shock. '*C'est la guerre européenne*', Sazonov exclaimed when he heard the news on the morning of 24 July,[4] and Sir Edward Grey, the British Foreign Secretary, described the Austro-Hungarian note as 'the most formidable document I had ever seen addressed by one State to another that was independent'.[5] The reaction of the Serb government was, not surprisingly, one of confusion and dismay. They were in the midst of a domestic political crisis (see Ch. 4) and were about to hold general elections. Their military position had not yet recovered from the efforts of the two Balkan wars. At the moment when the ultimatum was delivered, the Prime Minister, Nicholas Pašić, was away on an election campaign and indeed planning to take a few days holiday. It was only with some difficulty that he was contacted, and he arrived back in Belgrade early in the morning of 25 July. In the meantime, the instinct of the Serbian cabinet was to play for time and to place their hopes in the possibility of mediation, perhaps by the King of Italy, an uncle of the Prince Regent Alexander. But because of the rigidity of the Austrian time limit, their immediate problem was to decide whether they had any choice other than to accept the ultimatum in its entirety. There is some evidence to suggest that they considered doing this: but, in the event, the reply they sent, while extremely conciliatory in tone, raised objections to the participation of Austro-Hungarian officials in the Serbian enquiry into the plot to assassinate Franz Ferdinand. This was enough; for the Austro-Hungarian minister in Belgrade had been given precise instructions that any Serbian reply other than unconditional acceptance of the terms of the ultimatum would lead to the breaking off of diplomatic relations. The Serbian reply was delivered to the Austrian representative, Baron Giesl, just before the expiry of the time limit at 6 p.m. on 25 July. Giesl at once declared it unsatisfactory and left by the 6.30 train for Vienna.

There has been much speculation about Serbian policy in these crucial forty-eight hours and the topic is still one of controversy among Yugoslav politicians and scholars. Some people have argued that it was Pašić's fear that Austrian participation in the enquiry would reveal the extent of the Serbian government's complicity or connivance in the assassination plot which made him insist on the unacceptability of that part of the ultimatum. Others have suggested that it was an offer of Russian support which changed the mood of the Serbian ministers from one of resigned acceptance of the whole ultimatum to its acceptance with reservations. Certainly, on 24 July the Regent of Serbia addressed a personal appeal to the Tsar in which he complained that the Austrian terms were unnecessarily humiliating and the time limit too short. 'We cannot defend ourselves. Therefore we pray Your Majesty to lend help as soon as possible. Your Majesty has given so many proofs of your previous good will and we confidently hope that this appeal will find an echo in your generous Slav heart.'[6] Even before this message was received at St Petersburg, it was clear what the Russian response would be. As soon as Sazonov heard the terms of the ultimatum to Serbia from the Austrian ambassador, he accused the Austro-Hungarian government of deliberately provoking war: '*Vous mettez le feu à l'Europe!*'[7] He at once consulted the Chief of Staff, General Yanushkevich, with the result that on the next day, 25 July, the Tsar authorized preparations for partial mobilization, though the actual orders for mobilization were not yet issued. These measures were reported enthusiastically by the Serbian minister in St Petersburg to his government in Belgrade.[8]

It was on 24 July – nearly four weeks after the assassination of Franz Ferdinand – that the scale and implications of the crisis began to be realized outside Berlin and Vienna. Throughout the crisis the German and Austrian governments had accepted the risk that the Austrian demands on Serbia might well lead to the intervention of Russia which in turn might lead to a European war. However, they had believed that the more decisive Austrian action was and the firmer Germany's backing of her ally, the less likely the Russians would be to intervene. Yet the risk had to be run: by the Austro-Hungarians because, as Tisza put it to the German ambassador, 'The Monarchy must take an energetic decision to show its power of survival and to put an end to intolerable conditions in the south-east',[9] and by the Germans because many of the responsible leaders shared the view summed up by the Bavarian representative in Berlin after talks with the Under-Secretary and other senior officials in the Foreign Ministry that 'people are of the opinion that it is a moment of destiny for Austria and for this reason we have unhesitatingly agreed to any measures which might be decided on there, even at the risk of danger of a war with Russia'.[10] Over the next few days after the presentation of the Austrian note in Belgrade on 23 July, it became increasingly clear that those people in Berlin and Vienna who thought that vigorous action by Austria and a clear declaration of support by Germany would deter Russia were deeply mistaken.

By 24 July the British government began to be seriously worried about the situation. On the previous day, Count Mensdorff, the Austro-Hungarian ambassador in London, had given Grey privately some idea of the Austrian demands and in particular of the time limit which was to be set for Serbia's acceptance of them. For a moment Grey had a frightening picture of the implications:

> The possible consequences of the present situation were terrible. If as many as four great Powers of Europe – let us say Austria, France, Russia and Germany – were engaged in war, it seemed to me that it must involve the expenditure of so vast a sum of money and such an interference with trade, that a war would be accompanied or followed by a complete collapse of European credit and industry. In these days, in great industrial states, this would mean a state of things worse than that of 1848, and, irrespective of who were victors in the war, many things would be completely swept away.[11]

The result was that on the next day Grey began to explore the possibility that England, Germany, France and Italy 'who had not direct interests in Serbia should act together for the sake of peace, simultaneously in Vienna and St Petersburg'.[12] By the time he had spoken to the French and German ambassadors, Grey was already beginning to assume that a war between Austria and Serbia could not be localized, and he spent most of the next day trying to arrange some sort of joint mediation before setting off for his usual weekend's fishing in Hampshire. On 26 July in the afternoon he authorized, from his cottage at Itchen Abbas, the issue of a formal invitation to the governments of Italy, Germany and France to instruct their ambassadors in London to join him in a conference 'in order to endeavour to find an issue to prevent complications'.[13]

By the time Grey's invitation was despatched two of the countries directly concerned in the crisis were already planning military action, even though no irrevocable step had yet been taken. On 25 July, the German government was pressing for immediate Austrian military operations against Serbia because 'any delay in commencing military operations is regarded . . . as a great danger because of the interference of other powers'.[14] On the next day, however, General Conrad, Chief of the Austro-Hungarian General Staff, had to point out that his mobilization plans did not allow for an attack on Serbia before 12 August: and this raised the question of whether there was any point in a declaration of war if it were not accompanied by immediate action. By 27 July the views of Berchtold prevailed and it was decided that a formal declaration of war on Serbia should be made on 28 July; and Berchtold at least seems to have hoped that it might frighten the Serbs into total submission without the need of actual military measures. The declaration of war referred not only to the unsatisfactory Serbian reply to the Austrian note of 23 July, but also alleged that the Serbs had already attacked a detachment of the Austro-Hungarian army on the Bosnian border, an accusation based on an unconfirmed report subsequently shown to be false, although the Serbian army had been mobilized immediately on receipt of the news of the ultimatum. On 26 July the Tsar agreed to authorize partial mobilization in the military districts of Kiev, Odessa, Moscow and Kazan. However, although preliminary steps could now be taken, the actual mobilization orders were still delayed.

But even if the Austrian and Russian delays in mobilization or military operations left some room for the diplomatic negotiations suggested by Grey, the reply he received from the German government on the evening of 27 July, after the French and Italians had agreed to his proposal for a conference, put an end to the hopes that this particular attempt at avoiding war might be successful, since Jagow had maintained that the question was one which concerned Russia and Austria alone and should be settled by direct negotiation between them. As there did at that moment seem to be a chance of conversations between Russia and Austria beginning (on 26 July Sazonov had a calm and constructive talk with the Austrian ambassador in St Petersburg) and as Jagow did not rule out completely some sort of mediation later on, Grey was obliged to accept for the moment the failure of his proposal. On 27 July, even before receiving news of the German refusal of his conference proposal, Grey raised with the Cabinet, for the first time and still in a very hypothetical way, the question of Britain's entry into a war if France were to be attacked by Germany. The realization was growing that no armed conflict was likely to be localized. Although there was considerable opposition in the Cabinet to the idea that Britain might enter the war, it nevertheless approved the decision taken by the First Sea Lord that the British fleet which had been conducting manœuvres should not be dispersed to its peacetime bases and the crews should not be sent on the leave which they would normally have expected after the manœuvres.

French reactions to the crisis had been somewhat confused by the fact that the President and Prime Minister were at sea on their journey back to France from St Petersburg during these days in which tension was growing. Wireless telegraphy was still very imperfect, and Poincaré subsequently recorded his frustration at the incomplete and garbled radio messages which he and Viviani on board the *France* were receiving from the Eiffel Tower, so that it was only when they arrived in Stockholm on 25 July that they began to realize the seriousness of the situation, an impression confirmed by such messages as did get through to the ship as it crossed the Baltic towards Copenhagen. As a result, the French cancelled their state visits to Denmark and Norway and returned as fast as possible to France, landing at Dunkirk on the morning of 29 July. During the critical days immediately after the publication of the Austrian ultimatum, the leaders of the French government were therefore unable to exercise much control over events. In their absence, the Acting Foreign Minister, Jean-Baptiste Bienvenu-Martin, the Minister of Justice, was indecisive and hesitant and far slower than the Paris press in realizing the gravity of the situation, so that both the German and Austrian ambassadors formed the impression that France would not support Russia's position very firmly. The absence of the President and Prime Minister also meant that Maurice Paléologue, the French ambassador in St Petersburg, a man wholly committed to the Russian alliance, felt free to strengthen the resolve of Sazonov, whose changes of mood contributed to the complexity of the situation, by assuring him of France's readiness to fulfil her obligations as an ally. Moreover, he does not seem to have bothered to keep the Foreign Ministry in Paris fully informed of the many detailed developments in St Petersburg between the evening of 23 July when Poincaré and Viviani left and their arrival in France six days later.

In fact, the French had already taken some precautionary measures. Soldiers on leave were being inconspicuously recalled to their regiments; some units were being moved back from Morocco; the prefects were exhorting the editors of provincial newspapers to be patriotic and discreet. And on 27 July, General Joffre, the Chief of the Staff, and Adolphe Messimy, the War Minister, were expressing through the military attaché in St Petersburg their hope that should war break out the Russian high command would immediately take the offensive in East Prussia. The French military authorities were presumably worried by reports that the Russians were for the moment only preparing to mobilize against Austria. By the time the French cabinet met under the chairmanship of the President of the Republic on the evening of 29 July, they were confronted with further evidence of the deterioration of the situation. Not only had the Austrians declared war on Serbia on the previous day and had on 29th bombarded Belgrade from ships of their Danube flotilla, but the German government was now directly threatening France: the German ambassador had told Viviani as soon as he was back in Paris that the military precautions which France had begun to take would justify Germany proclaiming the *Kriegsgefahrzustand*, the 'state of imminent danger of war' which was the preparatory stage before mobilization.

By the evening of 29 July, the military actions of all the states concerned were becoming of major importance: Austria-Hungary and Serbia were already at war even though it would be some days before the Austrian army could commence operations, and general mobilization – mobilization against Russia – had not yet been ordered; the French had started taking precautionary measures; the British had kept their fleet concentrated. Most serious of all, the Tsar had that morning signed two alternative decrees, one for partial mobilization and one for general mobilization. That evening the German ambassador called on Sazonov and showed him a telegram from Bethmann Hollweg, the German Chancellor: 'Kindly impress on M. Sazonov very seriously that further progress of Russian mobilization measures would compel us to mobilize and that European war could scarcely be prevented.'[15] The result of this was the opposite of what the Germans presumably intended, for the Foreign Minister, the War Minister and the Chief of Staff agreed to order general mobilization at once. Yet the Tsar still hesitated: he had just received a telegram from the Kaiser (in English) which ended: 'I am exerting my utmost influence to induce the Austrians to deal straightly to arrive to a satisfactory under-standing with you. I confidently hope you will help me in my efforts to smoothe over difficulties that may still arise. Your very sincere and devoted friend and cousin Willy.'[16]

Indeed, the Kaiser and the Imperial Chancellor, Theobald von Bethmann Hollweg, had by now begun to have some misgivings. On 27 July Bethmann had received a telegram from Prince Lichnowsky, the German ambassador in London, which passed on a message from Grey asking the Germans to persuade the Austrian government to accept the Serbian reply to their ultimatum, as Grey believed this met the Austrian demands 'to an extent he would never have considered possible'.[17] Grey, whom Lichnowsky found depressed for the first time since the beginning of the crisis, had said that the whole future of Anglo-German relations depended on joint action to avoid war, that he had done what he could to urge moderation on the Russians and that the Germans must now do the same in Vienna. Bethmann at once passed the telegram to the Kaiser. On the afternoon of the next day the Kaiser replied that the Serbian answer had removed grounds for war but that, as 'the Serbs are orientals and so mendacious, false and masters of obstruction', the Austrians should occupy Belgrade as a pledge for the Serbs' fulfilment of their promises until these were satisfactorily carried out.[18] This proposal was passed on to Vienna later in the day; and as the Austrian government had already declared that they had no intention of annexing permanently any Serb territory, it looked like a possible basis for negotiation. But in spite of several reminders, Berchtold delayed replying, and when he finally did send an answer it was an evasive one. No doubt this was because the Austro-Hungarian government was getting contradictory advice from Berlin. Just when Berchtold was considering Bethmann's proposal for a 'halt in Belgrade', General Conrad was being urged by Field Marshal von Moltke, the Chief of the German General Staff, that any further delay in ordering Austria's mobilization would be disastrous. It is not surprising that at this point Berchtold is said to have flung up his hands and exclaimed: 'Who actually rules in Berlin, Bethmann or Moltke?'[19] Between 28 and 31 July, events were moving too fast for the diplomats because the decisions were now more and more being taken by the soldiers.

Sir Edward Grey, though discouraged, had not given up hope of mediation and he welcomed the possibility of a 'halt in Belgrade' which would give time for further negotiation between Austria and Russia.

But these hopes vanished as it became clear that the Austrians would not make any concessions to Serbia: late on the afternoon of 29 July, the British ambassador reported that the German Chancellor had passed on to the Austrians Grey's view that the Serbian reply was sufficiently conciliatory to serve as a basis for discussion, but he had been told 'that it was too late to act upon your suggestion as events had marched too rapidly'.[20] The result of the failure of Grey's initiative and the fact that Britain's room for diplomatic manœuvre was vanishing changed the nature of the problems confronting the British government. The British were now under increasing pressure from France and Russia to declare their support for them; and at the same time the Germans were insistently asking for a promise of British neutrality. As early as 25 July, Sir George Buchanan, the British ambassador in St Petersburg, had been told by Sazonov, 'If we [the British] took our stand firmly with France and Russia there would be no war. If we failed them now rivers of blood would flow and we would in the end be dragged in.'[21] This was to remain the constant theme of the French and Russian leaders over the next few days. On the evening of 30 July, President Poincaré put the same point to Sir Francis Bertie, the British ambassador in Paris, who telegraphed to London: 'He is convinced that preservation of peace between Powers is in the hands of England, for if His Majesty's Government announce that, in the event of conflict between Germany and France resulting from present differences between Austria and Serbia, England would come to the aid of France, there would be no war for Germany would at once modify her attitude.'[22] Grey's response was consistently to avoid commitment. As he had put it to Paul Cambon on 29 July:

> If Germany became involved and France became involved, we had not made up our minds what we should do . . . we were taking all precautions with regard to our fleet, and I was about to warn Prince Lichnowsky not to count on our standing aside, but it would not be fair that I should let M. Cambon be misled into supposing that this meant that we had decided what to do in a contingency that I still hoped might not arise.[23]

Nor was the language he used to the Germans much different. On the previous evening Bethmann had made a bid for British neutrality, promising that if Britain remained neutral, Germany would not make any territorial acquisitions at the expense of France – though such a promise would not include the French colonies. Sir Eyre Crowe, the Assistant Under-Secretary in the Foreign Office minuted: 'the only comment that needs to be made on these astounding proposals is that they reflect discredit on the statesman who makes them'.[24] Yet even then Grey still hesitated. While refusing to bargain about terms for British neutrality, he was still saying much the same as he was saying to the French: 'We must preserve our full freedom to act as circumstances may seem to require in any development of the present crisis . . .'[25] In the early stages Grey's reluctance to commit Britain to support France and Russia was based on a fear that any such support might make the Russian government more intransigent and reduce the chances of successful mediation. As one of the members of the government opposed to British involvement put it, 'If both sides do not know what we shall do, both will be less willing to run risks.'[26] By 28 July, however, Grey's hesitations were due to the realization that he could not carry his colleagues in the Cabinet with him in a positive policy. On 29 July the Cabinet agreed 'after much discussion' that 'at this stage we were unable to pledge ourselves in advance either under all circumstances to stand aside or on any condition to go in.'[27] And as late as 1 August the government decided 'that we could not propose to Parliament at this moment to send an expeditionary military force to the continent',[28] a reply which dismayed Paul Cambon. British hesitations were only finally resolved on 2 August. By that time Germany and Russia were already at war.

On 29 July the Tsar had still hesitated to order general mobilization, and on the same day Bethmann, supported by Moltke, resisted the proposal of General Falkenhayn, the War Minister, that Germany should at once proclaim the stage preparatory to formal mobilization, the *Kriegsgefahrzustand*. But by the next day, when it was clear that any further attempts at persuading the Austrians to suspend their action against Serbia were bound to fail, the military preparations were carried a stage further, with each side trying to put the blame for the escalation on the other. On the afternoon of 30 July, the Tsar's hesitations were finally and not without difficulty overcome and at 5 p.m. he issued the orders for the proclamation of general mobilization on the next day. As tension grew in Europe, so rumours spread: that same afternoon a report appeared in a Berlin paper that the Kaiser had ordered general mobilization, though there is no serious evidence to support the view that this influenced the Russian decision.

In fact, the paper's information was not totally wrong in so far as it reflected a new mood of resolution among the German military and civilian leaders. Once the Russians had ordered general mobilization the German government had no longer any need to delay their own military preparations. Bethmann and Moltke had succeeded in their aim that, if there were to be war, the Russians should make the first move. Late on the evening of 30 July Bethmann and Jagow accepted the advice of the Chief of the General Staff and the War Minister and agreed to issue next day the proclamation of the 'state of imminent danger of war'. The orders were accordingly issued on 31 July; and they were followed by a very strong German warning to Russia:

In spite of negotiations for mediation which are still in the balance, and although we ourselves up to now have taken no measures of mobilization, Russia has mobilized its whole army and fleet, that means against us. These Russian measures have forced us for the security of the Empire to proclaim the 'imminent danger of war' which does not yet mean mobilization. But mobilization must follow if Russia does not suspend all warlike measures against us and Austria-Hungary within twelve hours . . . [29]

On 30 July, before the final decision to start the mobilization process in Germany had been taken, Bethmann Hollweg had told a meeting of the Prussian cabinet* both of his hopes that Russia could be made to appear the guilty party and of his disappointment over England: 'Hopes of England are precisely nil.' But he ended with a remarkable expression of fatalistic irresponsibility: 'The great majority of the peoples are in themselves peaceful, but things are out of control (*es sei die Direktion verloren*) and the stone has started to roll . . .'[30] This feeling of helplessness was the sign that the crisis had reached a new intensity. The Austrians had believed that vigorous action against Serbia and a promise of German support would deter Russia: the Russians had believed that a show of strength against Austria would both check the Austrians and deter Germany. In both cases the bluff had been called, and the three countries were faced with the military consequences of their actions.

With the Russian mobilization and the possibility of the imminent outbreak of war between Germany and Russia, the Germans were anxious for the Austrians to play their part on the Galician front and were not particularly interested any longer in the Austrian punitive expedition against Serbia. Conrad, on the other hand, who had long advocated just such action against Serbia, was determined to complete it; and he hoped that the German mobilization might distract the Russians from action against Austria. The divergence of the military aims of the allies was apparent even before the war actually started, and it was only rather reluctantly and under German pressure that the Austro-Hungarian ministers recommended the Emperor Franz Joseph finally to sign the order for general mobilization on 31 July, though mobilization was not actually to start until 4 August. In the event therefore Germany declared war on Russia before Austria-Hungary, whose formal declaration was delayed till 6 August.

Although some of the civilians appeared to think that mobilization would not inevitably lead to war it soon became clear that at least for Germany it was not feasible to keep the armies poised on the brink without taking action. This was particularly the case with Germany because the plan for a two-front war devised by General Schlieffen some years before (see Ch. 4) was based on any war with Russia being accompanied by a war with Russia's ally France. The campaign was to open with an all-out attack in the west which would involve the passage of German troops through Belgium. German general mobilization was

---

*In Germany there was no imperial cabinet as such; the Chancellor was also the Prussian Prime Minister, while in some cases – notably that of the War Ministry – the Prussian minister concerned acted for the whole Empire.

therefore as much a threat to France as to Russia and meant that the war which now seemed imminent would inevitably be a European war; and indeed under the terms of her alliance with Russia, France was bound to mobilize if Germany did. But the illusion that something might still be done to avert the consequences of the military decisions already taken persisted a little longer. However, on 1 August even the Kaiser himself, the *Allerhöchster Kriegsherr*, found that he could not reverse the plans set in motion by his generals.

On that day Grey, still unable to achieve agreement in the British Cabinet on the necessity for British intervention on the side of France and Russia and still believing that there might be a last-minute diplomatic solution through a resumption of direct negotiations between Russia and Austria, was looking for some formula that might avert a German attack on France and so avoid England having to make a choice which the British government was very reluctant to make. This seems to have led to a genuine misunderstanding between him and Lichnowsky. On the morning of 1 August, Grey's private secretary, Sir William Tyrrell, told the ambassador that Grey hoped to be able to make a suggestion to him that afternoon after the meeting of the Cabinet and that he hoped this might avert the catastrophe. Lichnowsky formed the impression that Grey was going to propose that England would remain neutral and would guarantee France's neutrality provided that Germany did not attack the French. Lichnowsky at once telegraphed to Berlin and followed it three hours later with a second telegram saying that Tyrrell had later added that Grey would make proposals for English neutrality even in the case of a war between Germany and both France and Russia. The news was received with jubilation in Berlin. The Kaiser called for champagne, sent an enthusiastic personal message to King George V and summoned the Chief of the General Staff and the War Minister. But when he demanded that the troop concentration in the west should be stopped and the entire force of the German army used against Russia, he was obliged to learn the limits of his power. Moltke told him this was impossible and that, 'If His Majesty insisted on leading the whole army eastwards, he would not have an army ready to strike, he would have a confused mass of disorderly armed men without commissariat.'[31] In any case, it soon became clear that the Kaiser's enthusiasm was premature: Grey had clearly no more thought out the implications of the proposal than the Kaiser had; he had not consulted the French; and when at midnight the British ambassador in Paris received Grey's telegram saying, 'I suppose French Government would not object to our engaging to be neutral as long as German army remained on frontier on the defensive',[32] he was clearly amazed: 'I cannot imagine that in the event of Russia being at war with Austria and being attacked by Germany it would be consistent with French obligations towards Russia for French to remain quiescent . . . Am I to enquire precisely what are the obligations of the French under Franco-Russian alliance?'[33] In any case, at 3.40 p.m. that afternoon the French had proclaimed general mobilization, and the War Minister told the British military attaché, 'We rely on ourselves first and on you',[34] so that – as so often in this crisis – events had moved faster than the imagination of the politicians. By the next morning, 2 August, Grey had dropped his proposal and instructed Bertie to take no further action. While there is still some uncertainty where the misunderstanding about the scope and exact nature of Grey's proposal arose – whether through what Grey himself said or through Tyrrell's original message or Lichnowsky's interpretation of it – the importance of the episode is perhaps only as an illustration of both Grey and the Kaiser's refusal to give up hope and to accept the limitations imposed on their actions by strategic necessity.

In fact at the first of two meetings of the British Cabinet on 1 August Grey had introduced a new factor into the discussion and one which was to be important in finally bringing the Liberal Party round to accepting the necessity for war – the question of Belgian neutrality. The German plans for an attack on France were based on the movement of a German army through Belgium. Belgian neutrality had been guaranteed in 1839 by England, France, Prussia, Austria and Russia; and respect for Belgian neutrality had been reaffirmed at the time of the Franco-Prussian War in 1870 by both Prussia and France, while Britain had repeated that she accepted her responsibilities as a guarantor. In the years immediately before 1914 the Belgian government had kept outside the European alliance system and had repeatedly stressed its adherence to the strictest neutrality, so much so that in July 1914 the Belgians themselves appear to have been the last people to be worried about any threat to their neutrality and refused to the last to ask for support from any other state. However, on 28 July the Belgian government told the British minister in Brussels that they were 'determined to offer resistance to the utmost of their power should the integrity or neutrality of Belgium be assailed from any quarter'.[35] On 29 July a special courier brought the German minister in Brussels a sealed packet which he was not to open until instructed; the instructions were given on 2 August and he was told to demand from the Belgians the right of German troops to cross Belgian territory; at the same time the German government promised to respect Belgian sovereignty and territorial integrity. In the meantime, before the delivery of the German note to Belgium, the news of German military preparations had given Grey the occasion on the afternoon of 31 July to ask both the French and German governments whether they were prepared to respect the neutrality of Belgium as long as no other power violated it. The French replied affirmatively that same night: the Germans were non-committal and postponed giving a definite answer. At the same time Grey informed the Belgians what he had done, but the Minister of Foreign Affairs assured him that the relations between Belgium and the neighbouring powers were excellent and that there was no need to suspect their intentions.

The German refusal to give a direct answer led Grey to issue what was in fact the clearest warning to Germany he had yet given: he repeated that Britain could not give a promise to remain neutral but that 'our attitude would be determined by public opinion here, and that the neutrality of Belgium would appeal very strongly to public opinion here'.[36] The Cabinet had in fact agreed earlier in the day that this should be formally conveyed to the German government with an expression of their very great regret that the Germans had not yet given an assurance that they would respect Belgian neutrality. Yet the question of Belgian neutrality, important as it was to be in reconciling liberal opinion in Britain to the war, was not the immediate reason for the decision of the British to support France. The discussions in the Cabinet and the analysis of the situation by the Foreign Office occasionally revealed a concern with more general questions about Britain's position in the world and the nature of the balance of power. The view of Sir Eyre Crowe that 'the theory that England cannot engage in a big war means her abdication as an independent state'[37] was shared by those members of the Cabinet who had become convinced of the necessity of British intervention; and it was reinforced by a message from the Conservative opposition on 2 August: 'Any hesitation in now supporting France and Russia will be fatal to the honour and future security of the United Kingdom.'[38] Yet the issue did not often present itself in so generalized a form and the discussions in the Cabinet revolved round the nature of British commitments to France and the implications of a possible violation of Belgium, so that it was in these terms that the discussions were finally presented rather than in any more general categories.

From the moment of the return of Poincaré and Viviani from Russia, the French government had been very anxious to get the English to commit themselves to active support of Russia and France. They themselves had repeatedly asserted their loyalty to the Franco-Russian alliance and had made little attempt to moderate Russian policy or to delay Russian mobilization; both the French ambassador in St Petersburg, Paléologue, and the Russian ambassador in France, the former Foreign Minister, Isvolsky, were working hard to maintain that solidarity and to speed up French action. However, on 30 July Viviani did urge caution on the Russians and pressed them – too late – 'not to proceed to any measure which might offer Germany a pretext for total or partial mobilization'.[39] When this evidence of France's efforts for peace was passed to London, it was accompanied by a reminder of the exchange of letters between Grey and the French ambassador in 1912 (see Ch. 3) 'in which we agreed that, if the peace of Europe were threatened, we would discuss what we were prepared to do'.[40] At the same time Cambon gave Grey the latest information about German troop movements on the French frontier and pointed out that German military preparations were further advanced than those of France.

This meeting was followed by continuing indecision on the part of the British government and an increasing anxiety on Cambon's part about their intentions. Grey was under great strain: he knew how far the Cabinet were from agreement: he was aware of the courteous reproaches implied in every encounter with the French ambassador: though himself convinced that England was morally committed to France, he yet refused to accept the inevitability of war or to give up hope that there might still be some diplomatic way out. He was under pressure from his senior officials, notably Sir Arthur Nicolson, the Permanent Under-Secretary and Sir Eyre Crowe, the Assistant Under-Secretary, to accept the necessity of war, but he knew how reluctant to do so his political colleagues were. Like so many of the leading participants in the crisis, including Bethmann Hollweg, he gave the impression to those who saw him in these days of a man near the end of his nervous resources. The French government on the other hand, once the Russian decision to mobilize had been taken without any objection from France, had fewer choices open to it than the British. By the time the French cabinet met on the afternoon of 30 July, they seem to have been united in expecting war to break out. Military preparations had already started but, mainly in order to impress the British with France's peaceful intentions, the covering troops on the German border were instructed to remain 10 kilometres away from the actual frontier.

Within forty-eight hours, the French freedom of action was further limited by the German declaration of war on Russia. In St Petersburg the German ambassador had been working hard to persuade the Russians to revoke their mobilization measures: the Germans had invoked the principle of monarchical solidarity – a line they had consistently been taking to justify Austrian policy ever since the murder of Franz Ferdinand: they made much of the fact that the Austrians had undertaken not to annex any Serbian territory and suggested that this left room for further negotiations; but it was clear by 1 August that neither Austria nor Russia was prepared to give way. On that afternoon the German government formally declared war on Russia on the grounds that the Russians were not prepared to suspend their military measures directed against Germany and Austria. For France the German declaration of war meant that the provisions of her alliance with Russia obliged her to enter the war; and the government had a fairly clear idea that this would produce an immediate attack by Germany. The French government were above all concerned that the war which now seemed inevitable should find them in as favourable a situation as possible. This entailed first working for British support and second making the Germans appear clearly as the aggressors; and indeed the two aims were very closely linked.

The French government repeatedly reminded the British by all the means at their disposal that they regarded them as morally committed to France, while at the same time stressing – though how convinced they were themselves by the argument it is hard to say – that the only means of averting war was a clear declaration of British support. Late on the evening of 31 July, for instance, a special emissary arrived in London with a personal letter from President Poincaré to King George V which was delivered to the King at noon the next day, and which stated with studied moderation: 'It is, I believe, on the language and attitude of the English Government that the last possibilities of a peaceful solution now depend . . . I am deeply convinced that the more England, France and Russia at the present moment give a strong impression of unity in their diplomatic action, the more it will be legitimate to count on peace being preserved.'[41] But George V's reply was even more non-committal than the communications which Cambon had been receiving from the British government. By 1 August, indeed, Cambon was desperately hoping not only for diplomatic action but also for positive naval and military support. He was using all his personal influence in the circles in London in which he had been a familiar figure since his appointment as ambassador there in 1898. He was to be heard in the clubs asking if the word 'honour' was to be erased from the English dictionary: he complained in despair on 1 August to his old friend Sir Arthur Nicolson, at the moment when Grey was still apparently discussing with Lichnowsky conditions for British neutrality: '*Ils vont nous lâcher.*'[42] In a conversation that evening after the cabinet meeting, Cambon pointed out that France, had, for the sake of public opinion in England, kept her forces 10 kilometres from the frontier. But she had also (as agreed in 1912) concentrated her fleet in the Mediterranean and left her northern coasts exposed. And Grey yet again replied that Britain was under no obligation and that there were 'very grave considerations' involved.[43]

By the next day the air had cleared a little as far as Anglo-French relations were concerned. Grey had given up his approaches to the Germans about terms of neutrality. The Germans had invaded Luxemburg on the grounds that they needed to protect railway communications through the Grand Duchy against possible French attack. There were reports of German violations of the French frontier. It was on that afternoon that the British Cabinet finally reached a decision that 'if the German fleet came into the Channel or through the North Sea to undertake hostile operations against French coasts or shipping, the British fleet will give all the protection in its power'.[44] This was the action implicit in the exchange of letters of 1912, but even so it was still expressed in guarded terms, referring to the necessity of parliamentary approval and remaining non-committal about the despatch of a British

Expeditionary Force to the Continent. Thus even this Cabinet meeting, which one participant looking back later described as 'the Cabinet which decided that war with Germany was inevitable',[45] still had not come to an unequivocal decision. However, they had accepted some responsibility towards France and they had also accepted that a substantial violation of the neutrality of Belgium would constitute grounds for war. These decisions had not been taken unanimously and four members of the Cabinet (Morley, Burns, Simon and Beauchamp) announced their resignation, though two of them (Simon and Beauchamp) subsequently withdrew it.

During the two days of 2 and 3 August rumours were spreading about the actual state of military operations in the west. Both the French and German governments were denouncing each other. There were certainly cases in which patrols from both sides had crossed the border. Reports of other episodes, such as that French aeroplanes had bombarded Nuremberg, were published without verification and were later proved false, though some of them were used by the Germans as an excuse for their final declaration of war on France. The Germans had already drafted the declaration on 1 August, on the grounds that France was not prepared to remain neutral in a German-Russian war, but they had then instructed their ambassador in Paris not to deliver it. There was considerable disagreement in Berlin about the way to handle the outbreak of war with France. Moltke and Tirpitz, State Secretary for the Navy, saw no need for a declaration of war at all and believed that the French would be the first to take formal action. At the same time they believed that delay in the actual declaration of war would give longer time for the carrying out of German mobilization, ordered on 1 August. Bethmann on the other hand was anxious to observe the principles of international law as reaffirmed as recently as the Hague Conference of 1907, by which the opening of hostilities had to be preceded by a formal declaration of war. The French and German orders for general mobilization were issued within a few hours of each other on 1 August, but whereas the French could afford to wait, the Germans had to act in order to make their attack on France through Belgium. Accordingly, as we have seen, the ultimatum to Belgium was presented on the evening of 2 August and expired at 8 a.m. on the 3rd. It was firmly and unanimously rejected by the Belgian government and king, and at the same time they denied German allegations that there was any threat to Belgium from the French. Orders were at once given for the advance of German troops into Belgium. On that same afternoon the German ambassador in Paris was instructed to issue the declaration of war on France. One of the effects of the tension and the speed and number of diplomatic exchanges in these days was that the telegraphic services were becoming overstrained: there were often delays between despatch and delivery: ciphers were garbled in transmission so that the German ambassador

27

to France later wrote that he had to reconstruct the text of the final declaration of war himself and suspected that the original cable had been tampered with by the French. In fact, however, by now it was to the advantage of the French that they should be the passive recipients of a declaration of war by Germany, which had already put itself in the wrong by the threat to Belgium. What was now important for both Germany and France was to present their policies in such a way as to justify the war to their own public and to the neutral countries they were hoping to draw in. The Germans had been able, by stressing that the Russians had been the first to mobilize, to put some of the blame on the Russians even though it had been the Germans who had been the first to declare war. However, the attack on France weakened their position; and the declaration of war on France together with the invasion of Belgium made any further German appeal to England ineffective.

On the morning of 2 August, the British Cabinet had, as we have seen, accepted the necessity of protecting the northern coasts of France. By the evening, at the second Cabinet meeting of the day, they had, faced with the news from the Continent, agreed that a 'substantial' violation of Belgian neutrality would justify war. At their meeting on the morning of 3 August they were still not openly committed to any precise action, but they found that the logic of their decisions on 2 August and the pace of events left them with very little choice. By noon the news of the German ultimatum to Belgium and of Belgium's determination to resist reached London; and at 2 o'clock that afternoon Grey telegraphed to the ambassador in Berlin repeating his request for an assurance from Germany that they would respect Belgian neutrality and asking for a reply by midnight: 'If not, you are instructed to ask for your passports and to say that His Majesty's Government feel bound to take all steps in their power to uphold the neutrality of Belgium and the observance of a Treaty to which Germany is as much a party as ourselves.'[46] This ultimatum expired at midnight on 4 August – though even then hesitations continued and it was not until 6 August that the Cabinet finally agreed to the sending of the British Expeditionary Force to France.

From the start of the crisis, Italy, the ally of Germany and Austria-Hungary, had made it clear that she did not regard the circumstances as requiring her to support Germany and Austria under the terms of her alliance with them. They had not given the Italian government any prior notice of the Austrian ultimatum; and the Italians regarded Austrian action as aggression against Serbia. At the same time, they were already letting it be known to the Austrians that they might be willing to enter the war if Italy were to obtain 'an advantage commensurate with the risk and of a nature to overcome the opposition of public opinion to a war fought in the interests of Austria'.[47] What they had in mind was the Trentino, the Italian-speaking southern part of the

Austrian province of Tyrol, though for the moment they only hinted at this; and in any case at the start of a war fought to restore the image of Austria-Hungary as a Great Power, the Austrians were naturally reluctant to begin by handing over part of their territory to an ally. On 2 August, the Italian government formally declared that Italy would remain neutral: so did Germany's other ally Rumania on 3 August. The diplomacy of the first months of the war was to be devoted to efforts by both sides to win the support of these countries, as well as of Greece and Bulgaria which were still uncommitted.

In the succession of declarations of war from 1 to 4 August, the Austrians were almost overlooked: the final breach with Russia only occurred on 6 August (though the Austrian declaration had been drafted three days before); and it gave as its reasons both the threatening attitude adopted by Russia in the conflict between Austria-Hungary and Serbia and the erroneous assertion that Russia had opened hostilities against Germany. France and Britain declared war on Austria-Hungary on 12 August, rather reluctantly and with expressions of personal esteem and regret from both Grey and the Austrian ambassador. The terms and timing of the actual declarations of war had been largely determined by the efforts of all the governments concerned to present themselves in the best light so as to justify their actions to their citizens; and for the moment they had little difficulty in doing so. Almost everywhere war was accepted not only with resignation but in many cases with enthusiasm. Very few people foresaw what the nature, duration and consequences were likely to be.

It is because the consequences of the July crisis of 1914 were so profound and so prolonged that we tend to be dissatisfied with an explanation of the outbreak of war in terms of the immediate decisions and pronouncements of the politicians and diplomats directly involved. An account such as that just attempted may explain the chronology of events and expound the official actions and statements of members of governments, ambassadors and soldiers, but it cannot explain how they reached a situation in which the decisions they took seemed rational and inevitable, and it certainly does not explain how the public came to accept or even welcome the decision for war. A summary account of the crisis is bound to leave out a great deal (Luigi Albertini in his excellent detailed study *The Origins of the War of 1914* devotes some 1,400 pages to the period between 28 June and 12 August), and cannot convey the complexity and confusion in which the participants were involved, the effects of the strain of those long hot summer days on men often reluctantly summoned back from their country houses or the spas where they were spending their holidays. Then there are a number of dramatic episodes which complicate the picture without in themselves really having any effect. For example, on the evening of 10 July, Baron Hartwig, the Russian minister to Serbia called on his Austrian colleague in order to deny rumours that he had spent the evening of the Archduke's assassination playing bridge and that he had not flown the Russian flag at half-mast on the day of the funeral. He thereupon dropped down dead of a heart attack on the floor of the Austrian legation. Hartwig was given a magnificent funeral by the Serbs; a street was named after him and he immediately became a symbol of anti-Austrian feeling in Serbia and of Russian friendship for the Southern Slav cause. The sudden death of a man who was well known to be one of the inspirers of Serbian policy and the embodiment of Russian sympathies for the Serb cause was bound to cause rumours; and it was symbolic of the state of Austro-Russian relations even before the crisis became acute that Hartwig's daughter at once suggested that her father had been murdered by the Austrians even though it was well known that he had suffered from a serious heart ailment for a long time.

In a crisis such as that of July 1914 individual actions and encounters took on a significance which their actual importance hardly justified. For example, on 26 July the Kaiser's brother, Prince Henry of Prussia, had breakfast with King George V and returned to Berlin apparently convinced that he had been given an assurance of British neutrality, whereas it seems certain that the King had been just as cautious and non-committal as his Foreign Secretary. The only effect of this misunderstanding was to increase the Kaiser's annoyance with the British government. As well as the attempts of the sovereigns to influence the course of the crisis by using their personal and family ties, private individuals, too, sought to avert the catastrophe. On 1 August the old Lord Rothschild sent a personal appeal to the Kaiser, who described him as 'an old and much respected acquaintance of mine. Some 75–80 years old',[48] but the Kaiser's telegram of acknowledgement was never sent as by then the wires were closed. Albert Ballin, the head of the Hamburg-Amerika steamship line, maintained close links with British businessmen and politicians, and, in his hopes of finding a way out of the crisis, may have suggested to members of the British government that there were more differences of opinion within German government circles than there in fact were. Men are reluctant to give up hope; and the optimistic belief that all problems have solutions – the great heritage of the European Enlightenment – had not yet been abandoned.

We who know what happened later can perhaps see which were the crucial decisions in the crisis of July 1914 that determined that any optimism was unfounded. Each of these decisions limited or seemed to limit the freedom of action of the other governments and closed options, not only for those taking the decisions but also for those who were reacting to them. And if we are trying to understand the reasons why the war broke out, we must start at least by looking for the reasons which were given at the time for the choices actually made. Leaving aside the decisions taken before 28 June – for example the decision of

the students of the Young Bosnia movement to assassinate the Archduke, the decision of the Austro-Hungarian authorities to allow the
Archduke to visit Sarajevo, in spite of warnings and his own forebodings, on a day on which the Serbs solemnly commemorated a great
national disaster, their defeat by the Turks in 1389 – we can in the days
after the assassination recognize which were the decisions of particular
importance and consequence. Each of these – the Austrian decision to
take vigorous action against Serbia, the German decision to support
Austria-Hungary, the Serbian decision to reject part of the Austrian
terms, the Russian decision to back Serbia, the British decision to
intervene and, perhaps the most important of all, the decisions to
mobilize by Russia and Germany – all depended on a whole series of
previous decisions, plans, inherited attitudes and assumptions which
we must try to analyse if we are to understand what happened in July
1914. But even if we succeed in doing this, we shall also need to see
what the men of 1914 expected to follow from their decisions, for very
few of them expected the kind of war they actually started and fewer
still realized what the consequences would be. As the Russian
representative in Belgrade warned his Austrian colleague on 22 July,
'We know when and why a war starts but never where it stops.'[49]
General Conrad, the Austro-Hungarian Chief of Staff, admitted as
much when on 6 July he discussed the question of a war against Serbia
with Count Berchtold, the Foreign Minister, and Berchtold expressed
some anxiety that their German allies might want to know what would
happen after such a war: 'Then you must say', Conrad replied, 'that we
ourselves didn't know.'[50] Again, many of the responsible leaders
during the crisis, and especially the German Chancellor, Bethmann
Hollweg expressed the feeling that they were the victims of forces
stronger than themselves: 'I see a doom greater than human power
hanging over Europe and our own people.'[51] And Sazonov, the
Russian Foreign Minister told the Italian ambassador on 25 July that
he feared '*d'être débordé dans cette affaire*'.[52] Sir Edward Grey expressed the same sense of helplessness when he made his celebrated
remark as he looked out of the Foreign Office windows at dusk on 3
August: 'The lamps are going out all over Europe. We shall not see
them lit again in our lifetime.'[53]

This sense that men were carried away by the tide of history tempts
us to look for historical forces which will explain the decisions of
individuals as part of a broader and inevitable historical process, or at
least as part of a wider landscape than that provided by the view from
the chancelleries of Europe. The problem of relating these broader
explanations to the individual decisions taken in July 1914 remains a
major historiographical and philosophical problem which may indeed
be insoluble. However, in the following chapters we will try to look at
some of the explanations which have been suggested for the outbreak
of the First World War and to see how far these can be directly related

to the decisions taken in the immediate crisis which we have been discussing.

REFERENCES AND NOTES

1. The phrase was used by Count Taaffe. See e.g. Oscar Jaszi, *The Dissolution of the Habsburg Monarchy* (Chicago 1961) p. 115.
2. Karl Kautsky, Graf Max Montgelas and Prof. Walter Schücking (eds) *Die deutschen Dokumente zum Kriegausbruch*, Vol. I (Charlottenburg 1919) No. 50, p. 78. (Hereinafter referred to as *DD.*)
3. O. Hoetsch (ed.) *Die internationalen Beziehungen im Zeitalter des Imperialismus. Dokumente aus den Archiven der Zaristischen und der Provisorischen Regierung*, 5 vols (Berlin 1931–34) 1st series, Vol. IV, No. 245. (Hereinafter referred to as *Int. Bez.*) See L. Albertini, *The Origins of the War of 1914*, Vol. II (London 1953) p. 184.
4. Baron Schilling, *How the War began in 1914* (London 1925) pp. 28–9. See also Albertini, op. cit., Vol. III, p. 290.
5. G. P. Gooch and Harold Temperley (eds) *British Documents on the Origin of War 1898–1914*, Vol. XI (London 1926) No. 91, p. 73. (Hereinafter referred to as *BD.*)
6. *Int. Bez.* 1st series, V, No. 37; Albertini, op. cit., Vol. II, p. 350.
7. *Oesterreich-Ungarns Aussenpolitik von der Bosnischen Krise 1908 bis zum Kriegsausbruch 1914*, Vol. VIII (Vienna 1930) No. 10616, p. 646. (Hereinafter referred to as *OeD.*)
8. See Gale Stokes, 'The Serbian documents from 1914: a preview', Supplement to the *Journal of Modern History*, **48**, No. 3, Sept. 1976.
9. *DD* I, No. 49, p. 74.
10. *DD* IV, Appendix IV, No. 2, p. 127.
11. *BD* XI, No. 86, p. 70.
12. *BD* XI, No. 98, p. 77.
13. *BD* XI, No. 140, p. 101.
14. *OeD* VIII, No. 10648.
15. *DD* II, No. 342, p. 59.
16. *DD* II, No. 335, p. 51.
17. *DD* I, No. 258, p. 250.
18. *DD* II, No. 293, p. 18.
19. Feldmarschall Franz Conrad von Hötzendorf, *Aus meiner Dienstzeit 1906–1918*, Vol. IV (Vienna 1923) p. 153.
20. *BD* XI, No. 264, p. 171.
21. *BD* XI, No. 125, p. 94.
22. *BD* XI, No. 318, p. 200.
23. *BD* XI, No. 283, p. 180.
24. *BD* XI, No. 293, p. 186.
25. *BD* XI, No. 303, p. 193.
26. Herbert Samuel, quoted in Michael G. Ekstein and Zara Steiner, 'The Sarajevo crisis' in F. H. Hinsley (ed.) *British Foreign Policy under Sir Edward Grey* (Cambridge 1977) p. 401.

27. Asquith to King George V, quoted in Ekstein and Steiner, op. cit., p. 404.
28. *BD* XI, No. 426, p. 253.
29. *DD* III, No. 490, p. 9.
30. *DD* II, No. 456, pp. 177–8.
31. Helmut von Moltke, *Erinnerungen, Dokumente, Briefe 1877–1916* (Stuttgart 1922) pp. 19–21.
32. *BD* XI, No. 419, p. 250.
33. *BD* XI, No. 453, p. 263.
34. *BD* XI, No. 425, p. 252.
35. *BD* XI, No. 243, p. 160.
36. *BD* XI, No. 448, p. 261.
37. *BD* XI, No. 369, p. 228.
38. Quoted in Ekstein and Steiner, op. cit., p. 405.
39. *Documents diplomatiques français 1871–1914*, III série, Vol. XI (Paris 1936) No. 305, p. 263. (Hereinafter referred to as *DDF.*)
40. *BD* XI, No. 319, p.201.
41. Raymond Poincaré, *Au Service de la France: Neuf Années de Souvenirs*, Vol. IV (Paris 1927) pp. 438–40.
42. Harold Nicolson, *Sir Arthur Nicolson, Bart. First Lord Carnock: A Study in the Old Diplomacy* (London 1930) p. 419.
43. *BD* XI, No. 447, p. 260.
44. *BD* XI, No. 487, p. 274.
45. Walter Runciman, quoted in Cameron Hazlehurst, *Politicians and War* (London 1971) p. 93.
46. *BD* XI, No. 594, p. 314.
47. Quoted in Albertini, op. cit., Vol. II, p. 316.
48. *DD* III, No. 580, p. 77.
49. *OeD*, Vol. VIII, No. 10688.
50. Conrad, op. cit., Vol. IV, p. 40.
51. Kurt Riezler, *Tagebücher, Aufsätze, Dokumente* (Göttingen 1972) p. 192.
52. *OeD* VIII, No. 10688.
53. Viscount Grey of Fallodon, *Twenty-five Years 1892–1916* (London 1925) Vol. II, p. 20.

Chapter 3

THE ALLIANCE SYSTEM AND THE OLD DIPLOMACY

The Prussian victory over France in 1870 and the creation of the German Empire led to a change in the balance of power in Europe and to an international system in which Germany, by now the strongest military power on the Continent and one with large and expanding industrial resources, necessarily played a leading role. Consequently the methods of conducting international relations and the basic structure of international alignments were to a large extent those devised by Bismarck to meet Germany's needs in the 1870s and 1880s. Bismarck's name has become associated also with a particular style of diplomacy – an unprincipled and unscrupulous *Realpolitik*. 'It is the lees left by Bismarck that still foul the cup', Sir Edward Grey wrote in December 1906, and he accused German diplomacy of 'deliberate attempts to make mischief between other countries by saying poisoned things to one about the other'.[1] This is perhaps unfair: as A. J. P. Taylor has pointed out, Bismarck was no worse in this respect than some other nineteenth-century statesmen, notably Napoleon III.[2] But it was Bismarck who seemed to contemporaries and to subsequent historians to be the great master of diplomatic intrigue, bluffing and frightening the ambassadors and foreign ministers of other countries into doing his will, sometimes by a calculated indiscretion, as when in 1887 he read out to the Russian ambassador the exact text of Germany's alliance with Austria in order to persuade the Russians to agree to a 're-insurance' treaty with Germany which would guarantee Russian neutrality in the event of a Franco-German war without committing Germany to anything specific in return. On other occasions, he could accept the failure of his bluff with a certain bonhomie: 'All I can say is: consider carefully what you do', Bismarck said to the Austro-Hungarian Foreign Minister during the negotiations for the alliance between Germany and Austria-Hungary in 1879. 'For the last time I advise you to give up your opposition. Accept my proposal, or else . . . or else I shall have to accept yours.'[3] More serious, however, than the actual methods by which Bismarck conducted diplomacy was the underlying assumption that all international negotiations and all international undertakings were to be interpreted in terms of national interest, so that *raison d'état* could always provide an excuse for going back on international commitments. Bismarck believed that Austria and Prussia were states too great to be bound by the texts of treaties. No agreement could be expected to last for ever; and, as Bismarck put it, all treaties should contain the phrase *rebus sic stantibus*. Lord Salisbury's views were much the same: at the end of his life he wrote on the question of Belgian neutrality: 'Our treaty obligations will follow from our national inclinations and will not precede them.'[4]

The details of the alliance treaties and other international agreements were in many cases kept secret and were only published in full after the war; and, as even those which were published contained secret clauses, they were often believed to contain more than they actually did. Bismarck's 'Reinsurance Treaty' with Russia in 1887 was concluded without the knowledge of Germany's ally Austria-Hungary, and it was Bismarck himself in embittered retirement who revealed its existence and the fact that his successor Caprivi had not renewed it. The details – as opposed to the existence – of the Triple Alliance between Germany, Austria and Italy were learnt partially in 1915 when Italy declared war on her former allies, but were not published completely until 1920. Speculation about secret agreements and hidden commitments was encouraged by the press. The famous journalists – Sir Valentine Chirol of *The Times* or Theodor Wolff of the *Berliner Tageblatt* for example – and editors, in an age when the popular press was beginning to be regarded as a power which governments had to take into account, were on friendly terms with members of governments and were often used as a channel for deliberate disclosures; and this in turn encouraged further speculations. In France at least one Foreign Minister, Stephen Pichon, had been a journalist and returned to the profession on leaving office in 1911. 'The diplomacy of nations', the British Prime Minister Lord Salisbury wrote resignedly 'is now conducted as much in the letters of foreign correspondents as in the despatches of the Foreign Office.'[5]

If newspapermen were fishing for sensational disclosures, governments too were as anxious to find out the secrets of other foreign ministries as they were to discover details of military plans. The French Foreign Ministry had maintained, with brief interruptions, a *cabinet noir* since the time of Richelieu, a secret office which worked to break the diplomatic ciphers of other governments, and which from the 1880s was regularly doing so.[6] The Germans had a spy in the Russian embassy in London in 1914 who gave them information about – and seems to have exaggerated the importance of – the inconclusive naval talks between the British and Russian admiralties in June 1914; and this information strengthened the Germans' conviction that their opponents were tightening a ring around Germany and that it would be better to break out of this encirclement sooner rather than later. The secrecy of diplomatic agreements as well as of military plans encouraged the powers to spend money and energy on developing their secret services; but documentation is fragmentary and it was only when espionage started political scandals, of which the most famous is the Dreyfus affair in France, that something of these activities came to light.

Liberals and radicals all over Europe, but especially in England, denounced the secrecy of diplomatic methods, while at the same time the belief was spread by many diplomats that theirs was an arcane profession which no outsider was qualified to understand and whose members must come from a particular class or caste. As one senior British Foreign Office official put it in 1914:

> I think your Board of Selection will generally take what one may call perhaps one type of man, because he is the type of man who is fit for this international career called diplomacy. All . . . , speaking metaphorically, speak the same language; they have the same habits of thought, and more or less the same points of view, and if anybody with a different language came in, I think he would be treated by the whole diplomatic service more or less with suspicion.[7]

Whether international relations would have been more successfully conducted if the diplomats had been recruited from a less exclusive class or whether international tension would have been lessened by exposing diplomatic negotiations to full publicity or to close control by parliaments is very doubtful; but there is no doubt that the practitioners of what after the war came to be called the 'old diplomacy' contributed to the belief that there was always more to every international negotiation than met the eye.

With treaties of alliance often negotiated in an atmosphere of distrust and with many unspoken reservations on all sides, why were they considered important and what effect did these formal agreements have on the policies of the states involved? In what way can it be said that the existence of the systems of alliances contributed to causing the outbreak of war in 1914? The theory, if that is not too grand a term, by which contemporaries justified the alliance system was that it would maintain the balance of power. This phrase, which had been common in diplomatic language since the eighteenth century, could be interpreted both as an objective assessment of the actual military and economic strength of the powers and as a subjective evaluation by statesmen of where their own national interest lay. The idea was expressed by Sir Eyre Crowe of the British Foreign Office in a famous memorandum of 1907 as follows: 'The only check on the abuse of political predominance has always consisted in the opposition of an equally formidable rival, or of a combination of several countries forming leagues of defence. The equilibrium established by such grouping of forces is technically known as the balance of power.'[8] Bismarck, whose diplomacy after the achievement of German unification aimed at maintaining the balance of power in Germany's favour, put it more succinctly and with his usual realism: 'All politics reduces itself to this formula: Try to be *à trois* as long as the world is governed by the unstable equilibrium of five Great Powers.'[9] Many statesmen and diplomats believed that the maintenance of the balance of power would itself prevent war by deterring an aggressor, either directly or by providing machinery by which, as Bismarck himself believed, one power could control its allies and stop them doing anything to upset the balance.

This aspect of the theory of the balance of power was expressed in a leading article in *The Times* in April 1914 as follows:

> The division of the Great Powers into two well-balanced groups with intimate relations between the members of each, which do not forbid any such member from being on the friendliest terms with one or more members of the other, is a twofold check upon inordinate ambitions or sudden outbreak of race hatred. All Sovereigns and statesmen – aye, and all nations – know that a war of group against group would be a measureless calamity. That knowledge brings with it a sense of responsibility which chastens and restrains the boldest and most reckless. But they know, too, that to secure the support of the other members of their own group and to induce them to share the responsibility and risks of such conflict, any Power or Powers which may meditate recourse to arms must first satisfy those other members that the quarrel is necessary and just. They are no longer unfettered judges in their own cause, answerable to none but themselves.[10]

It was this system that broke down in 1914 when it became clear that the balance of power was not a built-in regulator of the international system and that the division of Europe into rival alliance systems would not necessarily work as beneficently as the editor of *The Times* hoped.

The two treaties of alliance which were of central importance in the July crisis of 1914 were the German–Austrian treaty which had been signed in 1879 and the Franco–Russian alliance of 1893. Italy had joined the German–Austrian alliance in 1882, so that it was known as the Triple Alliance; and it had been renewed as recently as 1912. These were formal alliances, but equally important were the less formal *ententes* reached between England and France in 1904 and England and Russia in 1907. If we look at the circumstances in which these various agreements were negotiated and the situations which they were intended to meet, we can see how in fact their nature changed over the years. At the same time, the fact of their existence led other countries to frame their own policies in accordance with what seemed to be the permanent alignments with which they might be confronted in a war. Thus both political expectations and military plans were conditioned by the existence of the alliance system and strengthened the divisions which the alliances themselves tended to produce.

The German–Austrian alliance had by 1914 changed its emphasis significantly since it was first negotiated by Bismarck in 1879. In the diplomatic circumstances of that year, when Russia was still suffering from what the Panslav publicists regarded as the humiliation inflicted by the other powers at the Congress of Berlin in 1878, Bismarck believed that an alliance with Austria-Hungary would have the effect of deterring Russia from any action against Germany, and that it would therefore sooner or later force Russia to seek improved relations with Germany – as indeed happened in 1881 and again in 1887. But Bismarck also always regarded the alliance as a means of restraining Austrian policy in the Balkans and of avoiding a situation in which Germany would be drawn by Austria into a war with Russia to defend Austro-Hungarian interests in south-east Europe. The alliance was therefore in Bismarck's mind an element of stability in Europe since it would both alarm Russia sufficiently to make her want better relations with Germany and also provide Germany with the power to control Austrian policy towards her Slav neighbours.

For Austria-Hungary the German alliance meant an additional guarantee of the Empire's stability. At least since 1815, the survival of the Habsburg monarchy had depended to a large extent on convincing the other Great Powers that Austria was an essential element in the European balance of power which they could not afford to allow to disappear. Moreover, there was also among the German-speaking inhabitants of Austria a sense of relief that the alliance meant an end to the fatal division between Prussia and Austria which had resulted from the war of 1866. The formal diplomatic terms of the alliance were reinforced by an emotional feeling that Germany and Austria were now bound together in a community of fate, a *Schicksalsgemeinschaft*. Thus the alliance met not only immediate diplomatic requirements but also an emotional need among many people in both countries at a time when, as never before, the public – or at least the press – responded immediately to diplomatic moves, so that treaties could acquire a significance with which their actual contents had little to do. The fact that an alliance existed was more important than its exact terms, precise details of which were still kept secret. The essential part of the German–Austrian alliance was in fact an agreement that if either were attacked by Russia, each would support the other 'with the whole strength of their empires'.

In Bismarck's day, then, both the Germans and Austrians had regarded the alliance as a way of ensuring stability; and indeed, as we have seen, Bismarck revealed the terms to the Russian ambassador in 1887 when he was hoping to maintain that stability by persuading the Russians to sign a treaty with Germany. But by the time this 'Re-insurance Treaty' became due for renewal in 1894 Bismarck had fallen from power and the international situation had changed fundamentally by the signature in August 1892 of a military agreement between France and Russia which was converted into a full alliance in the following year.

A *rapprochement* between France and Russia, in spite of the differences of political system between the Third Republic and the Tsarist
autocracy had been a logical consequence of the new balance of power
established in 1870. As Karl Marx had put it at the time of the
Franco-Prussian War, 'If Alsace and Lorraine are taken, then France
will later make war on Germany in conjunction with Russia.'[11] The
annexation by Germany of the two French provinces meant that there
could be in the long run no reconciliation between France and
Germany; and although at some moments the French government and
public temporarily forgot about the lost provinces, the hope of recovering them was always likely to ensure that in a European war
France would join the side opposed to Germany.

The advantages for Russia of a French alliance seemed clear: it
would give the Russians a freer hand in south-east Europe. Faced with
the possibility of a war on two fronts, Germany would be less likely to
back Austria-Hungary in a conflict with Russia and so Austria would
not be able to resist Russia's moves. The alliance would also give, it
was hoped, security for Russia in Europe while the Tsar's government
was engaged in vast operations to extend control across Siberia to the
Pacific. (The decision to construct the Trans-Siberian Railway was
taken in 1891.) But, independently of these strategic and diplomatic
considerations, closer financial links between France and Russia were
developing, from 1887 onwards, which were to give the Franco-
Russian alliance a firmer popular base than most other diplomatic
alignments of the period. The Russian government needed foreign
capital, not only for investment in its expanding industries and growing
transport system, but also to carry out a major conversion of Russian
government stock in order to rationalize and economize. French
bankers were interested in expanding their share of the Russian money
market and conducted active campaigns to sell Russian bonds to small
savers in France, to which the French middle classes responded enthusiastically. Although the French government had not expected or
intended that these loans would supply an essential element of support
for a military and diplomatic alliance, this turned out to be the case;
and the interest in Russia which the promotion of these sales had
aroused helped to prepare the way for the popular success of the visit
of the French fleet to Russia in 1891 and that of the Russian Navy to
Toulon in 1893. Bismarck, too, contributed to these developments. He
never showed much awareness of the wider political significance of
international financial links; and in November 1887 he banned the sale
of Russian bonds on the Berlin Stock Exchange because he was
annoyed with the Russian government for imposing a tax on foreign
owners of estates in Russia, a measure which affected important
members of the German aristocracy who owned properties on both
sides of the border between Russia and Prussia. Thus Bismarck unwit-
tingly encouraged Russia to turn to Paris in its search for funds.

It was, however, the military leaders in France and Russia who were most anxious to reach agreement. There had been some contact between them going back to 1870, and it was as a military instrument that the alliance was primarily regarded. The agreement negotiated in 1892 and ratified during the winter of 1893–94 laid down: 'If France is attacked by Germany or by Italy supported by Germany, Russia will use all her available forces to attack Germany. If Russia is attacked by Germany or by Austria supported by Germany, France will use all available forces to attack Germany. . . . ' By the mid-1890s the existence though not the precise terms of the alliance were widely known. The Dual Alliance of France and Russia was seen as confronting the Triple Alliance of Germany, Austria-Hungary and Italy. The immediate consequence of this confrontation was that the German General Staff at once began to make plans for a war on two fronts, but for the moment this still seemed a remote possibility. The Russians were preoccupied with their expansion across Asia: the Austrians were anxious for a period of calm while they tried to damp down the national tensions within the Monarchy: the French for the moment were more preoccupied with imperial rivalries in Africa and south-east Asia than with the question of Alsace-Lorraine; and the Germans under William II were eagerly looking for ways of asserting their position as a potential world power, and in 1897 took the first steps towards creating a large navy.

Throughout the 1890s the imperialist activities and interests of all the powers except Austria cut across the lines which the Triple and Dual alliances seemed to be establishing. In the Far East, the French and Russians were prepared in 1895 to work with the Germans to impose a settlement at the end of the war between Japan and China. In 1901 the French were even ready to send a contingent to an international force under the command of a German general to put down the Chinese nationalists (the 'Boxers') who seemed to be threatening the privileged position of Europeans in China. For the French in Africa and the Russians in the Far East, England seemed a more immediate rival than Germany.

At the same time it was the problems caused by her imperial commitments which brought England, gradually and unintentionally, into the European alliance system. Until the late 1890s, British governments had refused to consider any formal alliances with other powers. They had ignored suggestions by Bismarck for a closer association with his international system, limiting themselves to the so-called Mediterranean agreements of 1887, which remained secret and which did little more than declare England's already well-known interest in the stability of the eastern Mediterranean area and promise consultation and possible joint action with Austria and Italy in time of crisis. By 1900, however, after several years of cold war against the French in Africa, and faced by what was seen as a Russian threat to British influence in

China, the British also found themselves involved in the war against the Boer republics in South Africa. The strains of acquiring and running a world-wide empire were beginning to tell. Some British leaders, notably Joseph Chamberlain, the Colonial Secretary, were beginning to think that Britain might have to abandon the policy of isolation.

> All the powerful States of Europe have made alliances, Chamberlain said in May 1898: and as long as we keep outside these alliances, as long as we are envied by all, and as long as we have interests which at one time or another conflict with the interests of all, we are likely to be confronted at any moment with a combination of Great Powers so powerful that not even the most extreme, the most hotheaded politician would be able to contemplate it without a certain sense of uneasiness.[12]

There were indeed discussions in 1898 and again in 1901 about the possibility of an Anglo-German alliance, but the interests of both sides were too far apart. The British wanted diplomatic support against Russia in the Far East: the Germans wanted British help, or at least benevolent neutrality, in a possible war in Europe. Lord Salisbury, the British Prime Minister, in his last major foreign policy decision before his retirement, put a stop to these discussions in May 1901, with the words, 'This is a proposal for including England within the bounds of the Triple Alliance.' And he went on to talk of British isolation:

> Have we ever felt that danger [of isolation] practically? If we had suc-cumbed in the revolutionary war, our fall would not have been due to our isolation. We had many allies, but they would not have saved us if the French Emperor had been able to cross the Channel. Except during his reign, we have never been in danger and therefore, it is impossible for us to judge whether the 'isolation' under which we are supposed to suffer, does or does not contain in it any elements of peril. It would hardly be wise to incur novel and most onerous obligations, in order to guard against a danger in whose existence we have no historical reason for believing.[13]

But although British politicians continued to talk as if Britain could avoid continental commitments, they were, sometimes almost without realizing it, becoming increasingly involved in the alignments of the European powers. Britain's immediate need for diplomatic support in the Far East seemed in fact to be satisfied by an alliance with Japan, signed in January 1902. This was Britain's first formal move away from isolation, but it was one which seemed at the time to have few implica-tions for policy in Europe and to be limited to the Far East.

It was of course, or so it seems now, the Anglo-French *Entente* of April 1904 which marked a real turning-point in British policy – and indeed 'un grand tournant de la politique mondiale' as the head of the political division of the French Ministry of Foreign Affairs was later to describe it.[14] Yet this is not how it seemed at the time, and the agreement was another of those international arrangements which gradually changed into something different from what the people who had originally made them envisaged. Throughout the 1890s the British and French had been quarrelling over their colonial differences in West Africa, on the upper Nile and in Siam. In 1898 the crisis at Fashoda on the upper Nile, when a small French force had confronted a British army which had just re-established control over the Sudan, had led to talk of war between the two countries, and the British Channel Fleet was sent to the Mediterranean. At the same time, Théophile Delcassé, the new French Foreign Minister and the architect of French foreign policy until 1905, realized that France's ally Russia was not prepared to help her against England in Africa and that, with France in the midst of the domestic political crisis caused by the Dreyfus case, a direct confrontation with England would have to be avoided. Gradually – and reluctantly, because he had been closely involved with the anti-British colonial party in France – Delcassé came to realize that there might be advantages for France in a colonial deal with England. The basis for such a deal was provided by the fact that the French were hoping to extend their North African empire by gaining control over Morocco, while the British, who had been in occupation of Egypt since 1882, wanted to consolidate their position there and to carry out a reform of the Egyptian finances, a step for which French approval would be essential since the French occupied a key position in the *Caisse de la Dette*, the international commission responsible for supervising Egypt's financial affairs.

The Anglo-French agreement of 1904 was therefore essentially a settlement of outstanding colonial differences aimed at strengthening France's hand in an attempt to win Morocco and at confirming Britain's position in Egypt. There was also an agreement to leave Siam as an independent buffer state between French Indo-China and the British possessions in Burma. Small territorial adjustments were made in Africa; and a dispute about fishing rights off Canada which had lasted for nearly 200 years was settled. But this hard bargaining about specific points of dispute outside Europe has a different significance when it is seen against the changes which had taken place in the general international scene in the previous ten years.

By 1904 the British government had begun to realize that the creation of a large German navy might pose a serious threat to Britain's position as a world power. Whereas only a few years before it had seemed that England and Germany had no serious differences and that a formal alliance between them might be a subject for discussion, by 1904 many people in England believed that Germany was becoming a serious rival: in March 1903 the Admiralty with this in mind decided to create a North Sea fleet and to construct a base for it at Rosyth on the east coast of Scotland. Thus, although the agreement with France was strictly limited to a settlement of colonial differences, old and new, the changing position and policies of Germany were at the back of the

minds of both the French and British statesmen involved in the negotiations. Although Delcassé, in a moment of irritation after the French
withdrawal from Fashoda, had considered seeking German help
against Britain in Africa, he had by 1903 come round to the idea that
both France's ambitions in Morocco and her position in relation to
Germany could be best served by an agreement with England. At the
same time, important sectors of French opinion in commercial circles
and the press, which during the South African war had been uniformly
hostile to England, now began to welcome the idea of better relations
between the two countries; and so the successful visits of King Edward
VII to Paris in May 1903 and of President Loubet to London in July
seemed to be symbols of a new and improved climate of opinion in
both countries.

It was, however, the German government which was responsible for
the rapid development of the *Entente Cordiale* into something which,
though never becoming a formal alliance, seemed to be moving in that
direction. The presupposition of German diplomacy since the 1890s
had been that the imperial rivalries between Britain and France and
Britain and Russia were so deep that they could never be overcome,
and so Britain would sooner or later be obliged by the pressures of
power politics to seek an alliance with Germany on Germany's terms.
For this reason the German Foreign Ministry had not been too disappointed by the failure of the discussions about an alliance in 1898
and 1901. Time, the Germans believed, was on their side. The conclusion of the Anglo-French agreement in 1904 did little to shake this
belief. The German Foreign Ministry still believed that Anglo-French
differences were insuperable and that any *rapprochement* was bound
to be a superficial one which could easily be broken. Between 1904 and
1906 the Germans were trying to test the *Entente* and to demonstrate
its hollowness. At first it appeared indeed that France's existing
alliance with Russia might conflict with her new friendship with
Britain.

A few weeks before the signature of the *Entente*, war had broken out
in the Far East between Japan and Russia. It was an incidental episode
in this war which provided the first test of the Anglo-French *Entente*.
The Russian fleet, on its way from the Baltic to the Far East shot at and
sank some British fishing-boats on the Dogger Bank in the North Sea,
apparently mistaking them for Japanese submarines. There was a
moment of violent anti-Russian feeling in Britain, and the German
government suggested to the Russians that now was the moment to
form a continental league against England, which it was hoped the
French might also join. But Delcassé refused to choose between
France's ally Russia and her new friend England, and he used all his
diplomatic skill to mediate between England and Russia and to persuade the Russians to hold the enquiry and give the compensation the
British government was demanding. However, it was over Morocco –

an area specifically covered in the Anglo-French agreement – that the most serious test of the *Entente Cordiale* came, a test which the Germans had hoped would weaken the *Entente* but which only had the result of strengthening it. In March 1905, the Kaiser, who was on a Mediterranean cruise, was, somewhat against his will, persuaded by his foreign ministry to land at Tangier and, in an obvious criticism of French ambitions in Morocco, declare that he was visiting an independent sovereign state and that Germany demanded equal treatment for her commerce there. The effect was to produce the most acute crisis between France and Germany for nearly twenty years; and there was much talk of the possibility of a war. The result was that the British and French were obliged to think a little more closely about the implications of the agreement of the previous year. It is still not clear exactly what was said in the talks in the spring of 1905 between Lord Lansdowne, the British Foreign Secretary and Paul Cambon, the French ambassador in London, or between Delcassé and Sir Francis Bertie, the British ambassador in Paris, since Delcassé seems to have given his colleagues in the French cabinet the impression that the British had offered an offensive and defensive alliance, while the British were convinced that all they had promised was that the two governments would confer together to discuss what steps might be taken to meet any German threat. If Delcassé hoped to bluff his colleagues into adopting a tougher line with the Germans over Morocco by hinting at the promise of an English alliance, he failed, for by now Rouvier, the Prime Minister, was alarmed by the seriousness of German intentions and worried that France might be embroiled with Germany because of the British wish to ensure that the Germans did not gain a naval base on the Atlantic coast of Morocco – a sign of the way in which the new Anglo-German naval rivalry was beginning to affect Britain's position with regard to the Franco-German rivalry in Morocco in which up till then England had had little interest. Delcassé found himself isolated in the cabinet and was forced to resign.

There was, however, little change in French policy after Delcassé's resignation. The crisis was eventually resolved by an international conference held at the Spanish port of Algeciras in January 1906. It was, however, in the course of the Moroccan crisis that the first military staff talks were held between representatives of the British and French armies. The military implications will be discussed in Chapter 4. Here the important thing to note is that within two years of signing the agreement of April 1904, plans were being made for common military action against Germany so that, however much the British government protested that the staff talks were unofficial and implied no commitment, nevertheless some moral obligations were being assumed, and the *Entente* was already something much closer than the original settlement of outstanding colonial differences had implied. When the Conservative government fell in December 1905 and was succeeded by the Liberals, Sir Edward Grey, the new Foreign Secretary made it clear that the change of government would involve no change in foreign policy. He also accepted that there was a moral aspect to the agreement with France. He wrote in February 1906:

> If there is a war between France and Germany, it will be very difficult for us to keep out of it. The *Entente* and still more the constant and emphatic demonstrations of affection (official, naval, political, commercial and in the Press) have created in France a belief that we shall support them in war . . . If this expectation is disappointed, the French will never forgive us. There would also I think be a general feeling that we had behaved badly and left France in the lurch . . . On the other hand the prospect of a European war and of our being involved in it is horrible. [15]

At the same time, he allowed the unofficial talks between the War Office and the French military attaché to continue.

The crisis over Morocco died down after the Algeciras conference; and although France's influence in Morocco was confirmed at the conference and Germany suffered a diplomatic defeat, nevertheless the two countries were able to co-operate in various economic enterprises over the next few years and it was not until 1911 that their rivalry in Morocco led to a second acute crisis. But the consolidation of the Anglo-French *Entente* continued, though perhaps not as fast as some of the French leaders would have liked. In 1907 the apparent division of Europe into two rival camps was carried a stage further. On 31 August 1907 the British and Russian governments signed an agreement which was intended to settle old differences between them on the borders between their two empires, particularly in Persia, Afghanistan and Tibet. For more than ten years there had been people in the British Foreign Office who believed that it would be possible to achieve an agreement based on mutual recognition of spheres of influence and that this would be preferable to risking a major confrontation as a result of the escalation of minor incidents. There had been some discussions in 1903, but the outbreak of war in the Far East impeded their progress. However, the defeat by Japan made the Russian government anxious to improve relations with England, and at the same time Isvolsky, the new Russian Foreign Minister, was hoping that he might win British support for a revision in Russia's favour of the international regulations closing the exit from the Black Sea in time of war.

For Britain, the agreement was based on a more explicit realization than in 1904 that Germany was now a growing potential even if not immediate threat to British interests. 'An *entente* between Russia, France and ourselves', Grey wrote on 20 February 1906, 'would be absolutely secure. If it is necessary to check Germany it could then be done.' [16] It was also assumed that by now Germany might be a greater danger than Russia. Consequently there had to be a thorough reassessment of Britain's position in the Middle East and India. The demands of the military commanders in India that the army there should be strengthened to meet a threat from Russia were finally rejected, and it was now realized that Germany was likely to be England's main rival.

The Russians, although they knew that British consent would be essential to any attempt to revise the agreements about Constantinople and the Straits, were anxious if possible to avoid antagonizing Germany and were by no means as yet committed to challenging her, as they had still not recovered from the military, economic and political strains resulting from the defeat by Japan. The agreement with Britain remained for them primarily one which would strengthen their hold on their Asiatic empire without fear of British interference – even though in fact disagreements about Persia and the Far East never completely disappeared. The agreement, however, also gave the Russians hopes of British support for their aspirations in the Balkans. Within little more than a year it became clear that the satisfaction of these aspirations was bound to lead to a confrontation with Germany.

During the fifteen years after Bismarck's fall, the alliance between Germany and Austria-Hungary had been, so to speak, a passive factor in international relations, something which was taken for granted but which did not involve any positive action. The problems of south-east Europe and the future of the Ottoman Empire were temporarily less important than the imperial rivalries of the powers outside Europe, rivalries in which Austria-Hungary was not involved. As a result, with the Russian government concentrating on its expansion in the Far East, the crises in Turkey caused by the massacre of the Armenians in 1894–96, the revolt in Crete in 1897 and the war between Turkey and Greece which resulted from it did not cause a conflict between the Great Powers and could even lead to co-operation between them. After 1905 the situation was changing. The Moroccan crisis and the conference of Algeciras had shown the Germans that their alliance with Austria was all that stood between them and complete diplomatic isolation, since Austria alone gave them any support over the Moroccan question: the Kaiser, with characteristic tactlessness, had thanked the Emperor Franz Joseph by referring to his 'brillanten Sekundantendienst' (brilliant services as a second). The maintenance of Austria-Hungary as a Great Power became a major foreign policy goal for Germany, both on diplomatic grounds, since Austria was seen as Germany's only reliable ally, and because any internal crisis in Austria-Hungary might have repercussions in Germany. In 1906, as a result of a constitutional crisis over the relations of Hungary with the rest of the Monarchy, there was much talk of an impending dissolution of the Empire, so that the German Chancellor wrote to German representatives abroad, pointing out that it would in such an event be dangerous for Germany if the German-speaking Austrians were to become part of Germany:

We shall thereby receive an increase of about fifteen million Catholics so that the Protestants would become a minority . . . the proportion of strength between the Protestants and the Catholics would become similar to that which at the time led to the Thirty Years War, i.e. a virtual dissolution of the German empire . . . [the question] compels attention whether the German Reich, today so well balanced and therefore standing so strong and powerful ought to let itself be brought into such a horrible position. In the interests of the preservation of a powerful Germany this question must unconditionally be answered in the negative.[17]

The conclusion was that the Austrian Empire must somehow be preserved at all costs.

In 1908 the implications of the German–Austrian alliance became clearer. The internal crisis in the Ottoman Empire caused by the Young Turk revolution once more raised the question of the future of the Turkish possessions in Europe: and the Austro-Hungarian Foreign Minister Aehrenthal decided that this was an opportunity for the Monarchy to annex the two provinces of Bosnia and Herzegovina which Austria had occupied since 1878, but which were still formally under Turkish suzerainty. Aehrenthal was convinced that a vigorous foreign policy was one way out of the problems caused by the aspirations of the subject nationalities within the Monarchy and that the incorporation of the two provinces would be a blow to Serb ambitions to make Serbia 'the Piedmont of the Southern Slavs', to serve, that is, as a focus for the unrest among the Serbs and Croats inside Austria-Hungary. Aehrenthal also seems to have believed that a bold initiative would demonstrate that Austria was not wholly dependent on her German ally – and indeed the Kaiser was understandably irritated at learning of the annexation of Bosnia and Herzegovina from the newspaper. The result was in fact to demonstrate both Austria's dependence on Germany and also the extent to which initiative within the alliance had passed to Austria.

The Russian Foreign Minister, Isvolsky, who was hoping to restore Russia's international position by gains in the Balkans and at the Straits, had secretly agreed with Aehrenthal to accept the Austrian move on the understanding that Austria would support Russia's demands for a revision of the treaties governing the closure of the Bosphorus and Dardanelles. However Aehrenthal had announced the annexation before Isvolsky had had time to muster diplomatic support in the other capitals of Europe. Isvolsky was extremely indignant and felt, rightly or wrongly, personally betrayed by Aehrenthal. Relations between the two empires became very strained and there was talk of war. The result was an unequivocal declaration by the German Chief of Staff, Moltke, to his Austro-Hungarian counterpart Conrad von Hötzendorf that, 'The moment Russia mobilizes, Germany will also mobilize.'[18] This was followed by a German demand that Russia should accept the annexation; and the Kaiser was able to declare that he had stood by his ally the Austrian Emperor 'in shining armour'.[19] Much of this was bluff: neither the Austrians nor the Russians were militarily or economically in a position to go to war, but the effect was to show both the nature and the limitations of the alliance system because, while the extent of Germany's commitment to Austria was made clear, the Russians had found only lukewarm support in Paris and London for their ambitions at Constantinople.

In the years between the Bosnian crisis and the outbreak of the First World War, four things were forcing a reassessment and a tightening up of the alliance system in Europe: the upheavals in Turkey which encouraged Russian hopes of compensating for their humiliation in the Far East by gains in the Balkans and strengthened the Austrians' conviction that they must act vigorously against Serbia to prevent the danger of the dissolution of the Habsburg monarchy; the growing realization by many people in British government circles that German naval building was a threat to Britain's imperial interests; the German belief that they must take some foreign political action both for domestic reasons and in order to ensure that the world balance of power should be tilted in their favour; the hopes of the French – and especially of Raymond Poincaré, Prime Minister in 1912 and then President of the Republic from 1913 – that they could use the alliance with Russia eventually to obtain the return of Alsace and Lorraine and at the same time be in a position to establish their control of Morocco without German interference.

In April 1911, increasing internal unrest in Morocco gave the French the opportunity they wanted to send troops into Fez and to prepare for the establishment of a protectorate over the country. The Germans saw in this action a chance to win some colonial concessions from France, if not in Morocco itself, then in the French Congo; and at the same time the German government recognized that a successful confrontation with France would strengthen their hands in the parliamentary elections of 1912. They sent a gunboat to the Moroccan port of Agadir and demanded compensations from the French for what was claimed to be a breach of the Algeciras agreement of 1906. In fact the German plan misfired. It demonstrated that the alliance with Austria would not be worth much unless Austria's own interests were directly threatened, for the Austrian government refused even diplomatic support. On the other hand, the British government, in spite of the reluctance of some members of the Cabinet, proclaimed its solidarity with France in a speech by the Chancellor of the Exchequer, David Lloyd George, a man till then thought to be one of the ministers most opposed to any involvement in continental alignments. He issued a warning, assumed by everyone at the time to be directed at Germany, that:

If a situation were to be forced upon us, in which peace could only be preserved by the surrender of the great and beneficent position Britain has won by centuries of heroism and achievement, by allowing Britain to be treated, where her interests were vitally affected, as if she were of no account in the Cabinet of Nations, then I say emphatically that peace at that price would be a humiliation intolerable for a great country like ours to endure.[20]

Within a few months – in April 1912 – an informal naval agreement had been concluded between France and England, by which the British navy would be responsible for the security of the English Channel and the French fleet concentrated in the Mediterranean, and the *Entente* had become still more like an alliance.

The German leaders were probably not surprised by the lack of support from Austria-Hungary. A few months before the crisis, Bethmann had admitted to the Kaiser: 'If it comes to a war, we must hope that Austria is attacked so that she needs our help and not that we are attacked so that it would depend on Austria's decision whether she will remain faithful to the alliance.'[21] But England's support for France was a shock: and German nationalist opinion held the British responsible for the failure of Germany's African gamble. Although over the next two years the British government still hoped to improve relations with Germany and reached agreements on questions outside Europe, the Agadir crisis showed how deep the divisions between the two countries now were. It was therefore, as many of the senior officials in the Foreign Office realized, important for England to maintain her close relations with France as otherwise there might be a danger that, if the French felt isolated, they would do a direct deal with Germany at the expense of the British Empire.

The international recognition of France's predominance in Morocco was one of the things which encouraged Italy too to seek compensation: on 29 September Italy declared war on Turkey and sent troops to occupy the Turkish provinces of Libya and Tripolitania. This blow to the stability of the Ottoman Empire was followed within weeks by the signature of an agreement between Serbia and Bulgaria, directed against Turkey and aiming at the conquest of Macedonia and its partition between the two countries. In May 1912 Greece was brought into this alliance, which became known as the Balkan League. The negotiations between Serbia and Bulgaria had been actively encouraged by the Russians, and especially by their ministers in Belgrade and Sofia who worked hard to persuade the Serbs and Bulgars to forget their old feuds and to join forces against Turkey. The events of 1911 and 1912 therefore raised problems for the Great Powers: problems about their relations to the small states of the Balkans which were showing their capacity to take the initiative and which could not be immediately or easily fitted into the alliance system, and problems about the relations of Italy to its allies Germany and Austria-Hungary.

The Triple Alliance had been renewed three times since it was first signed in 1882. It was due for a further renewal in 1912. Italy's involvement in the Libyan War therefore made the exact timing of the renewal of some importance. Some members of the Italian government argued that after a successful war Italy would carry more weight in the renegotiation of the alliance. Others were worried that Austria might claim compensation in the Balkans for Italy's gains in North Africa, since the treaty specifically allowed for this if 'the maintenance of the status quo in the regions of the Balkans or of the Ottoman coasts and islands in the Adriatic and in the Aegean sea should become impossible',[22] and presumably it might be argued that Libya and Tripolitania counted as part of the Ottoman coasts. The Italians also believed that there might be an advantage in the early renewal of the alliance so as to make sure that this was completed before the death of the old Emperor Franz Joseph, now aged eighty-one, since his heir the Archduke Franz Ferdinand was believed, rightly, to be hostile to Italy. At the same time, the German and Austrian governments were annoyed by Italy's unilateral action against Turkey and by the fact that they were given no warning of Italy's formal annexation of Libya and Tripolitania in November 1911 or her occupation of the Dodecanese Islands. However, by the autumn of 1912 and the outbreak of the war between the Balkan League and Turkey, all three signatories saw some advantage in the renewal of the Triple Alliance and this was formally signed on 5 December 1912.

Italy's alliance with Germany and Austria can be seen as an extreme case of a treaty entered into with numerous reservations and considerable cynicism – at least on the part of Italy. The Italians had welcomed the original alliance in 1882 because it appeared to give the recently united kingdom the status and prestige of a Great Power; it had seemed to offer her the prospect of support in an attempt to win some colonial compensation for France's acquisition of Tunisia the year before: to the King of Italy it appeared to offer the chance, through association with the Austrian Emperor, the senior Catholic sovereign in Europe, of improved relations with the Pope and therefore of a greater likelihood of going to heaven when he died. For Bismarck, Italy's alignment with Germany and Austria was one more step in his policy of keeping France diplomatically isolated; and for Austria the alliance seemed to provide one way of controlling Italian nationalist hostility to Austria caused by the number of Italians still living under Austrian rule in *Italia irredenta*, especially the South Tyrol and Trieste.

For the Italians, then, the Triple Alliance had always been a means of using other powers to further Italian interests; and, as with the other European alliances, both those interests and the international situation which the alliance had originally been intended to meet had changed. By 1911, Italy was not only involved in establishing her own empire in North Africa and the eastern Mediterranean, she was also actively interested in what was happening in the Balkans and anxious to establish her influence there. Popular feeling against Austria had not diminished, although the strident new nationalism of the past decade was aiming more widely than just at the winning of *Italia irredenta* from Austria. It had always been understood that the Triple Alliance would in no case be regarded as directed against England – and indeed this had been declared formally at the time of the original signature of the alliance. Moreover, although the text of the treaty as renewed in 1891 had given it a specifically anti-French emphasis, by the beginning of the century the economic and colonial rivalry between Italy and France had so far abated that in 1902 the Italian Foreign Minister had declared that Italy would remain neutral if France were attacked; and in the following year a commercial treaty between the two countries had been signed. Thus, although the renewal of the Triple Alliance in 1912 might seem to be a success for German and Austrian diplomacy, there was still much uncertainty about the extent of Italy's actual commitment to it. Indeed, Conrad, the Austrian Chief of Staff is said to have thought the alliance 'a pointless farce', and as 'a burden and a fetter which he would fain cast off at the first opportunity'.[23]

During the upheavals in the Balkans in 1912–13, Italian and Austrian interests were often opposed, particularly in their rival attempts to establish a predominant influence in the newly created state of Albania. Yet the very existence of the alliance forced an uneasy compromise, with all three governments continuing to behave as if the alliance was an important element in their strategic planning. For either side to admit that the alliance had lost its meaning would have been an admission of diplomatic failure and the abandonment of a diplomatic instrument that might still have its uses. Italy's alliance with Germany and Austria-Hungary was indeed an example of an alliance which, for the Italians, was never intended to be more than a diplomatic device to help the Italian government to get its own way, while for Germany and Austria even an unreliable and unpredictable ally seemed preferable to no ally at all. In spite of some measure of military co-operation, it was never really envisaged as preparing for a war. As a recent historian of Italian foreign policy has put it, 'The Triple Alliance remained a diplomatic arrangement likely to work in peace and not in war.'[24]

The continuous crisis in the Balkans between 1911 and 1914 demonstrated both the nature and limitations of the alliance system and the nature and limitations of the 'Old Diplomacy'. The two Balkan wars – that between the Balkan League and Turkey was followed by one in which Bulgaria fought Serbia, Greece and Rumania in the hope of winning territories conquered from Turkey in the first war – were localized. They did not escalate into a European war, partly because the governments involved were not ready for a war and partly because, given the desire to find a solution, it was possible to create the diplomatic machinery to achieve one. Sir Edward Grey was able to take the initiative in organizing a conference of ambassadors in London which dealt with such questions as the frontiers of the new state of Albania and the unsuccessful attempts by Serbia to win a port on the Adriatic. But Grey's successful diplomacy – and the belief that he could repeat that success was an important factor in his policy in July 1914 – was only possible because, to the annoyance of the Austrians, the Germans decided that they would not put their whole weight behind the Austrian efforts to limit Serbia's gains. The German government was indeed convinced of the ultimate likelihood or even the inevitability of war: there was much talk in court and army circles about the forthcoming struggle between Teuton and Slav, and in December 1912 the Kaiser had given instructions for a propaganda campaign to prepare public opinion for war. But the Balkan crisis did not seem the right moment to risk a general war. This was partly because of the complexity of the local issues and the difficulty which any government would have in explaining to its subjects why they would justify a war, and partly too from a feeling that the small states were showing a dangerous amount of initiative. 'It is the first occasion in the history of the Eastern Question', a French diplomat wrote, 'that the small states had won a position so independent of the Great Powers that they feel they are in a position to act completely without them and indeed to carry them along with them.'[25] Then, of the Great Powers most involved, neither Russia nor Germany was militarily quite ready for war. The Russians needed three or four more years to complete their remarkable military recovery from the disasters of the Japanese War: the German Admiralty was insistent that war should be avoided until the completion of the widening of the Kiel Canal and the construction of a submarine base on the island of Heligoland.

German policy was also strongly influenced by the fact that, in the view of the Chancellor and the Foreign Ministry, there was still a chance of securing British neutrality in a war, since England's *ententes* with France and Russia had still not become a firm alliance. Bethmann believed that if war broke out in such a way that it could be claimed that Russia had made the first move, then England would not intervene. In February 1912 there had been an attempt, with the visit to Berlin of Lord Haldane, the Lord Chancellor, to reach an agreement on the limitation of naval armaments; and although this had come to nothing, negotiations on other questions – co-operation in the construction of a railway across Turkey to Baghdad, the disposal of the Portuguese colonies in Africa, should Portugal's financial collapse lead to these coming on the market – proceeded in an amiable atmosphere right down to the outbreak of war. Some people in the British Foreign Office were beginning to wonder whether a rearmed Russia might not after all be an even greater threat to the balance of power than Germany, so that it was not unreasonable for Bethmann to believe than an Anglo-German *rapprochement* might be possible and that it was worth avoiding a major crisis until this possibility had had time to develop. Both the French government and those people in Britain who remained convinced of the German danger were apprehensive about a policy of *rapprochement* with Germany and were anxious for still closer ties between Britain and France and for the relationship to be made even more explicit. Sir Eyre Crowe had written at the beginning of 1911:

> The fundamental fact of course is that the Entente is not an alliance. For purposes of ultimate emergencies it may be found to have no substance at all. For an Entente is nothing more than a frame of mind, a view of general policy which is shared by the governments of two countries, but which may be, or become, so vague as to lose all content.'[26]

Although since Eyre Crowe had written this, the Agadir crisis and the Anglo-French naval talks of 1912 had made common action in war more likely, the French were quick to see any improvement of relations between Britain and Germany as a sign of how precarious the Anglo-French *Entente* was.

The Austrians too, in the particular situation in south-east Europe in 1912–13, felt that even their formal alliance with Germany did not seem to be giving them the support they expected. Kiderlen-Wächter, the State Secretary in the German Foreign Ministry, remarked in October 1912 that the time had come to reassert German predominance within the alliance and to prevent 'the leadership in policy passing from Berlin to Vienna as Aehrenthal had unfortunately been able to achieve as against Bülow' [the German Chancellor at the time of the Bosnian crisis in 1908].[27] For the Austrians, however, more than ever determined to reduce the influence of Serbia, this attitude was very unsatisfactory and there seemed an ironical contrast between the regular references to the loyalty – the *Nibelungentreue*, whatever that meant – between the two countries and the actual support offered in a specific situation. Although the Germans had given the Austrians some diplomatic support at certain points in the crisis; the Balkan quarrels had not escalated into a European war because the Germans were not prepared to give their ally a free hand against Serbia. At the same time the Russians, whose Balkan diplomacy had failed to stop her Slav protégés Serbia and Bulgaria from fighting each other in the Second Balkan War, were at this time more concerned with the future fate of Constantinople than with supporting Serbia. In these circumstances, Grey's diplomacy was successful because none of the Great Powers wanted a war at that time and on those issues. For the last time the old nineteenth-century Concert of Europe worked.

The Balkan crisis demonstrated that even apparently firm formal alliances did not guarantee support and co-operation in all circumstances. It might be that in a final emergency the German–Austrian alliance guaranteed German support for Austria; in the meantime, in F. R. Bridge's words, 'the eternal problem of the Dual Alliance remained: how effectively could an alliance designed to cope with the contingency of war serve the Monarchy's interests in the day-to-day diplomacy of peace'.[28] In the autumn of 1913 it also became apparent that the Franco-Russian alliance too was no automatic guarantee of general support for Russia by France. In October 1913 the Germans sent a military mission under General Liman von Sanders to advise the Turkish government on the modernization of their army after its defeat by the Balkan League; and Liman von Sanders was appointed to command the army corps in Constantinople. The Russians at once protested, asserting that the mission was an openly unfriendly act, and looked to France and Britain for diplomatic support against Germany. The British, who already had an admiral in Constantinople commanding the Ottoman navy, were reluctant to press too hard and worked for a compromise between Germany and Russia.

The French were in a more embarrassing position. Poincaré had throughout the Balkan crisis reaffirmed French loyalty to the Russian alliance and was hoping as President of the Republic to exercise a more direct control over foreign policy than his predecessors had done. He was determined to make the Russian alliance a central element in his policy and, although not working directly for war, accepted the idea that if war between Russia and Germany were to come, then France would have a chance of recovering the provinces of Alsace and Lorraine. At the same time, he showed more interest in the Balkans than some other French leaders, and wanted to develop French economic interest there. He is reported – though he later denied it – to have declared to Isvolsky, now the Russian ambassador in Paris, just before the outbreak of the First Balkan War: 'If conflict with Austria brought intervention by Germany, France would fulfil her obligations.'[29] France, the implication was, might intervene on Russia's side without herself being directly attacked by Germany. By the time of the row over the Liman von Sanders mission, however, the French government was more cautious; although reaffirming their loyalty to the alliance and their willingness to support Russia's demands for some sort of compensation from Turkey, they in fact made any action conditional on British participation. By this time both the French and the British were worried that they did not really know what Russian intentions were or how far the Russians were prepared to go in support of their ambitions at Constantinople, and were therefore reluctant to encourage them. Once again the Great Powers in fact decided that this particular issue was not worth the risk of war; and even the Russian ministers themselves were divided on this point.

By the beginning of 1914, then, the alliance system in Europe looked as if it was in some disarray. Both Austria and Russia felt that they had, in the recent crises in the Balkans and at Constantinople respectively, not received the diplomatic support from their allies they had the right to expect. Italy's position still remained ambiguous. The subsidiary alliance between Germany, Austria-Hungary and Rumania first signed in 1883 and renewed as recently as 1913 seemed hardly likely to survive the repeated complaints about the oppression of the Rumanian inhabitants of the Hungarian province of Transylvania: and like Italy, Rumania eventually entered the war on the side opposed to its formal allies. As far as England was concerned, the exact nature and implications of the *Entente* with France remained obscure right down to the beginning of August 1914. Nevertheless the existence of the alliance system and of the less formal *ententes* provided the framework within which the diplomacy of the pre-war years was conducted. It roused expectations about the behaviour of other governments which conditioned the foreign policies and the military plans of the major countries of Europe. And even when the alliances did not provide the immediate diplomatic support for which the governments were hoping, this sometimes made the participants all the more anxious to ensure that the alliance would function more effectively next time. Russian anxieties about France's attitude during the Liman von Sanders crisis and about Britain's lukewarm support led during the next months to Russian attempts to consolidate the alliance with France and tighten up the agreements with Britain, by, for example, negotiations for naval co-operation between the two admiralties. The realization by the Germans that Austria-Hungary was her only reliable ally and that she must be supported at all costs in any policies which the Austrians thought essential for the survival of the Habsburg state, was an important motive for the German decisions of July 1914; and these decisions have to be seen in terms of the Austrian belief that Germany had not supported her sufficiently in the previous year.

Moreover, each Great Power had attempted to build up a clientele of smaller states. As the Balkan countries showed their capacity for initiative, so too the Great Powers were anxious to recruit them into their respective alliance systems; but the price was a promise of support for the local ambitions of the small states. A Great Power could have its policies to some extent determined by the need to retain the friendship of a small power and to keep it within its diplomatic system. The Russian government knew in July 1914 that they had failed to support Serbia in the previous year as warmly as the Serbs had expected and hoped; and failure to support Serbia again would mean, the Russians thought, the end of Russian prestige in the Balkans and the beginning of a possible new diplomatic alignment there. Once the governments of Europe came to believe that they were aligned in two rival camps, then the winning of an additional small state to their side seemed to be of great importance, while the wooing of partners in an alliance whose allegiance seemed doubtful or wavering, such as Italy, came to be a major objective of diplomacy.

The existence of the alliance system above all conditioned expectations about the form a war would take if it broke out, and about who were likely to be friends and who enemies. These expectations laid down the broad lines of strategic planning, so that the general staffs were taking decisions which often committed them to irreversible military actions if war threatened; and consequently in a crisis the freedom of action of the civilian ministers was often more circumscribed than they themselves realized. What to many diplomats still seemed a stately and esoteric ritual which only they were qualified to perform became something rather different when translated into the logistical calculations of the military planners. However much the foreign ministers and diplomats believed that they were making foreign policy and that foreign policy held prime place in all acts of state, there were many other forces in twentieth-century European society which were limiting their choices, determining their actions and creating the climate of opinion in which they operated.

REFERENCES AND NOTES

1. G. M. Trevelyan, *Grey of Fallodon* (London 1939) pp. 114–15.
2. A. J. P. Taylor, *The Struggle for Mastery in Europe 1848–1914* (paperback edn, Oxford 1971) p. 81, fn. 1.
3. E. Wertheimer, *Graf Julius Andrassy*, Vol. III (Stuttgart 1913) p. 284, quoted in W. L. Langer, *European Alliances and Alignments 1871–1890* (New York 1939) p. 284.
4. Quoted in Samuel R. Williamson Jr, *The Politics of Grand Strategy: Britain and France Prepare for War 1904–1914* (Cambridge, Mass. 1969) p. 21.
5. Salisbury to Canon MacColl, 1901; G. W. E. Russell, *Malcolm MacColl* (London 1914) p. 283, quoted in W. L. Langer, *The Diplomacy of Imperialism* (New York 1951) p. 85.
6. Christopher Andrew, 'Déchiffrement et diplomatie: le Cabinet Noir du Quai d'Orsay sous la Troisième Republique' *Relations Internationales*, No. 5, 1976.
7. Cmd. 7748. Fifth Report of the Royal Commission on the Civil Service 1914. See Zara S. Steiner, *Britain and the Origins of the First World War* (London and New York 1977) pp. 171 ff.
8. G. P. Gooch and Harold Temperley (eds) *British Documents on the Origin of the War 1898–1914*, Vol. III (London 1928) Appendix A, pp. 402–3. (Hereinafter referred to as *BD*.)
9. Bismarck to Saburoff 1878, *Nineteenth Century*, Dec. 1917, p. 1119. See also G. Lowes Dickinson, *The International Anarchy 1904–1914* (2nd edn 1937) p. 76.
10. *The Times*, 8 April 1914. See also *The History of The Times*, Vol. 14: *The 150th Anniversary and Beyond* (London 1952) Part I, p. 168.

11. Quoted in Karl Kautsky, *Sozialisten und Krieg* (Prague 1937) p. 200.
12. *The Times*, 14 May 1898.
13. *BD* II, No. 86, pp. 68–9.
14. Maurice Paléologue, *Un grand tournant de la politique mondiale 1904–1906* (Paris 1934).
15. *BD* III, No. 299, p. 266.
16. *BD* III, No. 299, p. 267. See also Beryl Williams, 'Great Britain and Russia 1905–1907' in F. H. Hinsley (ed.) *British Foreign Policy under Sir Edward Grey* (Cambridge 1977) pp. 133–47.
17. This passage was in 1928 omitted by the editors from *Die Grosse Politik*, Vol. XIX, Part II, No. 6305 on the grounds that 'this would mean a heavy blow to the policy of the *Anschluss*'. See James Joll, 'German diplomatic documents', *Times Literary Supplement*, 25, Sept. 1953.
18. Feldmarschall Franz Conrad von Hötzendorf, *Aus meiner Dienstzeit*, Vol. I (Vienna 1921) pp. 380–1; Gordon A. Craig, *The Politics of the Prussian Army 1640–1945* (paperback edn, New York 1964) p. 289.
19. Quoted in Michael Balfour, *The Kaiser and his Times* (London 1964) p. 295.
20. Quoted in R. C. K. Ensor, *England 1870–1914* (Oxford 1936) pp. 434-5. Some later writers have suggested that Lloyd George's warning was aimed as much at France as at Germany and was intended to frighten the French off making any agreement with Germany without British participation, though this does not seem to have been a view expressed at the time. For a discussion of the Agadir crisis, see Geoffrey Barraclough, *From Agadir to Armageddon: Anatomy of a Crisis* (London 1982).
21. Quoted in Erich Brandenburg, *Von Bismarck zum Weltkrieg* (Berlin 1939) p. 342. See also Fritz Fischer, *Krieg der Illusionen* (Düsseldorf 1969) p. 135.
22. A. F. Pribram, *The Secret Treaties of Austria-Hungary 1879–1914*, Vol. I, (Cambridge, Mass. 1920) p. 225.
23. Theodor Sosnosky, *Franz Ferdinand der Erzherzog Thronfolger* (Munich 1929) pp. 143–4, Quoted in Albertini, *The Origins of the War of 1914*, Vol. II (London 1953) p. 9. See also Richard Bosworth, *Italy, the Least of the Great Powers: Italian Foreign Policy before the First World War* (Cambridge 1979) p. 196.
24. Bosworth, op. cit., p. 215.
25. *Documents diplomatiques français* 3me série, Vol. III (Paris 1931) No. 466. See also Fischer, op. cit., p. 219.
26. Quoted in K.A. Hamilton, 'Great Britain and France 1911–1914' in Hinsley, op. cit., p. 324.
27. E. Jaeckh, *Kiderlen-Wächter* (Stuttgart 1924) Vol. II, p. 189, quoted in Fischer, op. cit., p. 226.
28. F. R. Bridge, *From Sadowa to Sarajevo: The Foreign Policy of Austria-Hungary 1866–1914* (London 1972) p. 360.
29. *Diplomatische Schriftwechsel Isvolskis 1911–1914* (ed. F. Stieve) (Berlin 1926) ii, No. 401, quoted in Taylor, op. cit., p. 488.

Chapter 4

MILITARISM, ARMAMENTS AND STRATEGY

All general staffs, war ministries and admiralties prepare for war. That is what they are there for. But the existence of plans for war does not necessarily mean that the officers who drew them up were themselves going to be responsible for ordering them to be carried out, nor does it mean that all the plans which survive in the archives were actually intended to be put into operation. Sometimes they were simply exercises to fill up the time when things were quiet, as when the German Admiralty in the late 1890s drew up plans for a landing on the east coast of the United States.[1] The relation between military plans and the actual decision for war is a complicated one which involves discussion of the position of the army in society, the degree of control exercised by civilian ministers, the nature and implications of armament programmes and strategic doctrines as well as of specific operational plans. These are all factors which have to be taken into account in analysing the decisions which were taken in July 1914; but behind the question of the constitutional position of the armed forces or of the contingency planning of the general staffs and admiralties lies the wider question of the degree to which a society is permeated by militarist – or anti-militarist – values, because on this depends the response which a government can expect if it decides to go to war and the kind of arguments it will have to use to justify a declaration of war to the public.

Such justification was all the more necessary at a time when the armies of all the powers except England were composed of conscript soldiers called up from civilian life to serve two to six years in the army. The numbers in these mass armies were substantial: by 1900 the Germans called up 280,000 men annually, the French 250,000, Russia 335,000, Italy 100,000 and Austria-Hungary 103,000, even though for financial reasons most governments did not in fact call up everybody who was liable for service. As the composition of the population and the balance between town and countryside changed, so the nature of the army changed too. As a result, governments began to be aware that they could no longer be sure that all the soldiers would necessarily obey orders without question or report to their depots on mobilization unless they were given some satisfactory explanations of why they were going to war. Moreover, both in France and Germany the authorities were by 1914 growing increasingly anxious about the possible influence of socialist and other revolutionary ideas on the soldiers and the spread of anti-militarist propaganda. By 1912 the German authorities were so worried when the Social Democrats won a third of the votes in the Reichstag elections and became the biggest single party in the imperial parliament, that some of them had serious doubts about increasing the size of the army, desirable though they felt this to be on strategic grounds, because it would mean diluting the old officer corps with people of middle-class origin and also risking the growth in the number of soldiers susceptible to socialist ideas. Systematic attempts were made to propagate anti-socialist ideas among the troops, and to stop soldiers attending socialist meetings in their spare time. Officers were encouraged to give lectures criticial of socialism, and on the eve of the war many senior officers, especially in the entourage of the Crown Prince, were talking of the necessity of more drastic measures to stop the growth of socialism, such as the abolition of universal suffrage and the banning of the Social Democratic Party.[2]

In France, too, the growth of a militant anti-militarism, especially among the revolutionary syndicalists, was a constant source of alarm in the years immediately before the war; and the syndicalist efforts to influence conscripts in the garrison towns were the object of repeated warnings from the government to the local authorities.[3] Moreover, the proposal to extend the period of military service from two years to three was one of the great political issues of 1913. The Socialist Party was bitterly opposed to any extension of military service and indeed was committed, largely under the influence of their leader Jean Jaurès, to a radical reform of the system of national defence, by which a citizens' militia would be substituted for a conscripted standing army, so that, it was argued, military action would be subject to popular control and a war of aggression would be impossible. Even if there was little chance of such proposals being adopted and although the government succeeded in 1913 in carrying the Three-Year Law through parliament, the anti-militarist movement was strong enough for any government to have to take into account the mood of the conscripts before starting a war. The fears that subversive influences would endanger mobilization and the smooth execution of military plans at the beginning of a war proved groundless in 1914. But when we examine the extent to which we can talk of a mood of militarism dominating European society in the decade before 1914, we must look at the question in relation to the various anti-militarist movements which both challenged and intensified that militarist mood.

In the case of Germany, the effectiveness of the socialist challenge was much exaggerated, but its existence, and the growing numerical strength of the social democratic movement, contributed to the feeling among the old Prussian ruling class that their values were threatened and that only vigorous action could preserve them. To the outside world, and indeed to the socialist opponents of the system inside, Germany seemed to be the country where military values influenced society more strongly than anywhere else. The Prussians formed the dominant element in the army of the new German Empire after 1870 and the Prussian War Ministry was responsible for the administration and supply of the army as a whole. The Prussian tradition of a strong army and strong military values continued to affect the whole of German society. As the Kaiser proclaimed in 1891: 'The soldier and the army, not parliamentary majorities and decisions have welded the Empire together. I put my trust in the Army.'[4] Many Germans at the turn of the century shared this view. To be a reserve officer was a mark of distinction for a member of the middle classes; and it was something which a Jew or a socialist could never hope to be. The behaviour of the army might be criticized by the Social Democrats who regularly voted against the military budget in parliament, but they were too well aware of the strength of the army in the German state to challenge it directly.

In 1906 there occurred a famous episode which seemed to demonstrate in farcical terms the position of the military in German society. An elderly ex-convict dressed up in a uniform of a captain of the 1st Foot Guards, ordered, 'auf allerhöchstem Befehl', some soldiers coming out of the military swimming-baths to follow him in the name of the Kaiser and arrested the Burgomaster and Treasurer of the small town of Köpenick on the outskirts of Berlin, making off with the petty cash and leaving the bewildered soldiers in occupation of the Town Hall for several hours until the superior authorities received a telegram, 'Town Hall occupied by the military. We urgently desire information as to the reasons in order to reassure the excited citizens.' Satirists might laugh at this episode, but it was a sign of the readiness of Germans to accept without question the orders of anyone in military uniform.[5] A British equivalent was the '*Dreadnought* hoax' in 1910 when a group of young people including the writer Virginia Woolf, with her face blacked and a false beard, succeeded in persuading the officers of HMS *Dreadnought*, the most up-to-date ship of the British navy and the latest product of the Anglo-German naval race, that they were the Emperor of Abyssinia and his suite, and were given a suitably imperial reception. Although this was conceived just as a practical joke, Virginia Woolf 'came out of it' as her biographer writes, 'with a new sense of the brutality and silliness of men'.[6] If the Captain of Köpenick demonstrated the awe in which the Prussian army was held, the hoaxers of the *Dreadnought* were deliberately teasing the British navy at a moment when it was the most prestigious symbol of England's imperial greatness.

A more serious example of the extent to which the German officer corps regarded itself as being above criticism and as a privileged caste – even if it also showed that there was a growing body of people ready to express such criticism – was the 'Zabern affair' of 1913.[7] A young officer in the garrison of this small town in Alsace insulted the civilian inhabitants and encouraged his men to beat them up; and when the citizens of Zabern protested and insulted the officers in their turn, the commander of the regiment finally arrested twenty-seven of them and locked them up in the cells of the barracks. The matter was raised in the Reichstag, but although a majority carried a vote of censure on the Chancellor for his handling of the matter, nothing much came of this, and the commander of the regiment in Zabern was acquitted by a court-martial of a charge of illegal arrest, though some of the officers concerned were transferred elsewhere. Although there were now more voices raised in criticism of the army than might have been the case twenty years earlier, they were unable to make any impact on military procedures or to control the conduct of the army. The War Minister, the Crown Prince and senior members of the officer corps expressed their contempt for parliament and politicians and made it quite clear that they would never allow the army to be subject to them.

While the general acceptance of military values by large sections of the German public may have contributed to the mood which made war possible and to the enthusiasm with which the outbreak of war was greeted (see Chapter 8), the most important aspect of the role of the German army in the coming of war was its freedom from civilian political control. The Kaiser was the 'supreme war lord' and the army leaders were responsible to him alone. He had a personal military staff which operated independently of his civil and naval staffs, and the Chief of the General Staff had direct access to him. It was thus possible for military decisions to be taken without the knowledge of the civilian branches of the government – or indeed of the naval authorities. There was no collective leadership or responsibility. The only co-ordinating power lay with the Kaiser himself; and William II was a wayward, capricious and unstable monarch incapable of pursuing a consistent course or controlling his advisers.

There was not even any co-ordination between the strategic planning of the German army and that of the navy. Ever since the signature of the Franco-Russian alliance the strategy of the army had been based on the need to fight a war on two fronts, and the plans of the General Staff for this contingency culminated in General Schlieffen's famous plan of 1905, by which France was to be defeated by what would later have been called a *Blitzkrieg* so as to enable the German armies subsequently to concentrate against Russia. But while the army was planning a war against France and Russia, the navy was planning a war against England. In 1897 the construction of a German high seas fleet was begun; and Admiral von Tirpitz, the State Secretary for the Navy, based his plans on the use of the fleet against England. Strategic planning for a war against Russia should have been accompanied by a foreign policy aimed at securing at least the neutrality of England. Strategic planning for a war against England should have involved a foreign policy aimed at securing the friendship of Russia. General von Moltke, Schlieffen's successor as Chief of Staff, realized the danger: 'As the Navy cannot wage war against England with any prospect of success, this war must accordingly be avoided', he wrote in June 1909.[8] But there was little even he could do about it. Because of the lack of machinery for co-ordinating German policy, the army and the Admiralty pursued their policies regardless of each other, with the result that by 1914 they both saw themselves as encircled by the enemies which their respective policies had created. The Anglo-German naval rivalry was a major factor leading Britain to back French policy in Morocco and aligned Britain on Russia's side in Russia's struggle with Austria-Hungary for control of south-east Europe.

The differing aims and needs of the German army and navy created a number of problems. At a time when the budget of the central government was constantly strained, the rival claims of the army and navy created additional financial difficulties. During the first years of the century the navy was given priority, but when in 1913 it was decided to increase the size of the army just after the passage of a supplementary navy law, the government was obliged for the first time to introduce an income tax, thereby disproving Tirpitz's assumption that it would be possible to build the navy without increasing taxation. This at the same time had the paradoxical result that the bill for the army increases was carried with the support of the social democrats, who approved of the income tax, against the votes of the conservatives, who approved of the army but did not want to pay for it out of their own pockets. It has indeed been argued by some historians that the cost of armaments and the strain on German public finance was so great that only a war in which the rules of orthodox finance could be suspended saved the German state from bankruptcy.

The building of a large navy had repercussions on most aspects of German policy at home and abroad. It was regarded by some German leaders as a means of integrating and reconciling the various conflicting social forces in Germany. It was the subject of a very intensive propaganda campaign supported by industry and by many middle-class people who saw the navy as a less aristocratic and exclusive organization than the army and whose national pride was aroused by the prospect of Germany becoming a *Weltmacht* – though the meanings they attached to the concept of world power were ill-defined and often inconsistent. In fact, however, Tirpitz's plans did not succeed. Although he had hoped to plan the construction of the navy in such a way that its development would be independent of recurrent parliamentary votes, the British reaction to what was regarded as a German threat to Britain's imperial position and the world balance of power was to increase the rate of her own naval construction so that the pace of naval armament was constantly accelerating; consequently parliamentary approval for further expenditure was required in both countries. Tirpitz believed that the building of the navy would, once it was through a 'danger zone' in which it would be vulnerable to a British pre-emptive strike, make Germany sufficiently strong at sea for England not to risk a confrontation. British naval building had since 1889 been explicitly governed by the 'two-power standard' by which the British navy had to be stronger than the combined fleets of the next two naval powers. Tirpitz's 'risk theory' presupposed that the German navy would be so large that Britain would face the permanent risk of being confronted by a German navy which could inflict such damage on the British fleet that Britain, even if victorious, would be too weak to face the navies of the other leading naval powers. Britain would thus be in a position in which the very existence of the German fleet would limit her freedom of action. In fact the British avoided this dilemma by increasing the rate of their own naval building – and with the introduction of the Dreadnought class of battleship in 1906 constructing new types of ship – and at the same time realigning their foreign policy so as to avoid the possibility of hostilities with France and Russia and to be free to confront the German threat. Even before the outbreak of war, Tirpitz's strategy had failed. When the war did break out the kind of naval building which both Germany and Britain had undertaken turned out to be inappropriate to the war at sea as it actually developed. The British and German admiralties only sent their high seas fleet into action once in what was intended to be a decisive battle off Jutland in May 1916; but the result was indecisive because neither side was prepared to risk the loss of their battleships by prolonging the fight. Both sides claimed a victory but the battleships spent most of the rest of the war at their bases; and the war at sea became primarily a war of submarines and destroyers.

The consequence of the German naval programme was not only the realignment of British foreign policy. It also led indirectly to a radical change in British strategic thinking. Throughout the nineteenth century the superiority of the British navy was taken for granted and the army neglected as a consequence. Although there had been moments of alarm, such as that which led to the naval programme of 1889, when it was realized that ships and equipment were growing obsolete, the German fleet was the first serious threat to Britain's hegemony since the Napoleonic Wars. The navy was popular in Britain – though this did not prevent the pay of the ordinary seamen remaining practically unchanged at a very low rate for some thirty years. It seemed the symbol of Britain's imperial greatness, but it could also be supported on good liberal grounds; it ensured the 'freedom of the seas' and thus the freedom of trade: it had played a humanitarian role in the suppression of the slave trade. Naval budgets had not been seriously opposed in Parliament – even by the Irish.

The British army, on the other hand, had performed a less glamorous role. 'The British Empire is pre-eminently a great Naval, Indian and Colonial Power'[9] the committee which in 1904 recommended far-reaching changes in the administrative arrangements for imperial defence stated. The army since the Crimean War had been primarily a force for the defence of the colonies or for dealing with uprisings or unrest there, for fighting Zulus in South Africa or Pathans on the north-west frontier of India. The Indian army, backed by units of the British army sent to India for regular tours of duty, was an almost autonomous force, and the India Office in London or the Viceroy in Delhi sometimes seemed to be pursuing a foreign policy of their own, particularly over such questions as the rivalry with Russia for the control of Afghanistan. By the beginning of the twentieth century all this was gradually changing. The war against the Boers in South Africa revealed the weaknesses of the British army and led to demands for reform. The *Entente* with France led during the Moroccan crisis of 1905–6 to the War Office considering for the first time for decades the problems of sending an expeditionary force to the continent of Europe.

As in Germany there was a difference of opinion between the army and the navy as to the right strategy to adopt. The War Office was from 1906 committed to planning for the despatch of an army to the Continent to take its place on the left wing of the French. The navy, and especially Admiral Sir John Fisher, the voluble and forceful First Sea Lord from 1904 to 1910, did not want the responsibility of protecting the army's crossing of the Channel and thought the role of the army should be to aid a close naval blockade of Germany by seizing one or more of the Frisian Islands and possibly landing on Germany's Baltic coast. However, the newly formed Committee of Imperial Defence presided over by the Prime Minister finally backed the army's view. The supremacy of the civilian government was never in doubt; and however much staff officers might complain that, for example, 'The whole idea of governing the army by a civilian, whose whole training has been political expediency . . . is vicious in theory and hopeless in practice',[10] the final decision rested with the Prime Minister and Cabinet, and this made a degree of co-ordination possible. At the same time the increase in naval construction and the growing naval arms race caused problems for Britain as for Germany. The Liberal government had to find money simultaneously for the ambitious programme of social reform to which they were committed and also for the building of the Dreadnoughts for which the press and public, led by the Conservative opposition, were clamouring ('We want eight and we won't wait' was the slogan launched by one Conservative MP). Various attempts were made to halt the naval race and reach some agreement with Germany but this proved impossible. The British refused to give up their naval superiority: 'If the German fleet ever becomes superior to ours', Sir Edward Grey wrote to King Edward VII in July 1908, 'the German army can conquer this country. There is no similar risk of this kind for Germany; for however superior our fleet was, no naval victory could bring us any nearer to Berlin.'[11] (It is a remark which shows incidentally how firmly Grey had rejected the views of Sir John Fisher and the Admiralty who held that British naval superiority could enable a British force to land on the Baltic coast.) And Winston Churchill, who became First Lord of the Admiralty in 1911, as the result of changes in the Cabinet intended to resolve the disputes between the War Office and Admiralty, made a similar point in March 1913: 'I must explicitly repudiate the suggestion that Great Britain can ever allow another naval power to approach her so nearly as to deflect or to restrict her political action by purely naval pressure.'[12] The German government was in fact hoping for just that and wanted political concessions in exchange for naval disarmament. When Haldane went to Berlin in February 1912 to try and negotiate a naval agreement, it was made quite clear to him that the Germans would only be satisfied with an undertaking that Britain would under all circumstances remain neutral in a European war. Tirpitz expressed his own position to a colleague as follows:

> England will stand by her obligations and promises to France . . . [our] political demand [is that] England must take no part in a war between France and Germany, no matter who the aggressor is. If we cannot get this guarantee, then we must continue with our armament so that we are as strong as the Anglo-French Entente, which has the *de facto* nature of an offensive alliance.[13]

Even when these ideas were expressed in more diplomatic language by Bethmann Hollweg and the German ambassador in London, they were quite unacceptable to the British; and although there were subsequent attempts to delay the actual execution of plans for naval building – proposals for a so-called 'naval holiday' – there was no serious diminution of the arms race and consequently no diminution of the underlying antagonism.

The British felt that the German fleet was a luxury – a phrase used by Churchill that gave much offence in Germany – but that the British fleet was a vital necessity. The Germans, on the other hand, felt aggrieved that Britain would not settle for the 3–2 ratio of capital ships in Britain's favour proposed at the time of the Haldane mission. The British uncertainty about Germany's intentions had some justification: Tirpitz, as we have seen, had from the start envisaged the German navy as a means of bringing political pressure to bear on Britain. British objections to the German naval programme seemed to Germans just a hypocritical refusal to allow any other country the privileges long enjoyed by England. To the British, German policy seemed an unacceptable threat to their security. In fact, Tirpitz's gamble of building a fleet large enough to act as a deterrent which would enable Germany to influence British world policy had failed by 1914 as he himself seems to have realized, but it had had the effect of conditioning opinion in both countries and so contributing much to the climate which made war possible.

The programme of naval armament developed a momentum of its own which was hard to stop. Tirpitz was deliberately planning naval construction over a long term so as to limit the Reichstag's opportunities for interfering. At the same time naval building on a new scale required new facilities: wharfs and docks had to be enlarged; the Kiel Canal had to be widened; private firms had to be called in to supplement the government shipyards when the pace of construction was accelerated to keep pace with the British; the works of Krupp and other heavy industrialists had to be extended. All this activity created vested interests both in Germany and Britain. It was, for example, the managing director of the Coventry Ordnance Works who first drew the attention of the British government to the fact that in 1906 Krupps was expanding its plant 'for the purpose of manufacturing very large naval guns and mountings quickly'.[14] No doubt he was hoping that as a result his own firm would receive orders from the Admiralty for guns and mountings. But without attributing too much importance to the role of individual armament manufacturers in exacerbating the international situation, there were enough built-in forces in the armaments and shipbuilding industries to make any slowing down in the rate of construction difficult.

The British and German admiralties were agreed on this. The British Admiralty was writing in 1907, when the question of disarmament was coming up for discussion at the Hague Conference:

> The vested interests concerned in war-ship construction are moreover nowadays very large with ramifications in almost every branch of manufacture and trade. The immediate effect of any proposal to limit naval armaments will be to deal a heavy blow at these interests, with the result that the latter would in all probability array themselves against the movement [for disarmament] and the consequent opposition thus created would be a formidable obstacle. And, again, this country more than any other has a supreme interest in the maintenance of her shipbuilding trade in a flourishing and healthy condition. Will it be advisable for Britain to enrol herself under the banner of 'limited naval armaments' if as seems inevitable, such limitation will react seriously upon one of our premier national industries?[15]

Again, early in 1914, when the proposal for a 'naval holiday' was being considered, the State Secretary in the German Foreign Office told the British ambassador that the Germans were opposed to the idea because 'the interruption for a whole year of naval construction would throw innumerable men on the pavement',[16] while Tirpitz told the

Reichstag that any postponement would mean that 'the omissions must be made good in the following year. This would upset our finances, dislocate work in the shipbuilding yards and also our military arrangements, i.e. the regular placing of ships in commission on their completion . . . We should . . . have to dismiss a large number of workmen and the whole organization of our shipbuilding yards would be upset.'[17] Thus the naval race not only created political and psychological attitudes which contributed to the mood of 1914; it also inaugurated economic and technical processes which were increasingly hard to reverse. As early as 1893, before the naval race had begun, the German socialist thinker Eduard Bernstein had summed up the situation, using a phrase that was still a commonplace nearly a century later: 'This continual arming, compelling the others to keep up with Germany, is itself a kind of warfare. I do not know whether the expression has been used previously, but one could say it is a cold war. There is no shooting but there is bleeding.'[18]

The structure of German society gave a special role to the army and produced a special respect for military values. The naval policies of the Kaiser and Tirpitz aroused British antagonism and began a naval race which had important social and economic effects as well as producing a radical change in British foreign and strategic policy. The nature of the German political system made the co-ordination of policy between the various branches of the government almost impossible, so that there was a lack of clear direction in Germany's overall political and strategic planning. At the same time, the British regarded German naval building as a direct threat to their naval hegemony and their world-wide empire, so that their strategy and foreign policy – although some members of the government never gave up hope of improved relations with Germany – became increasingly directed towards resisting the German challenge. This in turn forced Britain into close relations with France and to a lesser extent with Russia.

French military planning was dominated by the effects of the defeat of 1870. The first objective was always the recovery of the lost provinces of Alsace and Lorraine: but it was expected that at the start of a war, the French armies would have to withstand a German attack. However, the task of consolidating and expanding the French colonial empire in Africa and the Far East had, since the 1880s, given the army an opportunity of restoring its self-esteem after the débâcle of 1870 and provided a chance of promotion and distinction for ambitious officers. Until the turn of the century this colonial activity meant that the French army had to plan for a possible war against the British as well as planning for a war against Germany. However, after the crisis at Fashoda in 1898, it became clear that France was not in a position to challenge the British in Africa, and this contributed to the change in French foreign policy under Delcassé resulting in the Anglo-French agreement of 1904, which gave France the hope of achieving colonial gains with British approval. Once French colonial ambitions centred on Morocco, it was Germany who now seemed France's main colonial rival and consequently the Moroccan question was an issue which helped to consolidate the Anglo-French *Entente*, and to link the Anglo-German naval rivalry with France's imperial aims in North Africa and her long-term goal of recovering Alsace-Lorraine. There was no longer any conflict between the immediate aims of French imperialism and French desire for revenge, so that after 1904 French military planning could concentrate on Germany.

There were, however, considerable difficulties over the position of the army in French society and the relations between the government and the high command. In the immediate aftermath of the defeat of 1870, the two traditions of French nationalism, the one going back to the military glories of the *ancien régime* and the other deriving from the revolutionary defence of France in 1793 and the triumphs of Napoleon, had combined, so that the army and especially the officer corps had been a highly esteemed element in French society. By the time of the Fashoda crisis, however, the army had, as a result of the Dreyfus affair and the division between those who accepted the army's claim to be above criticism and those who saw the army's treatment of Dreyfus and its handling of the case as a shocking infringement of the rights of man, become the object of political dispute rather than of political consensus. The Dreyfus affair had been followed by a campaign on the part of the government between 1902 and 1905 to ensure that the army leaders had reliable republican views and that officers who were known to be actively practising Catholics should be denied promotion. These bitter divisions over the army's role also meant that left-wing and radical attitudes to the army were now highly critical and that a passionate anti-militarism became an important part of their revolutionary rhetoric.

These political divisions inevitably affected the relations between the government and the high command. When the Minister of War was a general, it was not always easy for him to work smoothly both with the professional politicians and with his military colleagues. When he was a civilian he had to overcome the prejudices of the generals against a politician. Some of the politicians tried to overcome the mutual suspicions between the army and the civilians left behind by the Dreyfus case and the attempts to purge the army of anti-republican elements. In 1907 Georges Clemenceau, the Prime Minister, in spite of having played a leading role in the campaign in favour of Dreyfus, approved the appointment of Colonel Ferdinand Foch as head of the École de Guerre – an appointment which would have been unthinkable a few years earlier, since Foch was known to be a devout Catholic whose brother was a Jesuit. Then in 1911 the post of Chief of Staff, who had been responsible for overall planning, was combined with that of 'Generalissimo', who was to take over command on the outbreak of war; and Marshal Joffre was appointed to the new post. Joffre combined impeccable republican credentials and links with republican politicians with a confidence in his national mission. 'Do you not think about war?' he was asked in 1912 and he replied, 'Yes, I do think about it, I think about it all the time. We shall have war, I will make it, I will win it.'[19]

The revival of some degree of national solidarity enabled the government in 1913 to extend the period of military service from two to three years, though in the face of vigorous opposition in and out of parliament from socialists and radicals. The Moroccan crisis of 1911 and the German army increases of 1913, as well as the need to show the Russians that France was playing her part in the alliance at a moment when the Russians had also made substantial increases in their army, gave the government the opportunity to improve the equipment of the army as well as increasing the size of the reserves through the three-year law. French hopes of a victory over Germany had become increasingly dependent on the alliance with Russia. Just as German plans aimed at knocking out the French so as to concentrate their forces against Russia, so the French hoped that Russian action in the east would make victory in the west possible. Consequently the French were constantly impressing on their Russian allies the need for rapid mobilization and an offensive strategy so as to bring the weight of Russian manpower to bear against the German armies in the east as quickly as possible, and so relieve the pressure in the west. The French population was increasing much more slowly than that of Germany; and the French military planners were always aware of French demographic weakness, so that the Russian alliance was important both for its immediate strategic effect and because it would make available Russia's reserves of manpower. To some extent France's demographic inferiority was compensated by the fact that she called up each year a higher percentage of the men liable for military service than Germany did, but once the full weight of German manpower was mobilized, then France would inevitably be the weaker.

There were, however, difficulties in making the French-Russian alliance militarily effective. The Russians, at least until 1910, were reluctant to undertake an offensive against Germany. They realized that they too had to face a war on two fronts, against Germany and against Austria-Hungary. But there were other problems which complicated and weakened Russia's military position. The most obvious of these was the defeat in the Far East in 1904–5, which had largely destroyed the Russian navy and revealed serious defects in the strategy, organization and equipment of the army.

The attempts to reform the Russian army were only partially successful.[20] They were hampered by personal rivalry between cliques of officers and between those who came from the nobility and those – a large proportion – who came from humbler origins. The efforts of the

War Minister, Sukhomlinov, to change the structure and strategy of the army were made less effective by the atmosphere of corruption surrounding many members of his staff and entourage. Above all, these disagreements led to confusion about the strategy to be adopted against Germany and the type of armament which would be required. Should Russia's effort be concentrated on holding a number of fortresses which, in a situation in which it was expected that German mobilization would be completed first, would defeat an initial German attack? Or should the fortresses be demolished and plans made to build a mobile army and to develop the railway network to this end? In the event, neither policy was carried out thoroughly: an invasion of East Prussia at the start of the war was defeated because of the greater mobility and more efficient railway system of the Germans, while in 1915 the fortresses were quickly captured by the German army. The Russian army, in spite of attempts to create a general staff, lacked central direction. In the last resort all decisions ultimately rested with the Tsar; and Nicholas II, as we have seen from his conduct during the July crisis, was uncertain, vacillating and incapable of exercising the control over all aspects of military planning which the system demanded of him.

There were also, as in other countries, difficulties over the rival demands for expenditure by the army and the navy. The reconstruction of the Russian navy after its defeat by the Japanese seemed to be an important symbol of Russian recovery, but its actual strategic use was less clear. Certainly the French believed that the Russians should be concentrating on land armament instead of, for instance, spending money on Dreadnoughts (ordered from a British firm for construction in Russia) and in 1913 embarking on a substantial programme of further naval expansion. When the Russian government requested naval talks with England in the spring of 1914, the British Admiralty was not convinced that they would serve any useful purpose. As Grey wrote subsequently, 'To my lay mind it seemed that, in a war against Germany, the Russian Fleet could not get out of the Baltic and the British Fleet would not get into it.'[21] Russian foreign policy and strategic planning in the years immediately before 1914 and during the July crisis were not determined by a privileged officer corps or the predominant influence of the military leaders but rather by the uncertainties resulting from the weakness of an autocratic system in which the ultimate decisions rested with an inadequate autocrat. They were also the result of the need to satisfy certain presuppositions, emotional as much as strategic, about Russia's relations with the Balkan Slavs and her historic claim to Constantinople. But because these were likely to antagonize Austria-Hungary who was assured of the full military support of Germany, Russia needed to strengthen her alliance with France; and this in turn entailed meeting French wishes for an offensive against Germany on the outbreak of war. Therefore a two-front war, against the Germans in East Prussia and Prussian Poland and against the Austrians in Galicia, seemed inevitable, while the Russian leaders had also to be prepared for a possible campaign in the Balkans, since the position of Rumania and Bulgaria was still uncertain. At the same time, the speed of Russia's recovery after the defeat in the Far East and the revolutionary upheavals of 1905 together with the scale of her rearmament programme – even if this was not very effectively executed – impressed the other powers with Russia's potential for war, reassuring the French but alarming the Germans.

In Austria-Hungary the army was one of the strongest unifying forces in a multinational state whose existence as a Great Power depended on maintaining sufficient internal stability for the Empire to be taken seriously by other governments as an irreplaceable element in the international system. The officers were inspired by a genuine loyalty to the Emperor Franz Joseph in his dual role as Emperor of Austria and King of Hungary. They were recruited from a fairly broad section of society: as in Russia only a minority came from the aristocracy, though they were often given the ennobling prefix 'von' as a reward for long service. Nevertheless, they formed a recognized caste; often several generations of the same family served as officers, and they developed their own social and ethical codes which could be seen as either expressions of folly and arrogance, or else as loyalty and self-abnegation depending on the viewpoint. (In fiction, Arthur Schnitzler's short story *Leutnant Gustl* expresses the former view and Joseph Roth's *Radetzky-Marsch* the latter; Schnitzler in fact lost his position as a reserve officer because of his satire on the fatuous moral values of the junior officers in the army.) Many of the officers spoke several of the Monarchy's ten languages, following the example of the Archduke Franz Ferdinand, the Inspector-General of the army, who, in spite of being reputed a bad linguist, spoke seven of them.

On the other hand, the Austro-Hungarian army suffered from the principal defect of the Monarchy as a whole, an enormously cumbrous and complicated administrative system. Because of the *Ausgleich* of 1867 and the establishment of the Dual Constitution which gave the Hungarian government equal powers with that of the Austrian half of the Monarchy, three different ministries were responsible for different parts of the military system. The main field army was run by the Joint Austro-Hungarian Minister of War, one of the three ministries (the others were Foreign Affairs and Finance) with jurisdiction over both halves of the Monarchy; but the two reserve armies, the *Landwehr* in Austria and the *Honved* in Hungary, were run by the Austrian and Hungarian Ministries of Defence respectively. There was considerable friction between the Austrian and Hungarian governments about the number of conscripts to be raised each year from each half of the Monarchy; and for this reason, as well as because of a chronic shortage of money made worse by each international crisis when precautionary military measures had been taken as in the Bosnian crisis of 1908 and the Balkan crises of 1912–13, only a comparatively small proportion of the men available were in fact called up. One historian has estimated that the field army in 1914 contained fewer infantry battalions than in the war against Prussia in 1866, in spite of an increase of some 20 millions in the population.[22] Moreover, for all the claims that were made that the army was a truly unifying force that somehow embodied the essence of Austro-Hungarian national consciousness independent of the claims of the individual nationalities, there had been, less than ten years before the outbreak of war, a bitter dispute between Germans and Hungarians about the retention of German as the language of command in the army. (Instruction of recruits was carried on in the language of any national group which formed more than 20 per cent of any regiment, but German remained the language of command in spite of the Hungarian claim for the use of Magyar.)

The Austro-Hungarian armed forces faced other problems too. Their armament programme was restricted for financial reasons, and even though the country had an efficient arms industry – the Skoda factory at Pilsen did a flourishing international trade and was a rival of the great German firm of Krupp – the equipment of the army was not always adequate and reserves of munitions insufficient even for a very short war. It was clear that the main enemy was likely to be Russia; but the Chief of Staff, General Conrad von Hötzendorf, was also planning for a campaign to crush Serbia, as well as talking about the possible necessity of launching a preventive attack against Austria's nominal ally Italy. By 1914, therefore, the Austro-Hungarian army was, like so much else in the Monarchy, in a paradoxical and contradictory situation. It had an important role as a symbol of unity which was supposed to stand above the conflict of nationalities within the Empire; yet that conflict was a potential source of weakness within the army itself. It had many able and dedicated officers: yet their effectiveness was hampered by a cumbersome bureaucratic administrative system. Above all, as events in 1914 were to show, its general staff never succeeded in clarifying their strategic priorities. They assumed that they would not have to face a simultaneous war with Russia, Serbia and Italy, but by the spring of 1915 this is just what they were obliged to face.

In one other country directly involved in the outbreak of war, the role of the military was very important and of a rather different nature. In Serbia a group within the army in 1903 murdered the King and replaced him with a monarch from a rival dynasty, so that the new King owed his position to the army. The army was bitterly disappointed by the government's acceptance of the Austrian annexation of Bosnia and Herzegovina in 1908, but it gained enormously in prestige and influence as a result of its success in the two Balkan wars. It claimed the right to administer the newly acquired territory in Macedonia and resented the appointment of civilian officials. In December 1913 there was a direct clash between a representative of the government and the local regimental commander at a reception at the Russian consulate in the Macedonian town of Bitolj when the colonel claimed precedence over the civilian official in proposing the health of the Tsar. The government then issued an order giving precedence to the civilian authorities at all public functions. As a result of these and other disagreements, early in June 1914 the Chief of Staff persuaded the King to dismiss the Prime Minister, Pásić; and it was only the support for Pásić from the Russian government and Crown Prince Alexander which kept him in office. The King withdrew from politics and Alexander became Prince Regent, while Pásić announced the dissolution of parliament and new elections for 1 August. Thus, because of tension between the army and the civilian government, Serbia was in the midst of a major political crisis at the moment of the assassination of the Archduke Franz Ferdinand.

The intense national feeling in Serbia at the time of the Bosnian crisis had led to the foundation in Belgrade of a nationalist association, the Narodna Odbrana, which soon had branches in other towns as well as links with Serbs in the United States. This organization encouraged young people to volunteer for military training and undertook cultural activities to foster the Serb national spirit. But in addition a secret society, Union or Death, called by its opponents the Black Hand and with members among officers and civilians of all classes, was founded by an army officer, later to become head of Serbian military intelligence, Colonel Dragutin Dimitrević, better known by his code name of Apis. Apis had been one of the regicides of 1903. He was a man who stopped at nothing, including murder, to attain his national and revolutionary ends. 'This organization', the constitution of the society ran, 'prefers revolutionary action to cultural';[23] and this marked the difference between Union or Death and the Narodna Odbrana, though a number of people were members of both organizations. The illicit activities of Apis and his group exacerbated the feud between the army and the civilian government; shortly before the murder of Franz Ferdinand, Pásić had ordered an enquiry into the illegal smuggling of arms over the frontier into Bosnia. There was a whole network of conspiracies and intrigues which have still not been unravelled and which created bitter and lasting feuds within the Southern Slav movement. Although there was a moment of unity in July 1914 in the face of the Austrian attack, one of the reasons which led Pásić's government to reject part of the Austrian ultimatum may well have been the realization that the participation of Austrian officials in any enquiry in Serbia into the assassination of the Archduke might have revealed the extent of the influence of Apis and his organization on the whole political and administrative life of the country. The feud between Pásić and Apis was never healed. Three years later Apis was arrested and condemned to death on charges of plotting to murder the Prince Regent, his activities and motives obscure to the last, so that his role has been the subject of wild speculation and rumour ever since. He certainly had links with the Young Bosnia group who were responsible for the assassination of the Archduke; the guide who led the assassins across the Serbian border into Bosnia was one of Apis's agents, though the same man also reported what he had done to the local representative of the Narodna Odbrana, who in turn reported the fact to the government. On the other hand, Apis already knew that he was under investigation on the orders of the Prime Minister; and there is some evidence to suggest that he tried to stop the assassination after the conspirators had already left for Sarajevo. As with later interacting terrorist groups, the links between them are hard to disentangle.

What is more important than the details of the conspiracy and the various secret societies is the light which Apis's career throws on the nature of Serbian society and politics. In a small poor country where nationalist feelings were growing in intensity, the army was regarded as a symbol of national aspirations; but there was room for much rivalry and difference of opinion about how those aspirations might best be realized. At the same time the interests of the army were not necessarily the same as those of the politicians who were basing their careers on the establishment of a parliamentary and democratic system. Traditions of terrorism and conspiracy going back to the years of Turkish rule contributed an element of instability in both domestic and foreign policy. Even if Apis and his organization were involved with the planning and execution of the murder of the Archduke, it was without any real idea of what the long-term consequences might be. It was enough to remove someone whom they regarded as an enemy and oppressor of the Serb people; and in any case, the war with Austria-Hungary was coming sooner or later. Apis believed, as his newspaper put it in 1912:

> The war between Serbia and Austria . . . is inevitable. If Serbia wants to live in honour, she can only do this by war. This war is determined by our obligation to our traditions and the world of culture. This war derives from the duty of our race which will not permit itself to be assimilated. This war must bring about the eternal freedom of Serbia, of the South Slavs, of the Balkan peoples. Our whole race must stand together to halt the onslaught of these aliens from the north.[24]

Yet the summer of 1914, when the Serbian army had not yet recovered from its efforts in the Balkan wars, was hardly the moment for Serbia to provoke such a war; and the evidence does not suggest that either the Serb government or the army command wanted to do so. However, the conspiracies and intrigues in which so many officers and politicians were involved served to give a *prima facie* plausibility to the

Austrian accusations of Serbian complicity in the murder of Franz Ferdinand and provided the excuse needed by the Austro-Hungarian government to launch the war against Serbia which both sides had for different reasons come to regard as inevitable. The case of Serbia in 1914 is a striking example of the way in which a fanatical nationalism will inspire actions which are not based on any rational calculation of profit and loss, actions whose consequences are unpredictable and unintended.

The nature of the social and political position of the army and navy and the role of the military leaders in deciding policy varied from country to country. Nevertheless, whatever the influence within each country of the officer corps and the respect paid to its moral values, the actual military and naval plans of each country necessarily affected the policies of others. Each government reacted to the military and naval preparations of its neighbours: a move to increase armaments was never isolated but was followed by increased military expenditure in other states, regardless of their political system. The arms race itself contributed to the feeling that war was inevitable; and although governments claimed that their preparation for a defensive war was a sign of their wish for peace and their will to deter aggression, deterrents in fact often provoke as much as they deter. While some governments were more ready than others to start or at least risk a war in pursuit of their policies, no government felt able to exclude the possibility of war and therefore took action which made its outbreak more likely. The pace was set by Germany trying, for a variety of reasons, to shift the world balance of power in her favour even if it involved the risk of war: but the European Great Powers were so bound up with each other that armament programmes and militaristic propaganda in one necessarily led to armament programmes and militaristic propaganda in another. German naval expansion provoked British naval expansion: the Navy League in Germany was paralleled by the Navy League (and its rival the Imperial Maritime League or 'Navier League') in Britain. Russian military expenditure provided the excuse for German army increases and these in turn provoked the French three-year law. Calls for a national revival and greater preparation for the coming struggle became the common currency of political rhetoric – whether in the Ligue des Patriotes, the National Service League or the Narodna Odbrana – even if in many cases these were counterbalanced by the old liberal slogans of peace, retrenchment and reform or the socialist assertions that the working man has no country and that war between classes was destined to replace war between states. Some of these factors which contributed to the atmosphere in which the decisions of 1914 were taken will be examined in later chapters; but there is one area in which strategic decisions took precedence over all others and limited the choice of the civilian politicians. This was in the actual course and immediate consequences of the July crisis itself.

The war plans which were put into operation in the crisis of 1914 were conditioned by many things: strategic doctrine, technological capacity, the structure of command. They were revised from time to time as the diplomatic situation changed, so that when war did come the nature of the opening moves had been fairly clearly foreseen and carefully worked out by the general staffs. What could not be foreseen – and what made the war very different from what its instigators had envisaged – were the consequences of those opening moves. Moreover, political hesitations, loss of nerve and tactical blunders often made the effect of the military plans other than what had been intended by the planners. In general, however, the speed with which the final crisis developed in the last week of July 1914 meant that there was little chance of changing the military plans once their execution had been ordered. The case of Austria-Hungary – the first of the powers to start military action – shows clearly the difficulty of reconciling the ideal world of the staff officer with the reality of hundreds of thousands of soldiers on the move.

The problem for Conrad, who was to a very great extent responsible for Austria-Hungary's strategic planning, was, as we have seen, that he had to allow for a war on at least two fronts and perhaps more. He was himself passionately determined to use the first possible opportunity to inflict a crushing military defeat on Serbia; and he seems at times to have hoped that Russian support for Serbia might turn out to be bluff: 'We are not yet clear', he said as late as 31 July, 'whether Russia is only threatening so we must not let ourselves be distracted from our action against Serbia.'[25] On the other hand, for the Germans an essential point of the Austro-German alliance was that it would provide for an immediate Austrian offensive against Russia while Germany was concentrating on the campaign against France. To complicate the position still further, although Italy was officially allied to Austria-Hungary, it was by no means certain what her attitude in a war would be, and Conrad had indeed sometimes envisaged a preventive war against her too; in any case it would be prudent not to leave the Italian frontier unguarded. In addition, Rumania, although also nominally an ally, had to be regarded as a potential enemy, and the Hungarian authorities were worried that there might be a rising among their Rumanian subjects in Transylvania in the event of war. A Rumania opposed to Austria-Hungary would also be of direct advantage to the Russians and would release for use against Austria the divisions which were kept on the Rumanian frontier.

By the spring of 1914 the Russians had improved their railway transport to such an extent that it was very possible that their mobilization would take less time than the thirty days on which Conrad had previously reckoned, so that his hope that, by mobilizing the Austro-Hungarian forces for use against Serbia in fifteen days, there would be time to deal with Serbia before Russia could open the campaign in

Galicia, was unlikely to be realized. In a war which started as a punitive expedition against Serbia it would in any case be difficult for reasons of prestige and public opinion to postpone operations against Serbia so as to concentrate on the Russian front. Conrad and the Austro-Hungarian government were, as Norman Stone has convincingly shown,[26] the victims both of their obsession with Serbia and of the endemic military weakness of the Monarchy. Conrad had made an attempt to deal with the situation in March 1914, when he had tried to change the plan of campaign against Russia so as to evacuate some Austrian territory in the initial stages of a war and thus concentrate on a defensive battle. But – quite apart from the fact that such a strategy was directly contrary to the interests of Austria's ally Germany – he was told by the transportation division of the War Ministry that the requisite revision of the railway timetables would take far too long.

Accordingly, on 25 July, when the Austrian ultimatum was running out, and three days before the actual declaration of war on Serbia, the mobilization of the army intended to defeat Serbia was begun. The Russian threat was ignored and it was planned to direct the bulk of the Austro-Hungarian army against Serbia. When it became clear that Russia was not bluffing, and under pressure from the Germans to speed up the start of the Austrian offensive in Galicia, Conrad found that to switch a large part of the army from the south to the north was impossible within any reasonable length of time. The railway time-tables and the capacity of the rolling-stock did not allow it. The head of the transportation in the War Ministry assured Conrad that to attempt the operation would only end in a 'Tohowa-Bohu' – a complete mess.[27] Conrad was thus stuck with the war which he had unleashed against Serbia and was forced to open hostilities against both Serbia and Russia in circumstances so unfavourable that the first months of the war were a disaster from which few people expected Austria-Hungary to recover to the extent she did. The fault did not lie just with Conrad's planning or the risks he was willing to run: the whole administrative system of the Monarchy made a more rapid or a more flexible mobi-lization unlikely. The Austro-Hungarian government had been deter-mined to crush Serbia at all costs; they had realized that the cost might be a war with Russia and had chosen to proceed with their military plans against Serbia all the same. The results were that Austria was unable to overcome Serbian resistance until 1915, when Bulgaria had entered the war on the side of Germany and Austria and substantial German forces and a German commander had been sent to the Serbian front. Austria also had to face initial defeats by the Russians which led to a steadily increasing predominance of German influence over Austria-Hungary. The gesture that was to have demonstrated Austria-Hungary's strength and to maintain her position as a Great Power only in fact led to the loss of that status and her ultimate downfall.

The Russians had slowly and rather reluctantly come round to the idea pressed on them by the French that they would have to open a war with an offensive. Even then their preparations were somewhat inconsistent and confused: part of the additional expenditure authorized in 1913 was still used to add to the artillery in the dilapidated fortresses in Poland. Still, they had made much progress with their strategic railway building; and in May 1912 they had modified their Plan 19 – the plan for a war against Germany and Austria-Hungary combined. The original plan made in 1910 had been for an attack on the Germans in East Prussia by the main bulk of the Russian army while the remainder would follow a defensive strategy against the Austro-Hungarians. In 1912 it was decided that if Germany attacked France, then the larger part of the Russian forces available would attack Austria-Hungary, on the assumption that Germany would be too busy in the west to intervene effectively on the eastern front and that it would still be possible to conduct a successful offensive in East Prussia with a reduced force. In the autumn of 1912, at a moment when most of the governments of the Great Powers were thinking that war might be imminent as a result of the crisis in the Balkans, the Tsar, the senior ministers and the commanders concerned considered whether it might be possible to carry out a partial mobilization for a war against Austria-Hungary alone, and so avoid provoking Germany. The idea was abandoned, largely because of the arguments of Kokovtsev, the Prime Minister, who saw – rightly as things turned out – that 'No matter what we call the projected measures, a mobilization remained a mobilization, to be countered by our adversaries with actual war.'[28]

Because of the size of the Russian armies and the distances involved, the timing of the Russian mobilization was essential to the success of Russia's initial plans on the outbreak of war. It was the decision of the Russians to mobilize in July 1914 that was seized on by Germany as providing the justification for their declaration of war, giving rise to the belief which was taken for granted in the years between the two world wars, that 'mobilization means war'. On 24 July 1914, after the Serbians had appealed to the Tsar for support, the Chief of Staff and the Foreign Minister again considered a partial mobilization of the military districts of Kiev, Odessa, Moscow and Kazan with a view to action against Austria-Hungary. However, the Russians proceeded cautiously, partly from prejudice, partly from divided counsel. On 25 July they decided to recall officers on leave and to return troops on manœuvres to their depots; and early the next day the 'Period preparatory to war' was proclaimed. This in fact meant that the first steps towards general mobilization could be taken without the use of that fatal phrase. The decision also gave the Russians several days' advantage over Germany, since the equivalent German measures – the proclamation of the 'State of imminent danger of war' (*Kriegsgefahrzustand*) – were not ordered till 31 July.

There has been much subsequent discussion as to whether the Russians could or should have carried out the partial mobilization discussed on 24 July; and to some historians it has seemed yet another example of the way in which mobilization plans and railway timetables inexorably determined the development of the crisis. But, as L. C. F. Turner has shown,[29] this possibility was not very seriously considered in 1914 and was rejected for the same reasons as it had been in 1912 – namely that it would at once provoke Austrian general mobilization. In fact the announcement of the 'Period preparatory to war' and the measures already taken gave the Russians additional time for their mobilization while at the same time apparently leaving room for further diplomatic negotiations. The Austrians had always feared a situation in which the Russians would delay mobilization until the Austro-Hungarian army was tied down on the Serbian front; but it was just this situation that Conrad had created by his rash decision to risk everything on preparing an immediate attack on Serbia.

The period between 25 July and the final decision to proclaim general mobilization was marked by the hesitations and divisions which were characteristic of the way in which Russia was governed. While suggesting to the Tsar – and to the Germans – that mobilization against Austria-Hungary could be carried out without threatening Germany, Yanushkevich, the Chief of Staff, was already telegraphing to his subordinates to regard 30 July as the first day of general mobilization. It was thus possible for Sazonov to assure the German ambassador that no mobilization had taken place, since the formal orders for it had not yet been issued even though the preparations had begun. How far Sazonov himself understood the implications of the military measures already taken is by no means clear: 'Surely mobilization is not equivalent to war with you either. Is it?' he asked the German ambassador on 26 July when the first reports of Russian military measures were reaching the German embassy. The German ambassador was apparently less innocent, at least according to his own subsequent account, and replied, 'Perhaps not in theory. But . . .once the button is pressed and the machinery of mobilization set in motion there is no stopping it.'[30]

This is in effect what happened. By the afternoon of 29 July, Sazonov was sufficiently alarmed by German reactions to Russia's preparations that he was prepared to go along with the proclamation of general mobilization. Yet, just as the orders were about to be telegraphed to the military districts, there was another hitch, when the Tsar late that evening changed his mind yet again after a personal telegram from the Kaiser. 'I will not be responsible for a monstrous slaughter', he exclaimed;[31] and he considered again the idea of a partial mobilization. The result, however, was much the same, since by now the Austrians, under pressure from the Germans, had decided to mobilize anyway and issued the order for general mobilization on 31

July. The Russian general mobilization was only postponed for twenty-four hours: by the evening of 30 July the orders had gone out and this gave the Germans the opportunity to start their own mobilization on the pretext that the Russians had made the first move.

Events were moving too fast for the diplomats to keep pace with the realities of military planning. Again and again during the last days of peace we have the impression that the politicians and diplomats were taking decisions about situations that had already changed without their realizing it. In this connection it is interesting to speculate how much the French government was kept up to date with the progress of Russian military preparations. In theory the terms of the Franco-Russian alliance imposed on the Russians the obligation of consulting with the French before mobilization if the reason for mobilizing was action by Austria-Hungary; and Paléologue, the French ambassador in St Petersburg, certainly seems to have known what was going on and to have welcomed it. President Poincaré and the Prime Minister, Viviani, seem, however, to have gone out of their way to pretend ignorance of Russian mobilization as long as possible, presumably so as to free themselves from the criticism that they could have done more to restrain the Russians from a step which would certainly lead to war.

In any case, French military planning was now based on the assumption that the Russians were prepared to attack the German armies by the sixteenth day after mobilization. It was an undertaking which the Russians had been somewhat reluctant to give. In 1910 they had hoped to improve their relations with Germany, and the Tsar and the Kaiser had had a much publicized and friendly meeting at Potsdam. Early in 1911 the French had been alarmed to discover that their allies had, without telling them, withdrawn two army corps from the Polish frontier. However, in August of that year a French military mission found the Russians more willing to commit themselves; and although they said that they would not be ready for war for two years, they now agreed to open their campaign with an offensive. President Poincaré visited St Petersburg in 1912 and the Grand Duke Nicholas, the Tsar's uncle and the Inspector-General of Cavalry (who became Supreme Commander on the outbreak of war), attended the French army manœuvres. His Montenegrin wife, an enthusiastic supporter of the alliance and of Russia's role as protector of the South Slavs, endeared herself to the French by insisting on taking home with her a bag containing soil from Lorraine.

Plans for collaboration were carried further and formalized when Joffre visited Russia in the summer of 1913. He reported that he was satisfied with the progress made in the construction of Russia's strategic railways; and in September 1913 a military convention was signed by which the French and Russians both undertook to open offensive operations on the outbreak of war with Germany, France on the eleventh day and Russia after the fifteenth. These plans were based on the assumption that 'Germany will direct the greatest part of her forces against France and leave only a minimum of troops against Russia'.[32] At the same time the French government made the Russians a further substantial loan for railway building and armaments.

Since the Moroccan crisis of 1911, the French in addition to strengthening their links with Russia had been considering and revising their strategic plans as well as making changes in the high command. When Joffre became Chief of Staff and Commander-in-Chief, he began work on a new plan of campaign, Plan XVII. This not only relied on a Russian attack in the east, but also allowed for the presence of a small British force on the left of the French line; and in fact the talks between the two general staffs had led to closer co-operation than the more cautious political contacts between the two foreign offices, as well as being more frequent and more detailed than the military talks with the Russians. However, Joffre's plans were based on faulty intelligence about German intentions: he believed that the bulk of the German forces would be concentrated on the frontier in Lorraine and that any move by the Germans through Belgium would be limited to the area to the south of the Sambre and Meuse rivers, in part because he did not realize that the Germans were prepared to use their reserve divisions for immediate action in the same way as regular divisions, and that this would provide the manpower for a major operation through Belgium. The French hope was that an all-out attack on the main German forces could achieve a quick decision. The prevailing doctrine among French military leaders, in spite of a few critical voices, was that victory was as much the result of moral as material superiority and that the will to attack was bound to make the attack successful. Foch's teaching at the Ecole de Guerre laid down that 'If defeat comes from moral causes, victory may come from moral causes also';[33] and his disciple, Colonel de Grandmaison, one of the younger officers who had been influential in securing the appointment of Joffre as Generalissimo, put it even more strongly: 'The French army, returning to its traditions, no longer knows any other law than the offensive . . . All attacks are to be pushed to the extreme . . . to charge the enemy in order to destroy him . . . This result can only be obtained at the price of bloody sacrifice.'[34] Grandmaison was right about the price but wrong about the success. These doctrines found expression in the formulation of Plan XVII itself: 'Whatever the circumstances, it is the Commander-in-Chief's intention to advance with all forces united to attack the German armies.'[35]

Before deciding early in 1914 that this all-out attack would be made in Lorraine, Joffre had considered an attack through Belgium, and in 1912 had pressed the idea on the Supreme War Council. However, Poincaré and the majority of the members of the government realized that any breach of Belgian neutrality by France and any move into Belgium before German forces crossed the frontier would run the risk of putting an end to any prospect of British intervention on the side of France; and Joffre was obliged to accept this decision. Here at least the authority of the civilian government over the military leadership was clearly asserted. When the crisis came in July 1914, this subordination of the military to the civilians continued, and the final decisions always rested with the government rather than with the high command however much the latter might press for action. However, Joffre did with the agreement of the War Minister, take some preliminary measures before the President and Prime Minister had returned from their visit to Russia. As soon as Poincaré and Viviani returned on 2 July, Joffre was pressing them to authorize further measures and to allow the army to take up its positions on the German frontier. The cabinet agreed on 30 July, but they insisted that the troops should remain 10 kilometres from the frontier because they were determined to impress on the English and Italians that their intentions were purely defensive.

By 31 July, Joffre was even more alarmed and he seems to have had an exaggerated view of the military measures so far taken by the Germans and of the number of reservists called up. That afternoon he told the cabinet that any delay in French mobilization might mean having to start the war by abandoning French territory and that 'the Commander-in-Chief must decline to accept this responsibility'.[36] The cabinet authorized further troop movements, but not the calling up of reserves, as they were still anxious to avoid any step which might be misinterpreted by the British before British intervention was assured. In fact, although each government claimed that its own mobilization was ordered as a reaction to the preparations of others, the respective military machines were set in motion largely independently of each other once the gravity of the crisis was realized. Thus Joffre finally succeeded in persuading the government to allow him to issue the mobilization orders on the afternoon of 1 August, with the next day Sunday 2 August as the first day of mobilization. Although the French government later implied that this decision was taken in response to the German proclamation of the *Kriegsgefahrzustand*, news of this was not actually received in Paris till after the French decision had been taken.

'Mobilization is not war' the official French statement announced; and it is true that most of the mobilizations ordered in the last days of July and the beginning of August did not necessarily mean that there would be immediate hostilities; and in most cases there was in any case bound to be a delay of two weeks or more between ordering mobilization and being ready to start fighting. The one state whose military plans involved immediate aggressive action as soon as mobilization was proclaimed was Germany. German strategy on the outbreak of war had been determined in its general lines by the plan for a two-front war prepared by General von Schlieffen, the Chief of Staff from 1891 to 1906. He had been working on various versions of it since 1892 when he took the crucial decision to begin the war with an attack in the west rather than in the east. The plan was given its final form at the end of 1905, just before Schlieffen's retirement and at the moment of Russia's greatest weakness.[38] In order to achieve a rapid victory over France, the German armies were to move through Belgium and the Netherlands so as to cross the French frontier where the fortifications were weakest and thus envelope the French armies and eventually surround Paris. Finally, the French armies would be cut off from Paris, forced back against the fortresses on their eastern frontier and annihilated. (In fact, although the French General Staff had some idea of the German intention to move through Belgium at least as early as 1905, their plans for an attack in Lorraine meant that they would do more or less what Schlieffen wanted them to do since he hoped by an attack on Nancy to draw them away from reinforcing their northern front.) On Schlieffen's calculations the initial victory could be achieved in about a month, and indeed the whole plan was a gamble on the German ability to move swiftly and defeat the French before they had time to regroup their armies to meet the German advance from Belgium, so as to knock France out before the Russians could launch an offensive in the east.

Schlieffen did not bother about possible political complications: 'the neutrality of Luxemburg, Belgium and the Netherlands must be violated',[39] he wrote. Perhaps the Dutch might be prepared to agree to the passage of German troops; perhaps the Belgians would fight, but in any case Germany must not be deflected from pursuing her strategic goals by political and diplomatic considerations, any more than she would be by the possibility, which Schlieffen foresaw, that Britain might intervene and land an expeditionary force. He needed the room to manœuvre so as to launch an attack on a broad front; and this could only be obtained by a move through Belgium; and he needed to cross Dutch territory and use the Dutch railway system in order to capture the key Belgian railway junction of Liège and its surrounding forts.

It was this last point which was to be the object of an important modification by Schlieffen's successor, General von Moltke. He was convinced by the political objections to the violation of Dutch neurality and decided not to cross Dutch territory in order to launch the attack on Liège. Instead, the campaign was to open with a sudden surprise attack on Liège and the surrounding forts; and it was essential for the whole subsequent development of the German plans that this risky *coup de main*, involving as it did a very rapid advance on a narrow front so as to take the Belgians by surprise, should be carried out immediately war was declared. (It was in fact successfully launched on the night of 4–5 August 1914.) Thus, to the general necessity inherent in the Schlieffen plan for the violation of Belgian neutrality and offensive action as soon as possible after mobilization, the attack on

83

Liège required even more immediate action, since it was scheduled to take place on the third day of mobilization with such troops as were immediately available. It was therefore, as Moltke was to argue in a long meeting with Bethmann on the evening of 31 July 1914, essential to launch the attack in the west the moment Russia proclaimed mobilization, so as to carry out the onslaught on France before Russian mobilization was complete and before fighting began on the eastern front. And to launch the attack in the west, it was equally essential to capture Liège within three days. The attack on Belgium had therefore to be launched almost immediately after the proclamation of mobilization and there was no margin for any delay between mobilization and the start of hostilities. The Liège operation had been kept a deep secret, and it looks as though the Kaiser himself had not been told about it and that Bethmann only grasped its implications on 31 July. While the other powers could order mobilization and wait to decide what to do next, in the case of Germany mobilization inevitably meant war.

Although the violation of Belgian neutrality gave the British government a convincing reason to explain to their Liberal supporters why they declared war on Germany, the decision had, as we have seen, been taken on more general political and strategic grounds. Nevertheless, the involvement of Belgium had been foreseen by the British military planners ever since the first staff talks with France started late in 1905. Indeed at this stage there were even talks with the Belgians themselves, though these were not followed up once the immediate crisis over Morocco had abated; and the Belgian authorities reverted to a dogged insistence on their neutrality, rejecting any suggestion of co-operation with the French and British. The contacts between the British and French military staffs continued, however. The British government had taken a rather ambiguous attitude to the growing collaboration between their military planners – notably General Sir Henry Wilson, the Director of Military Operations at the War Office since 1910 – and the French. On the one hand, it was the job of the military to plan for all contingencies; on the other, it was the job of the political leadership to decide when those plans were to be put into operation. As Grey told Asquith in 1911, referring back to the staff talks of 1906, 'The military experts then convened. What they settled I never knew – the position being that the government was quite free, but that the military people knew what to do if the word was given.'[40] It was presumably this belief that military arrangements need not necessarily be implemented that enabled Asquith to tell the House of Commons after the Agadir crisis: 'There is no secret arrangement of any sort which has not been disclosed.'[41] Some of his closest advisers were less convinced. 'I reminded him [Asquith]', Lord Esher had written in his diary six weeks earlier, 'that the mere fact of a War Office plan having been worked out in detail with the French General Staff

. . . had certainly committed us to fight whether the Cabinet likes it or not.'[42] This was also the view of Sir Henry Wilson who had gone ahead with detailed plans for the despatch of an expeditionary force to France, and who in July 1911 had worked out the zone of concentration for the British forces on the left of the French armies and made precise agreements about port facilities and supply lines. Yet, however much these agreements may have contributed to the frame of mind of the British political and military leaders which led to Britain going to war at the side of France, in the final days of the crisis it was still the civilians who had the last word: even when the cabinet decided to intervene, the decision to order the despatch of the British Expeditionary Force (BEF) still had not been taken. General Wilson protested and fumed to the Foreign Office, members of the government and leaders of the opposition, and recorded scornfully in his diary that 'Grey's delay and hesitation in giving orders is sinful' and that Asquith had written to the Chief of the Imperial General Staff (CIGS) 'putting on record' the fact that the government had never promised the French an expeditionary force.[43] It was only on 4 August that the order to mobilize was given and the movement of the BEF to Europe was only ordered two days after the declaration of war; and even then there were still debates about its strength and destination and suggestions that the plans prepared by Wilson and Foch should all be changed. Finally on 12 August the original plans were put into operation, but the existence of the plans does not seem to have determined the government's policy or the timing of their decisions.

The British machinery of government had delayed the execution of the army's plans for collaboration with the French rather than hastening it. The case of the navy was somewhat different. It had been decided some months earlier that, in order to save money, there should be no full-scale manœuvres of the fleet in the summer of 1914 but that instead there should be a practice mobilization. As a result, by 17 July the whole fleet was mobilized and assembled for a grand review at Spithead. It had only started to disperse on 23 July. When the news of the Austrian ultimatum to Serbia became known on 26 July, the First Sea Lord, Admiral Prince Louis of Battenberg, at once issued orders to stop the dispersal. This was approved the next day by his political boss, Winston Churchill, the First Lord of the Admiralty, though it was not till 29 July that the Cabinet authorized the navy's preparations. Thus the British navy was able to complete its preparatory measures and concentration at their wartime base at Scapa Flow in the Orkneys by the time war was actually declared. This has been interpreted by some historians[44] as showing that it was in fact England which started the process of mobilization which was to escalate the crisis and lead to war, but there seems to be no evidence to suggest that it was any more than an accidental stroke of good fortune or that Battenberg acted in any other way than any responsible officer would have done in his position and that the initiative for the decision was his alone. Churchill later said that he had hoped that this step might remind Germany and Austria-Hungary to act prudently; and Grey used it in conversation with the Austrian ambassador as a sign of the seriousness with which the government regarded the situation, but it was a decision taken by the naval authorities without consultation with the government. It also seems to have been taken before learning of the Kaiser's order on 25 July to bring back the German fleet from its summer cruise in Norway – a step regretted by the German Foreign Office for fear it might alarm the British. Yet although in theory the decision enabled the British navy to be in a high state of readiness when war was declared, it made very little difference to their operations at the start of the war and certainly does not seem to have influenced British political decisions in the final days of the crisis.

How far then can one attribute the outbreak of the war to the arms race or to the primacy of strategic planning over political decisions? The major powers were all increasing and re-equipping their armies and navies, and, notably in the case of the Anglo-German naval race, a step by one at once provoked a step by another. Armaments bred armaments; and an armament programme once started was not easy to stop, for its reversal would have wide social and economic consequences. Yet at the same time governments were confronting the alternatives of cutting down their arms programme or else increasing taxation if they were not to face bankruptcy. The Germans introduced an income tax in 1913 to meet the cost of their navy and army increases; in France the introduction of an income tax was one of the major political issues immediately before the war, while in Britain the Liberal government risked a major political and constitutional crisis by including in the 1909 budget provisions for increasing death duties and duties on increments in land values, a political *tour de force* which attempted to pay both for the fleet and for the government's welfare programme but which bitterly alienated the Conservative opposition.

The influence of strategic planning depended on the role of the army in society and on the position which the general staffs occupied in the process of decision-making; and these differed widely from country to country. Such an influence could be both positive and negative. The negative influence was to restrict the freedom of action of a government in an international crisis; the decision to mobilize and the military and naval steps which mobilization involved inevitably increased the danger of war and provoked counter-measures by those governments which felt themselves threatened. The positive influence was felt in cases such as Germany and Austria where the General Staff was able to demand or persuade the government to take aggressive military action or where the army was virtually free from civilian control. All general staffs, war ministries and admiralties existed to plan for action in an international crisis, but not in all cases did they have the last word, and not in all cases did their plans include immediate aggressive action. However, in Austria-Hungary both Conrad and most of his civilian colleagues were convinced of the importance of an early attack on Serbia, and in Germany Schlieffen's plan as modified by Moltke required an immediate invasion of Belgium.

All governments envisaged the possibility of war: that was why they kept general staffs and spent vast sums on armaments. But some were more willing to contemplate starting a war than others. The Austrians had become convinced by 1914 that they must crush Serbia at whatever risk. The Germans believed that time was no longer on their side and that a war which many of their leaders said was inevitable had better be fought sooner rather than later – though there was some difference between the army and the navy as to which would be the most favourable moment.

Conrad had talked of the need for a preventive war for several years (and had been temporarily removed from office in 1911–12 for this reason) and the campaign against Serbia had been prepared since 1908, in spite of the problem of combining it with a campaign against the Russians. Serbia's successes in the Balkan wars gave renewed urgency to Conrad's pleas for action. He was clearly ready to take the first chance which presented itself for an attack on Serbia; and the assassination of Franz Ferdinand gave an unusually favourable opportunity. Some historians have placed the German decision for war in December 1912:[45] and it is certain that at a meeting between the Kaiser and the military and naval leaders at which neither the Imperial Chancellor nor the War Minister were present, Moltke expressed his desire for 'war – the sooner the better', even though Tirpitz demanded at least another year and a half. In fact, few new specific preparations for war were made as a result. Even the Kaiser's orders for a press campaign to prepare the nation for the coming conflict were not taken very seriously and to at least one observer the discussion was an example of the uncertainty and vagueness of German policy-making. Yet the accounts which we have of this meeting are convincing proof that at least by this date Germany's leaders were anticipating war in the near future and were quite ready to risk it when the moment seemed propitious, even if they were not planning for a particular war at a particular moment.

The attitude of the other belligerent powers was more complicated. They prepared for war; and in many ways they expected it. The British hoped it would not come and within limits tried to prevent it. The French, and especially President Poincaré, believed that a war at the side of Russia might lead to the recovery of the lost provinces; but they were not prepared to start it. The army had planned its strategy based on the all-out attack, but they were not going to put it into operation until Germany moved first. The strategic initiative remained with the Germans.

The situation of Russia was more complicated still. The recovery from the defeat by Japan had been surprisingly rapid, and both the British and the Germans believed that Russia would be capable of fighting a major war by 1916 or 1917. Some of the Russian leaders had talked as if they were ready to go to war over the question of the German military mission to Constantinople in 1913, without apparently having any clear idea how they would set about it, since it soon became clear that it would be impossible to mount an expedition to seize the Straits while at the same time facing a war with Germany and Austria. However, by 1914 some at least of the Russian ministers were confident that Russia, now that she had embarked on the big army and naval increases approved in 1913, was strong enough to confront Germany and Austria-Hungary without waiting till 1917. The Germans, on the other hand, believed that they had better have the expected war with Russia as soon as possible before the Russians were militarily even stronger. But in any case the Russians felt bound to act in 1914 for reasons affecting their general international position and influence in the Balkans, and so believed that they must respond to Serbia's appeal for help. They believed that they could risk a war, even though they still hoped that a firm diplomatic stand and eventually mobilization might avert the Austro-Hungarian attack on Serbia.

The degree to which each government was prepared to risk a European war by taking the initiative in starting military action varied; but German and Austrian plans involved the highest danger of general war. What is more important than the immediate responsibility for the actual outbreak of war is the state of mind which was shared by all the belligerents, a state of mind which envisaged the probable imminence of war and its absolute necessity in certain circumstances. Still, the war they expected and the war for which the general staffs and admiralties planned was not the war which they actually got. Very few people inside or outside government circles expected a long and destructive world war. None of the governments involved had made adequate economic plans for war: within weeks of its beginning they were already running out of munitions. In Germany, the banker and industrialist Walter Rathenau warned the government in September 1914 that the war would be long, and persuaded Bethmann Hollweg to put him in control of stockpiling strategic raw materials. Lord Kitchener, England's most famous soldier, summoned to be Secretary for War on 4 August 1914, startled his colleagues by saying that Britain must be prepared 'to put armies of millions into the field and maintain them for several years', but there were no plans to do so. Grey later commented: 'It was never disclosed how or by what powers of reasoning he made this forecast of the length of the war';[46] and it took the government a long time to act on Kitchener's brief: conscription was not introduced till 1916.

All the governments and most of their subjects were the victims of what one historian has called 'the short-war illusion'.[47] The consequences of this miscalculation were to make the First World War a far more significant turning-point in European history than those who embarked on it – some light-heartedly like the German Crown Prince who exhorted the German people to take part in a bright and jolly war, some with regret, like Sir Edward Grey who saw the lights going out all over Europe – ever imagined.

REFERENCES AND NOTES

1. H. H. Herwig and B. F. Trask, 'Naval operations plans between Germany and the USA 1898–1913' in P. M. Kennedy (ed.) *The War Plans of the Great Powers 1880–1914* (London 1979).
2. See H. Pogge von Strandmann, 'Staatsstreichpläne, Alldeutsche und Bethmann Hollweg' in H. Pogge von Strandmann and Imanuel Geiss (eds) *Die Erforderlichkeit des Unmöglichen: Deutschland am Vorabend des ersten Weltkrieges* (Frankfurt-am-Main 1965). For anti-socialist measures in the army see Martin Kitchen, *The German Officer Corps 1890–1914* (Oxford 1968), Ch. VII.
3. See Jean-Jacques Becker, *Le Carnet B: Les pouvoirs publics et l'antimilitarisme avant la guerre de 1914* (Paris 1973).
4. Quoted in Michael Balfour, *The Kaiser and his Times* (London 1964) p. 158.
5. *The Times*, 18 Oct. 1906.
6. Quentin Bell, *Virginia Woolf*, Vol. I (London 1972) p. 158.
7. For a detailed account of the Zabern affair and its implications, see David Schoenbaum, *Zabern 1913: Consensus Politics in Imperial Germany* (London 1982).
8. A. von Tirpitz, *Politische Dokumente*, Vol. I. *Der Aufbau der Deutschen Weltmacht* (Stuttgart and Berlin 1924) p. 160. See also Gerhard Ritter, *Staatskunst und Kriegshandwerk*, Vol. II (Munich 1965) p. 197.
9. Quoted in Franklyn Arthur Johnson, *Defence by Committee* (London 1960) p. 68.
10. Henry Wilson's Diary, 31 Dec. 1901; quoted in C. E. Callwell, *Field-Marshal Sir Henry Wilson*, Vol. I (London 1927) p. 47.
11. G. P. Gooch and Harold Temperley (eds) *British Documents on the Origins of the War 1898–1914*, Vol. VI (London 1930) Appendix III, p. 779. (Hereinafter referred to as *BD*.)
12. Hansard, 5th series, Vol. I, cols 1749–91. See E. L. Woodward, *Great Britain and the German Navy* (Oxford 1935) p. 408.
13. Tirpitz, op. cit., Vol. I, p. 282. See also Arthur J. Marder, *From the Dreadnought to Scapa Flow*, Vol. I. *The Road to War 1904–14* (London 1961) p. 156.
14. Quoted in Marder, op. cit., Vol. I, p. 156.
15. Marder, op. cit., Vol. I, p. 158.
16. *BD* X (2) No. 500, p. 736. See also Marder, op. cit., Vol. I, p. 315.
17. *BD* X (2) No. 501, p. 737.

18.   E. Bernstein, 'Die internationale Bedeutung des Wahlkampfes i
       Deutschland', quoted in R. A. Fletcher, 'Revisionism and empire' (ur
       published Ph.D. thesis, University of Queensland 1981) p. 406.

19.   Quoted in Jean-Jacques Becker, *1914: Comment les Français sont entre
       dans la guerre* (Paris 1977) p. 43, n. 174. For accounts of civil–militar
       relations in France see David Ralston, *The Army of the Republic* (Cam
       bridge, Mass. 1967) and especially Douglas Porch, *The March to th
       Marne: The French Army 1871–1914* (Cambridge 1981).

20.   See especially Norman Stone, *The Eastern Front 1914–1917* (Londo
       1975) Ch. I.

21.   Viscount Grey of Fallodon, *Twenty-five Years 1892–1916*, Vol.
       (London 1925) pp. 284–5. See also Marder, op. cit., Vol. I, pp. 309–11

22.   Stone, *Eastern Front*, p. 71.

23.   Vladimir Dedijer, *The Road to Sarajevo* (London 1967) p. 378.

24.   Dedijer, op. cit., p. 415.

25.   Quoted in Norman Stone, 'Die Mobilmachung der österreichisch
       ungarischen Armee 1914', *Militärgeschichtliche Mitteilungen*, **2**, 1974.

26.   Stone, *Easter Front*, Ch. 4. See also Stone, 'Moltke and Conrad
       relations between the Austro-Hungarian and German General Staff
       1909–1914', *The Historical Journal*, ix, No. 2, reprinted in Kennedy, op
       cit., pp. 222–251. For the details see especially Stone, 'Mobilmachung'

27.   Stone, 'Mobilmachung', p. 79.

28.   L. C. F. Turner, 'The Russian mobilization of 1914' in Kennedy, op. cit.
       p. 255.

29.   Turner, 'Russian mobilization'. See also L. C. F. Turner, *Origins of th
       First World War* (London 1975).

30.   Friedrich Graf Pourtalès, *Meine letzte Unterhandlungen in Sankt Peters
       burg* (Berlin 1927) p. 27, quoted in L. Albertini, *The Origins of the Wa
       of 1914* (London 1953) Vol. II, p. 481.

31.   Quoted in Turner, 'Russian mobilization' in Kennedy, op. cit., p. 266.

32.   *Documents diplomatiques français*, 3 série, Vol. VIII (Paris 1935), N
       79. See also Turner, 'Russian mobilization' p. 257.

33.   Quoted in Sir Basil Liddell Hart, 'French military ideas before the Firs
       World War' in Martin Gilbert (ed.) *A Century of Conflict 1850–195C
       Essays for A. J. P. Taylor* (London 1966) p. 138.

34.   Liddell Hart, op. cit., p. 140.

35.   Quoted in S. R. Williamson, 'Joffre reshapes French strategy 1911–191:
       in Kennedy, op. cit., p. 147.

36.   J. J. C. Joffre, *The Memoirs of Marshal Joffre*, 2 vols (London 1932) Vo
       I, p. 125. See also Albertini, op. cit., Vol. III, p. 105.

37.   Raymond Poincaré, *Au Service de la France: neuf années de souvenirs
       10 vols (Paris 1926–33) Vol. IV, p. 484.

38.   The various versions of the Schlieffen plan were first published in full i
       1956 and are printed in Gerhard Ritter, *The Schlieffen Plan* (Eng. tr
       London 1958).

39.   Ritter, *Schlieffen Plan*, p. 136.

40.   Grey of Fallodon, op. cit., Vol. I, p. 94. See also Samuel R. Williamso
       Jr, *The Politics of Grand Strategy: Britain and France Prepare for Wa
       1904–1914* (Cambridge, Mass. 1969) p. 139.

41.   Hansard, 5th series, Vol. XXXII, col. 107.

2. M. V. Brett (ed.) *The Journals and Letters of Viscount Esher*, 2 vols (London 1934) Vol. II, pp. 61–2. Williamson, *Grand Strategy*, p. 197.
3. Callwell, op. cit., Vol. I, pp. 154, 156.
4. Most recently by Erwin Hölzle, *Die Selbstentmachtung Europas* (Göttingen 1975).
5. See John Röhl, 'Admiral von Müller and the approach of war 1911–14', *Historical Journal*, xii (1964); *1914: Delusion or Design* (London 1973); 'An der Schwelle zum Weltkrieg: eine Dokumentation über der "Kriegsrat" vom 8 Dezember 1912', *Militärgeschichtliche Mitteilungen*, 1 1977; 'Die Generalprobe. Zur Geschichte und Bedeutung des "Kriegsrates" vom 8 Dezember 1912' in Dirk Stegmann, Bernd-Jürgen Wendt and Peter-Christian Witt (eds) *Industrielle Gesellschaft und politisches System* (Bonn 1978). See also Fritz Fischer, *Krieg der Illusionen* (Düsseldorf 1969) pp. 232 ff, but cf. Bernd F. Schulte, 'Zu der Krisenkonferenz vom 8 Dezember 1912 in Berlin', *Historisches Jahrbuch*, **102** Jahrgang Erster Halbband (1982) 183–97.
6. Grey of Fallodon, op. cit., Vol. II, p. 69. See also Barbara W. Tuchman, *The Guns of August* (New York 1962) pp. 195–7.
7. Lancelot L. Farrar Jr, *The Short War Illusion* (Santa Barbara 1973).

Chapter 5

THE PRIMACY OF DOMESTIC POLITICS

In the previous three chapters we have looked at the decisions to go to war in the light of the diplomatic and strategic factors which influenced them. It has been assumed that each government was largely motivated by foreign political purposes – to preserve the balance within the international system, to gain territory or influence, to protect the fatherland against attack or encirclement. But there is another dimension to all foreign policy decisions, that provided by domestic politics and internal social and economic pressures.

Each of the European Great Powers was passing through a political and social crisis in 1914; and in some cases the problems which confronted them were solved or at least postponed by the outbreak of war. It does not necessarily follow, however, that it was in order to solve or postpone these problems that governments declared war. Indeed, many of them were well aware that a declaration of war might create more social problems than it would solve. In the period before the war as well as at the moment of its outbreak the governments of Europe had had to pay some attention to public opinion in formulating their foreign policies, but this does not necessarily imply that they used foreign policy primarily in order to manipulate public opinion or to achieve internal political aims. In some cases, notably that of Germany, as we shall see, foreign policy was sometimes used as a way of providing a focus for national feelings so as to distract attention away from the divisions and tensions in German society. However, the relation between domestic and foreign policy was a very complex one; and it was often by no means clear whether a policy which risked involving a country in war would be more likely to create a mood of national solidarity or to provoke a revolution.

The foreign policy of one country at least, Austria-Hungary, was wholly the product of its internal problems. Austria-Hungary depended for its very existence on its international relations. Since the days of Metternich, it had been essential for the Austrian government and the House of Habsburg to persuade other countries that the preservation of the Empire was an international necessity and that its disappearance would produce a situation in central Europe which would be fatal to the stability of the international system. By 1914 this international consensus was beginning to break down. Some of the subject nationalities of Austria-Hungary were looking for outside support for their national claims and in some cases were in contact with foreign governments.

By the early twentieth century the growing influence of independent national states on the borders of Austria-Hungary gave a new focus for national movements within the Monarchy. The Southern Slavs – Serbs, Croats, Slovenes – began to look to Serbia for support and to forget their own religious and cultural differences because of their grievances against the Habsburg state. The mood was expressed at its simplest by a Croat sergeant on trial for desertion in 1916: 'The Croats were always loyal to the Emperor, but he did not love them and delivered them over to the Magyars, so that they were forced to turn to the Serbs, who at least spoke their language.'[1] The Rumanian and Italian governments were being forced to decide whether their desire to 'redeem' their compatriots in Transylvania or the South Tyrol was stronger than the pull of their alliances with Germany and Austria-Hungary. Of the national problems confronting the Habsburg state, it was the Southern Slav question which had the most serious inter-national repercussions. The relations between Czechs and Germans in Bohemia and Moravia were more intractable but they did not yet have an international dimension; and negotiations for some compromise at a local level were unsuccessfully dragging on in 1914. Yet although a few of the Czech and Slovak national leaders looked to Russia and were even in secret contact with the Russian government, the majority were not yet seeking outside support for their claims; and the Russians were not yet prepared to take the risk of giving them open and practical encouragement.

The Southern Slav question was different. Although there were plans with which Franz Ferdinand himself was involved for the grant of some form of autonomy to the Croats, any change of this kind was bitterly opposed by the Magyars, so that by 1914 very little had been done to meet the grievances of the Croats, and consequently they had increased their contacts with other Southern Slavs. In 1905 a number of Croat and Serb politicians inside the Monarchy had agreed on a common programme, but this had achieved little. Then in 1908 the annexation of Bosnia had increased Serb discontent both within and outside Austria-Hungary so that, with the growth of national feeling inside Serbia and the movement towards Southern Slav unity, Serbia seemed to the Austrian government an increasing threat to the very existence of the Habsburg state. As a conflict between Austria and Serbia was likely to involve Russia, anxious to use her traditional role as protector of the Balkan Slavs for her own ends, the Austro-Hungarians' failure to solve their internal national problems inevitably had international ramifications. The Austro-Hungarian governmen believed that the establishment of some sort of control over Serbia wa essential for the survival of their state. After trying economic pressur between 1906 and 1910, they decided to use more direct methods, an the decision for war in 1914 was the result of a mistaken belief that onl vigorous action against Serbia could solve the problem of the Sla nationalities within the Empire and that Austria-Hungary's interna problems could only be solved by an active and aggressive foreig policy. For all the complexities of the Austro-Hungarian state, th relation between its domestic problems and its foreign policy is com paratively clear, even if one may be surprised at the misconception and illusions which led Conrad, Berchtold and their colleagues to thinl that an attack on Serbia would solve the Habsburg monarchy's dif ficulties. In Britain and France the situation was more complicated.

A Liberal government had been in power in England since 1905 an there were many among its supporters who held to the tradition o Richard Cobden, John Bright and to some extent Gladstone himself and believed that the balance of power was a dangerous concept, tha expenditure on armaments was both wasteful and wicked and tha Britain's policy should be to maintain the freedom of trade and to kee herself free of foreign entanglements. Although there had bee inroads on these liberal beliefs, the issue was still very much alive i 1914. There had been bitter debates within the Liberal governmen about the priorities of expenditure between social welfare and nava construction; and in those tense discussions in the Cabinet in the las days of July 1914 it was uncertain almost to the last minute whether th government might not break up if a decision were taken to go to war o the side of France and Russia.

The British government in the years before 1914 faced a series o internal political crises. There had been a major constitutional conflic caused by the House of Lords' rejection of the budget, and th consequent passage, in the face of bitter opposition, of a bill to limit it powers. There had been an increase in industrial disputes and signs of a new militancy in the trade unions. The tactics adopted by the radica wing of the movement for women's suffrage introduced new problem in the administration of justice, since women arrested after violen demonstrations – chaining themselves to railings, disrupting publi functions, setting fire to official buildings and to mail boxes – then wen on hunger strike, obliging the authorities either to feed them forcibl or to release them only in order to rearrest them, both proceeding repugnant to a liberal society and a Liberal government. Finally, th introduction of a bill to grant Home Rule to Ireland led to a deadlocl over the future of the province of Ulster. By 1914 the constitutiona crisis over the House of Lords had been resolved, but the othe problems were still far from solution. The outbreak of war meant tha some of them could be suspended for the time being; and when the wa nded their nature had changed.

It is, however, hard, in the years before 1914, to find any links between these domestic problems in Britain and decisions about foreign policy; and divisions within the government on questions of foreign policy did not always correspond to divisions on other questions. Sir Edward Grey, for example, was regarded by the radicals in the government as taking too hard a line over commitments to France and antagonism to Germany, but was criticized by more conservative colleagues for his support of women's suffrage. Domestic issues tended to distract attention from international affairs, so that the conduct of foreign policy was left to the Foreign Office and the professional diplomats, and for much of the time criticism of that policy was limited to the small group of radicals whom A. J. P. Taylor has called the troublemakers'.[2] There were disputes within the government about the rival claims of expenditure on naval armaments and expenditure on social services, and, while the Conservative opposition was pressing for still more naval increases, the government's main problem was with its own radical supporters who called for arms reduction and an understanding with Germany.

At the time of the Moroccan crisis in 1911 there was a moment of anxiety in the Liberal Party that their leaders were undertaking commitments of which the public was ignorant. 'There is a considerable amount of discontent against Grey in the Liberal Party', Lord Sanderson, the retired Permanent Under-Secretary of the Foreign Office, noted in January 1912. 'A good deal of it is the inevitable result of the enthusiastic philanthropy which insists in messing about in other people's affairs which it does not understand. But part also arises from lack of information.'[3] Lloyd George later complained bitterly that Grey did not inform the Cabinet about the European situation, but one suspects that at the time Lloyd George did not always pay attention when foreign affairs were being discussed, at least until after the Agadir crisis. Still, Grey sometimes certainly preferred to discuss his policies with a small group of close colleagues rather than in the Cabinet as a whole, and, as a result of his failure to communicate with a wider circle, he was on at least one occasion, in November 1911, obliged to reassure Parliament that he had not been committing England to go to war without the knowledge of his colleagues and his party: 'No British government could embark upon a war without public opinion behind it, and such engagements as there are which really commit Parliament to anything of that kind are contained in treaties and agreements which have been laid before the house. For ourselves we have not made a single secret article of any kind since we came into office.'[4]

Opinions differ as to the extent of Grey's own disingenuousness and capacity to mislead his colleagues; and his refusal to enquire into the details of what had been arranged by the military leaders (see pp.84–5) has been interpreted both as a sign of incompetence and as evidence of dishonesty. The fact remains that the political pressures to which Grey was most directly subjected were against any policy which might involve Britain in a war on the Continent, even though he himself envisaged circumstances when this might be necessary.

At the outbreak of war the worst domestic problem confronting the British government was that of Ulster, and it was a problem which had direct implications for Britain's defence policy. Resistance to the government's proposals for Home Rule for Ireland was growing with the active support of the Conservative opposition in Parliament, so that a civil war between the Protestant Ulster Unionists, determined to resist government by a Roman Catholic majority in Dublin, and the supporters of Home Rule seemed probable. General Sir Henry Wilson, the Director of Military Operations at the War Office, noted on 31 December 1913: 'Ulster rapidly becoming the sole governing and immediate factor in the national life.'[5] With the coming of the July crisis, the relation between Ulster and the international situation was much in Asquith's mind: 'We are within measurable, or imaginable, distance of a real Armageddon, which would dwarf the Ulster and Nationalist Volunteers', he wrote on 24 July. 'Happily there seems to be no reason why we should be anything more than spectators. But it is a blood-curdling prospect, is it not?'[6] And two days later he noted: 'It is the most dangerous situation of the last forty years. It may incidentally have the effect of throwing into the background the lurid pictures of civil war in Ulster.'[7] This does not however suggest that the government's actions in July 1914 were deliberately intended to use the international crisis to distract attention away from the conflict in Ireland.

The crisis over Ulster reminded the British government how vulnerable Ireland would be in the event of war and what a strain on the loyalty of the subjects of the United Kingdom the Home Rule problem had imposed. The officers of the garrison at the Curragh, the military base outside Dublin, had made their position quite clear early in 1914 when they had threatened to resign their commissions rather than impose by force a solution on the Protestant majority in Northern Ireland. By the middle of 1914 the situation had become even more acute. As far as the south of Ireland was concerned, the government had recognized that the assumptions of five years earlier no longer applied. In 1909 the general commanding in Ireland had written: 'The time has now come when the Irish soldiers can safely be entrusted with the local defence of Ireland.'[8] But in 1914 it was accepted that the 24,000 Irish reservists should be used for service abroad, while troops from England should go to garrison Ireland. The result was that a substantial portion of the BEF was Irish, and their conduct belied any fears which might still have been felt on the subject.[9]

Still, there was in July 1914 a real threat of revolt in Ireland. On 26

July, when the full gravity of the international situation was becoming apparent, 25,000 German rifles were landed near Dublin. The arms had been bought in Hamburg by the militant Irish nationalist Erskine Childers, ironically enough the author of the most effective of the popular novels dealing with German machinations against Britain, *The Riddle of the Sands*. But on the Ulster side, too, activists had been busy buying arms in Hamburg at least as early as January 1914, and in April a cargo of 30,000 rifles had been delivered. Unionist politicians, including members of Parliament, had not been above using phrases such as: 'If the Ulstermen were put out of the Union . . . I would infinitely prefer to change my allegiance right over to the Emperor of Germany or anyone else with a proper and stable government.' Or again: 'Germany and the German Emperor would be preferred to the rule of John Redmond, Patrick Ford and the Molly Maguires', a view summed up in the phrase: 'If Protestant Georgie won't, then Protestant Willie will.'[10] In fact, the German government, although following the Irish question with interest and indeed concern, rejected suggestions made in some quarters – notably by Irish Americans – that they should intervene in order to foster the incipient civil war in Ireland; and the purchase of arms in Germany by both sides to the Irish dispute seems to have been a purely private enterprise.[11]

The strongest pressures that the Liberal government had to face were pressures for peace not pressures for war. Grey had never had any doubts in his own mind that, if it came to a conflict between France and Germany, Britain would have to support France. His reasons were based not on internal political pressures but on conventional thinking about foreign policy and Britain's place as a world power. However, one effect of the British system of government is that it forces ministers to be devious and disingenuous. A liberal statesman in a liberal democracy – and we have had the more recent examples of Franklin Roosevelt in 1939–41 and of Lyndon Johnson in the Vietnam War – who is himself convinced that circumstances demand entry into a war, often has to conceal what he is doing from those who have elected him. The charge levelled against Grey by the radicals on the left of his party was that those who had voted for a Liberal government had not realized the extent of the commitments in foreign policy which that government had undertaken. However much the British government stressed that the arrangements with the French did not commit England to war on the side of France, many of the members of that government believed that they did, but that their supporters would not stand for it if they knew the whole truth. In 1914 the German violation of Belgian neutrality gave the British government the moral grounds they needed for calling on their Liberal followers to support the war. If we look for the responsibility for the First World War in the political and constitutional arrangements of the belligerent states, then the structure of the British government can be held responsible for Grey's reluctance openly to commit Britain to support France and Russia before he was absolutely convinced he could carry his party with him.

For this reason, his attitude to the staff talks and the naval agreement with France and the naval discussions with Russia was deliberately ambiguous. He had to take account of the political attitudes and traditions within his own party; and the government's tactics in the crisis were in part determined by the need to reconcile what Grey, Asquith, Haldane and some others believed to be necessary on grounds of foreign policy with the pressures inside the Liberal Party which placed obstacles in the way of that policy. The government's decision to go to war was based on their view of Britain's international standing and their belief that it was essential to intervene in order to maintain it. This decision had to be presented to the members of the Liberal Party both inside and outside the government in such a way as to overcome their instinctive repugnance to a policy of involvement on the Continent. In the immediate crisis of July 1914 domestic politics were acting as an obstacle to the execution of foreign policy rather than as a spur to warlike action.

In France the relationship between domestic and foreign policy was a complex one. The period between 1911 and the outbreak of war was a period of considerable political tension not only because the industrial unrest, which had reached its peak in the rail strike of 1910, continued to smoulder, but also because French politics were dominated by three major controversies. These were the debate about electoral reform and the proposal to introduce proportional representation, the question of an income tax and, above all, the move to introduce, or rather reintroduce, a three-year term of compulsory military service instead of the two-year period adopted in 1905. The fragmentation of the centre groups in parliament because of these issues meant that between January 1912 and the outbreak of war there were seven different governments and six different prime ministers – a rapid turnover even by the standards of the Third Republic. It was only in the elections of May and June 1914 that the lines appeared, perhaps misleadingly, to become clearer, with a marked swing to the left and notable gains for the Socialist Party.

Since the Agadir crisis in 1911 there had been a revival of popular nationalism directed against Germany, reawakening memories of the loss of Alsace-Lorraine. As the atmosphere of tension in Europe grew during the Moroccan crisis and the Balkan wars, many Frenchmen became more aware of their restless neighbour across the Rhine and more sensitive than for several years about the lost provinces. The German representatives in Paris were constantly reminded of this by the success in the Paris theatres of patriotic shows with titles such as *Cœur de Française* or *Servir* or *Alsace* (in which, as the British ambassador also noticed, the tirades against the Germans were 'received with rapturous applause')[12], and by the nervousness of the French public over episodes such as the forced landing of a German zeppelin near Lunéville in April 1913 and the attacks on German businessmen in Nancy which followed. On the other hand the vociferous opposition to the Three-Years Law and the repeated assertions by the Left that they would resist what they regarded as a threat of militarism might suggest a different conclusion about the state of public opinion in France. Any French government if it was to survive had somehow to base its foreign policy on a balance between these two extremes of opinion.

The revival of popular nationalism had found expression in the election of Raymond Poincaré to the Presidency of the Republic in January 1913. Although Poincaré's move from the office of Prime Minister, which he had held for the past year, was the result of the usual political intrigues and parliamentary manœuvres, to the French public his election seemed to promise a tough line towards Germany and the assertion of France's position in Europe. Poincaré was a native of Lorraine, a fact which explains much about his foreign policy both before, during and after the war. As Prime Minister he had aimed at strengthening the army and tightening the links with France's ally Russia. While anxious to ensure immediate military action by the Russians in the event of war with Germany, at the same time he wanted to avoid involving France in a war in the Balkans in circumstances which would not be popular in France and would only serve Russian interests. If war was to come, it would have to be over an issue which would appear to the French public as involving a direct threat to France. For this reason, the French government sometimes appeared to the Russians to be rather unreliable allies in the crises in the Balkans or at the moment of the arrival of the German military mission at Constantinople (see p.54), just as the Russians had seemed to the French to be unreliable allies in the Agadir crisis. Poincaré was convinced that the Russian alliance was essential for France, and that if war was provoked by Germany France would, with Russian support, stand a chance of recovering the lost provinces. He needed, therefore, to reassure the Russians that, even if France seemed lukewarm about some of Russia's Balkan concerns, she nevertheless was serious about her obligations to the alliance. This was the reason for the new loan to Russia in 1913 intended to enable the Russians to extend their strategic railways; it was also one reason for the alacrity with which the French government seized on the German army increases in January 1913 to expand the period of conscript service; and it perhaps also explains Poincaré's willingness, after a year as Prime Minister, to run for the Presidency of the Republic, even though this might seem to be giving up real political power for purely ceremonial functions. He was convinced that he could produce a mood of national unity and was prepared to use his presidential prerogatives as far as they could possibly be stretched in order to do so. Domestic politics were to be subordinated to foreign policy.

Accordingly in March 1913 the government announced that it would introduce a bill in the Chamber to increase the length of military service to three years. Much was made of the widespread public fear of a mass invasion by the Germans; and the military leaders had more precise anxieties. They were worried that the Germans, with more troops immediately available on mobilization, might be able to launch a sudden attack before the French army was organized and ready to open the all-out offensive envisaged by Plan XVII, so that it was essential for the French to have more trained soldiers actually serving in the army on the outbreak of war. The passage of the bill would also give definite proof to the Russians of France's loyalty, determination and military capacity.

The bitter public debate which followed seemed to some people, both at the time and subsequently, to reflect a division in French opinion as deep as that over the Dreyfus case. The German ambassador in Paris, for example, reported in June 1914:

> The struggle for and against the three years service has in fact become identical with the guaranteeing of a strong state system respected at home and abroad or else the socialist state of the future with the breakdown of the concept of patriotism, just as at the time the decision for or against Dreyfus had become identical with declaring allegiance to reaction or to republican progress. France then stood at an important decisive point of her internal development which was also bound to affect her foreign policy.[13]

Yet for all the vigour with which the Left opposed the Three-Years Law, the situation was more complicated than it at first appeared to be. Some people were prepared to support the law as a short-term emergency measure to be repealed in due course: the army leaders themselves would have been satisfied with a less drastic increase of the number of men with the colours and they were worried that they would not have enough barracks available to house the new conscripts. Many socialists, including their leader Jean Jaurès, were in favour of national defence, but wanted a measure that would be part of a complete reorganization of the whole system. The supporters of an increase in the size of the army were divided between those who thought that a shorter extension of the period of service would be enough or that the call-up could be more selective; while others were totally opposed to any measure which appeared to distinguish between one class of citizen and another. Moreover, the problem of cost meant that the prolongation of the period of service was closely connected with the need to increase revenue by means of an income tax, so that there were, especially among the various radical groups, many people who willed the end but were not prepared to vote the means.[14]

But even if the division of opinion over the Three-Years Law was not as clear-cut as it sometimes seemed, there is no doubt that the result of the 1914 elections was extremely worrying for the supporters of the law and especially for President Poincaré himself, who sometimes talked of resigning if there were any move to repeal the law. In choosing a Prime Minister in June 1914 he was determined to find one who would, in spite of the socialist gains in the new Chamber, wholeheartedly commit himself to the maintenance of the three years' period of service. However, when Poincaré's first nominee had been defeated in parliament after only three days in office, the President was forced to settle for René Viviani, a former socialist and now an independent, whose commitment to the cause of the Three-Years Law was somewhat ambiguous, and whose vacillation, moodiness and inexperience in foreign affairs Poincaré was to criticize bitterly over the next few weeks. (A typical example is Poincaré's diary entry for 27 July 1914, while at sea on the way back from his and Viviani's visit to St Petersburg, which runs: 'I passed part of the day explaining to Viviani that weakness towards Germany always resulted in complications and that the only way to remove the danger was to show firm perseverence and impassive *sang-froid*. But he is nervous and agitated and doesn't stop pronouncing imprudent words or phrases which reveal a black ignorance of matters of foreign policy.'[15]) Up to the outbreak of the war, the future of the Three-Years Law still seemed to be in doubt, since Viviani's government, in order to secure the support of the Chamber, announced that it envisaged an eventual shortening of the period of service.

Even if the extreme anti-militarism of the previous decade was now on the wane, a sufficient number of people had signed petitions against the Three-Years Law to give the authorities ground for anxiety, while the trade unions and the Socialist Party were, in theory at least, committed to a general strike against war. It is, however, easy to overemphasize the significance of the extreme expressions both of militarism and anti-militarism in France in the three years before the war. Perhaps that shrewd observer of the French political scene Baron von Schoen, the German ambassador, was right when he wrote in February 1914: 'The bellicose desire for revenge . . . is now outmoded. It only exists to a certain extent in theory. The wound of 1871 still burns in all French hearts, but nobody is inclined to risk his or his son's bones for the question of Alsace-Lorraine, unless circumstances arose which might open up exceptionally favourable, and reasonably comfortable prospects for the venture.'[16] The aim of Poincaré's policy was to ensure that if war came it would be in a situation that would provide just the 'exceptionally favourable and reasonably comfortable prospects' to which the German ambassador referred. In Poincaré's view and that of the ministers who consulted him assiduously after he had become President, such prospects could only be obtained by strengthening the alliance with Russia and consolidating the ties with England. But he was also committed to the creation of a mood of national unity, and the two aims of his policy sometimes appeared to be incompatible. In any case, domestic and foreign policy were inextricably intermixed and it is very hard for the historian to give primacy to one over the other. The opposition to the Three-Years Law and the success of the Left in the elections of 1914 showed how essential it was for any French government to present its policies in a peaceful light. Poincaré's policy seems to have been accurately summed up in a remark reported by the Russian ambassador in 1912 even though Poincaré himself later denied having made it: 'France is unquestionably peace-loving: she neither seeks nor desires a war, but the intervention of Germany against Russia would immediately alter this frame of mind.'[17]

The limitations on Poincaré's foreign policy and his freedom of manœuvre were imposed by the political divisions in the country at large, but the events of July and August 1914 showed that his policy had been after all successful, and that the divisions in French opinion were not as deep as had been feared. The murder of Jaurès on 31 July by a nationalist fanatic, even though Jaurès had publicly supported the government's handling of the crisis, gave Poincaré and Viviani the chance of making sentimental gestures towards the socialists as well as depriving the Left of their most effective leader, but when the government decided not to arrest the militant agitators on the Left whose names were on the list of those to be detained when mobilization was declared, it was already clear to them that the strength of anti-militarism had been exaggerated and that mobilization would proceed without interference from socialists or syndicalists. However, these internal divisions had till then made it logical for Poincaré to adopt a passive waiting attitude in order to achieve his goal, so that in a sense the initiative had been left to Russia and to Germany to create a situation in which France could decide that the moment was favourable. The French government had not provoked or worked for a war but Poincaré's policies aimed at ensuring that when the expected war came it would be under circumstances which offered France the greatest chance of victory.

In Russia both the internal situation and Russia's foreign relations were dominated by the effects of the disastrous experiences of 1904–5 – the defeat by Japan in the Far East and the revolution at home. Although the Tsar's autocratic authority had been largely re-established after the revolution and the liberals' demands for a parliamentary system only very partially satisfied, the existence of the State Duma provided an organ for the expression of opinion to which the Tsar and his advisers had to pay some attention. The franchise was a narrow one and the upper house – the Council of State – could nullify much of the work of the Duma, but parliament had some control over the budget and could express views on a wide range of topics. Outside parliament, too, public opinion was more vociferous and more broadly based than before, even if there were still restrictions on the freedom of expression which would have seemed intolerable in western Europe. On the other hand, the experience of revolution had left the conservatives and the Tsar himself extremely apprehensive about a possible new outbreak and deeply suspicious of any demands for an increase in the power of parliament. However, in spite of recurrent and growing industrial unrest – there was a major strike in St Petersburg at the moment of the French President's visit in July 1914 – the Russian economy had by the outbreak of war expanded remarkably since 1905, while some political and social stability seemed to have been attained, especially as a result of the land reform carried out by Stolypin, President of the Council of Ministers from 1906 to 1911, though his assassination in 1911 was perhaps a reminder of how precarious the apparent stability was.

Because of the structure of the Russian governmental system, it is hard to evaluate the relative strength of the various pressures forming Russian foreign policy. The Tsar was still 'autocrat of All the Russias' although the liberals had objected to the use of the title).[18] Nicholas II was both obstinate and impressionable, sometimes easily swayed by the latest advice he had received, sometimes clinging stubbornly to a decision rather than face argument and confrontation. The Council of Ministers had no collective responsibility and the ministers individually were not responsible to the Duma but only to the Tsar. Their influence therefore depended very much on their personalities and on their relations with their colleagues. Stolypin while President of the Council of Ministers had been able to carry through his policies and had also tried to work to some extent with the Duma. His successor, Kokovtsev, had been a competent Minister of Finance, but he was increasingly criticized by his colleagues for being insufficiently reactionary and he had lost the confidence of the Tsar, or rather, even more important, that of the Tsarina, because he had dared to criticize the influence at court of Rasputin, a dissolute sectarian monk on whose healing powers and apparent ability to control the haemophilia of the young Tsarevich the future of the dynasty was believed by the royal couple to depend. Kokovtsev was replaced by a former President of the Council of Ministers, an elderly nonentity, I. L. Goremykin, who was described by a British observer as being 'acceptable to both the sovereigns for his attitude of a butler, taking instructions to the other servants',[19] and who described himself as 'like an old fur coat. For many months I have been packed away in camphor. I am being taken out now merely for the occasion, when it is passed I shall be packed away again till I am wanted the next time.'[20] Although he succeeded in maintaining reasonable relations with the Duma, he certainly did not determine the general lines of Russian policy. A minor episode in March 1914 is a good illustration of the confusion within the Russian government. A German newspaper had published an article attacking Russian rearmament and accusing Russia of aggressive intentions. Two replies were published in the Russian papers, one directly inspired by the War Minister, Sukhomlinov, the other by the Foreign Minister, Sazonov. The first said that 'Russia desires peace but is prepared for war' and that the Russian army would at once take the offensive if necessary; the second was much more conciliatory and argued that Russo-German friendship should be maintained in spite of the press war. As the British ambassador commented: 'It is not perhaps surprising that the Ministers of War and Foreign Affairs should advocate different methods of meeting the attack by the German Press; but it is curious that they should both have been received in Audience by the Emperor on the 10th of this month and that two such contradictory articles should have been published two days later.'[21]

The Tsar was also receiving recommendations of a contrary kind from members of his own family and household (including of course Rasputin) as well as from various unofficial advisers. Moreover, however reluctantly, he also had to take account of the opinions of the Duma, where, even after Stolypin had held fresh elections under a much restricted franchise and curtailed its powers, critical opinions were expressed, including comments on the competence of ambassadors and military and naval commanders, even when these were members of the imperial family. But there were also a number of other bodies – councils of representatives of trade and industry and of finance and agriculture, the Council of the United Nobility and others – which were expressing their views and hoping to exercise influence, while a vigorous press reflected the views of the various parties represented in the Duma.

The Fourth Duma was elected in the autumn of 1912 and seemed to provide a basis of support for the existing regime. The two liberal parties – the more conservative Octobrists and the more radical Kadets – were divided from each other and among themselves. The former were prepared to accept the limitations of the existing constitution and to work within it whereas the Kadets (Constitutional Democrats) were committed to constitutional reform which would give the Duma real power over the Council of Ministers. Even the most moderate demands for reform were too much for the various conservative groups which formed the largest section of the Fourth Duma; and some of them were repeatedly urging the Tsar to reduce yet further the powers of parliament and – as some of their German counterparts were pressing on William II – to make a *coup d'état* from above to deal with the opposition once and for all. This was advice which the Tsar was tempted to take, especially after there had been some criticism in the Duma of the influence which Rasputin was exercising at court, but he finally accepted the warning of the majority of his ministers not to act against the Constitution. Thus in 1914 Russia was still an autocracy, but an autocracy in which there was opportunity for the expression of a number of views and a number of channels by which influence could be exerted on the Tsar with whom in the last resort the final decisions lay and who believed himself to be directly responsible to God and to his people, who were certainly not in his view the same as their parliamentary representatives. (Indeed one of the sources of Rasputin's hold over the imperial family was that the Tsar tended to regard him as 'just a good religious, simple-minded Russian' who kept him in touch with 'the tears of the life of the Russian people'.)[22]

While almost everybody in the political class in Russia was convinced of the intimate connection between domestic stability or domestic reform and foreign policy, there were considerable differences of view about what that connection actually was. Thus there were many people on the Right who were suspicious of a close association with France and Britain because of the danger that such an alignment might encourage liberal ideas in Russia, and who would have preferred, in the interest of monarchical solidarity, an alliance with Germany against what they would have called western Jewish liberalism.[23] Many of them also believed, with the example of the war with Japan in mind, that war might once again lead to revolution. Stolypin was convinced that it would 'not be desirable to be drawn into a European war',[24] while Kokovtsev told the British ambassador in 1913 'that the reports current about the internal situation are much exaggerated, and said that there was nothing to fear so long as peace could be maintained'.[25] On the other hand, many conservative nationalists were also convinced that if Russia was to survive and the autocracy was to be maintained, she must reassert her position as a Great Power to compensate for the humiliation of the defeat by Japan. Such a recovery of Russia's prestige so as to strengthen the system both internally and externally involved a revival of Russia's traditional goal of establishing Russian control over Constantinople and the Straits.

The liberals, on the other hand, hoped that a strengthening of the ties with France and England would increase the pressures for internal reform and were also prepared to envisage concessions in Poland, for example, in order to win liberal support in France and Britain where left-wing opinion had remained critical of the Russian alliance, especially since the curtailment by Stolypin of the initial gains of the 1905 revolution. Both liberals and conservatives believed that Russia had a direct interest in the Balkans, though for rather different reasons. These different attitudes have come to be labelled Panslav and Neoslav. For the Panslavs, in the tradition of their predecessors of the 1870s and 1880s, the aim of Russian policy should be to spread Russian influence to the Straits and to exercise the role of protector of the Christian Slavs so that the Slavs freed from Turkish rule would be wholly dependent on Russia. A new generation of liberals on the other hand saw Russia's relations with the other Slavs in a more flexible way and had visions of Russia taking the lead in a free association of independent Slav peoples. For them support of Slav aspirations abroad was linked with the idea of reform at home. As a Russian journalist remarked to the French ambassador, 'Le parti panslaviste est réactionnaire, le parti néoslaviste est constitutionnel.'[26] The Tsar himself was sometimes influenced by similar ideas for the reconstruction of central Europe. He told a rather bewildered British ambassador in April 1913 that he believed the disintegration of the Austrian Empire was only a matter of time.

> He spoke of the day when we should see a kingdom of Hungary and a kingdom of Bohemia, while the southern Slavs might be absorbed by Servia, the Roumanians of Transylvania by Roumania and the German provinces incorporated in the German Empire. The fact that Germany would then have no Austria to entangle her in a war about the Balkans would, His Majesty said, make for peace.[27]

By 1914, therefore, there was an influential body of opinion in Russia convinced that Russia must expand her influence in south-east Europe. There were differences about when Russia might be ready for war; there were differences about whether Russia's goals were better pursued in co-operation with Germany or with France and Britain; but within the ruling circles of Russia, however apprehensive some politicians were about the effects of war, there was a growing feeling that Russia's internal development depended on a successful and expansionist foreign policy. The Foreign Ministry had been working to extend its influence in the Balkans and to encourage the alliance between the two rival Slav states in the Balkans, Bulgaria and Serbia; and this alliance had led to the outbreak of the First Balkan War. The victory of the Balkan League states was welcomed by the Russians and the Duma passed an enthusiastic motion congratulating the Bulgarians on their success. The breakdown of the Balkan alliance and the war between Bulgaria and her former allies made the Russian government all the more anxious to re-establish a new base for their influence in the Balkans. The Foreign Ministry tried to persuade the French to make a loan to the Bulgarians, but the Germans got in first. The lack of support shown by Russia's French allies at the time of the Liman von Sanders mission was regarded as a serious blow to Russian policy, while the failure, because of international pressure, to give Serbia total backing in the territorial negotiations at the end of the Second Balkan War convinced many Russians in July 1914, including the Tsar himself, that the government's credit both internally and internationally depended on Russia giving Serbia her unequivocal support this time. If he made any concessions, the Tsar believed, 'Russia will never forgive the sovereign.'[28] For the rest, 'If you see me so calm, it is because I have a firm and resolute faith that the fate of Russia, of myself and my family is in the hands of God who has placed me where I am. Whatever happens, I shall bow to his will conscious of having had no other thought than that of serving the country He has entrusted to me.'[29]

The complicated balance between a belief that a vigorous foreign policy and even a war might bring out reserves of loyalty to the Tsar, the opposite belief that a war might provoke a revolution, a conservative preference for a traditional alliance of the Three Emperors – the Tsar, the German Emperor and the Emperor of Austria – as opposed to a liberal hope that an alliance with France and England would benefit the cause of domestic reform, all these considerations make it very hard to assess the relative weight of the pressures to which the Tsar was subjected. However, by February 1914, when Kokovtsev was replaced by Goremykin as President of the Council of Ministers, there seems to have been a general belief in government circles that war was inevitable. At a conference on 21 February 1914 detailed plans were discussed for a Russian landing to seize Constantinople in the event of the collapse of the Ottoman Empire, though it was hoped that this was not immediately imminent. Sazonov, the Foreign Minister, pointed out that 'we could not assume that our operations against the Straits would proceed without a European war', while the military leaders declared that it would not be possible to launch an attack on the Straits at the same time as fighting on the western front. Nevertheless, 'a successful outcome to the struggle on our western frontiers would decide the question of the Straits in our favour'.[30] While they still hoped that it might be possible to seize Constantinople before the outbreak of a European war and agreed to go ahead with plans for such an expedition, it is clear that the Russian Foreign Minister and military leaders now felt a general war to be very likely and that it might enable them to win their long-desired control of the Straits, even though they would prefer the crisis to be delayed for two or three years so as to complete their preparations.

The immediate background to this meeting was a growing fear that the Balkan situation was still very unstable and that internal developments in Turkey would lead to the final collapse of the Ottoman state. However, more important perhaps was the growing popular belief, as in Germany, of the inevitability of a conflict between Slav and Teuton. For some months, the Russian press had been carrying anti-German articles: for example at the beginning of 1914, *Novoe Vremya*, the leading right-wing daily, was writing: 'The chief object of our foreign policy should from now on be to break the tightening Teutonic ring around us which threatens Russia and the whole of Slavdom with fatal consequences. . . . '[31]

The atmosphere in which decisions on Russian foreign policy were taken was one in which the rational calculations of profit and loss played little part. Vague beliefs, hopes and fears about the consequences of a war and its effect on the internal situation were more important than accurate assessments of Russia's strategic position, and, since in the comparatively small circle of what can be called public opinion in Russia attitudes towards foreign policy and Russia's relations with the outside world were inextricably linked with attitudes to the domestic situation, it is hard to distinguish between a 'primacy of internal policy' and a 'primacy of foreign policy' or even to say which of the opposing influences to which the vacillating and fatalistic Tsar was subjected was the more important in the decision for war. Almost more than in the case of any of the other Great Powers, it is difficult to point to any single factor determining Russia's entry into the war or to fit Russia into any model which can also be applied to the other states which went to war in 1914.

The supporters of the view that it was domestic political and social pressures which determined the nature of foreign policy and consequently the decision for war have made their strongest case in the analysis of the situation in Germany; and it is into the relation between foreign policy and domestic politics in Germany in the forty years before the war that the most research has been done.[32] Certainly the internal political situation and constitutional arrangements have features which are not to be found in the other belligerent countries. We have already seen that in the crisis of 1914 it is not easy to determine where the final responsibility for taking decisions lay, with the Emperor formally being the ultimate authority and receiving advice from civil and military officials who were not bound by any principle of collective responsibility. As in Russia the situation was complicated by the personality of the Emperor who regarded himself as the ultimate power but who was influenced in contrary directions by his own successive whims and the policies of some of his advisers, and still more by his belief that he represented and embodied the aspirations of most of his subjects. Nevertheless the constitutional position in Germany was sufficiently complex for there to be a number of ways in which public opinion, including opinion critical of government policies, could make itself felt. The German Empire was not a unitary state. The individual *Länder* still possessed important powers over the day-to-day life of their citizens: the susceptibilities of their rulers and governments had to be respected by the imperial authorities: their financial contributions to the central exchequer were essential for the functioning of the Empire. There is evidence that, at least from the 1890s, members of the imperial government believed that a vigorous foreign policy and the encouragement of an aggressive nationalist spirit would be one way of overcoming the particularist sentiments in the individual states and producing a mood of national unity comparable to that of 1870.

More important still was the existence of the imperial parliament, the Reichstag, elected by universal male suffrage. Its powers were limited, however. This was partly because many of the functions of government were still performed by the *Länder*, so that the policies of

Prussia, the largest and most powerful of them, were in many respects as important as those of the central government; and in several states, notably Prussia again, the local diet (the *Landtag*) was elected on a very restricted franchise which guaranteed a majority to the conservatives. The imperial government – or rather the Chancellor and the state secretaries, since they were not constitutionally a collective body – was not responsible to the Reichstag, so that there was no parliamentary government in the sense in which it was known in Britain and France. Nevertheless, the Reichstag was important because its vote was needed for the passage of legislation and, more important still, for the passing of the budget, while Reichstag elections provided some sort of indication of the political mood in Germany. From Bismarck onwards, therefore, the successive imperial chancellors had needed to secure and maintain majorities in the Reichstag: and on several occasions an initiative in foreign policy had been an effective means of doing so. Bismarck had deliberately made the most of the crisis in the Balkans and the talk of *revanche* in France in the elections of 1887 so as to secure a majority for the passage of an increased military budget. Bülow had successfully fought the Reichstag elections of 1907 with slogans which combined nationalism, colonialism and anti-socialism.

However, the supporters of the view that it was concern for domestic politics that determined the conduct of German foreign policy would argue that this was more than just a matter of using foreign political issues for the immediate purpose of winning a particular election, and that foreign policy was deliberately used as a means of manipulating public opinion so as to create a sense of solidarity among the German people and overcome the social and political divisions which were seen as a threat to the very existence of the German Empire. The attraction of a colonial empire, a large fleet and an active foreign policy would serve both as a basis for rallying the 'loyal' (*Staatserhaltende*) elements around the Kaiser and government and as a means of countering the threat of a growing socialist movement. It might even also serve as a means of integrating the socialists themselves into German society. (One of the problems of this explanation is indeed to determine which of these contradictory aims was foremost in the minds of those who pursued this policy: were imperialism and *Weltpolitik* being used to rally opposition to the socialists or were they intended to integrate the socialists into the German *Volksgemeinschaft*?)

There are two distinct phases in which the question needs to be discussed. First there is the general problem of the motives which led the German government in the 1890s to take the decision to embark on *Weltpolitik* and to construct a fleet which could if necessary challenge the British navy – a decision which, as we have seen, changed the whole basis of Anglo-German relations and contributed much to the atmosphere which made war possible in 1914. We also need to look at the pressures on the German government immediately before the war, and especially after the Reichstag elections of 1912 which had shown that one elector in three was voting socialist and that the Social Democratic Party was the biggest single party in the new Reichstag.

The decision by the Kaiser and his advisers to build a large navy and to turn Germany into a world power makes a clear dividing line in German foreign policy, so that Germany's imperialism seems to be the result of a specific decision rather than of a chain of events over at least several decades as was the case with Britain and France. It is true that Bismarck had in the 1880s given limited encouragement to colonial activity as a means of winning popular support; and it has been argued[33] that this was part of an overall strategy to weaken the appeal of the socialists by a combination of expansion abroad and social welfare at home. However, the imperialist movement of the 1880s in Germany, although it led to the foundation of what was to develop over the next years into an influential pressure group, did not go very deep or last very long and its immediate political consequences were not very important. But the decision for *Weltpolitik* and the introduction of the first Navy Law in 1897 had profound effects on both domestic and foreign policy. How far was this explicit decision to turn Germany into a world power the result of domestic political pressures and was it intended to serve the purposes of internal as much as of foreign policy?

In trying to find the profounder causes of the decision for *Weltpolitik* one must be careful not to underestimate the effects of the personal and contingent, and in this case particularly the position and predilections of the Emperor William II himself. Some historians[34] have talked about the 'personal rule' of the Kaiser and have overlooked the extent to which his powers were nevertheless dependent on the collaboration of others within the German constitutional system; but it is certain that the circle of his immediate advisers and confidants was a small one (so that his critics accused him of running Germany through a *camarilla*), and that, particularly in the early years of his reign, his own prejudices and caprices were very important. It is unlikely that German naval building would have been pursued so enthusiastically without the Kaiser's personal commitment to the creation of a German battle fleet. This was no doubt partly the result of his own psychology – his emotional need to show himself the equal of his royal British relatives, and his country the equal of the England which he both loved and hated – partly the result of his own superficial strategic thinking influenced by the reading of Mahan's work on the role of sea power in history. Without William II's personal backing, Admiral von Tirpitz, whom he appointed State Secretary for the Navy in 1897, would never have been able to carry through his programme and win the public support required to overcome the political opposition to the idea of a big navy.

However, a policy of naval and imperial expansion was in the late

1890s just what large sections of the German public seemed to want, and both politicians and industrialists were quick to see the advantages which they could derive from it. The sense that the fall of Bismarck in 1890 marked the end of an era led many people, especially the supporters of the National Liberal Party, to look for a new national cause to support and new national goals for which to work. The answer lay in *Weltpolitik*, though there were several different ideas of what this meant in practice. The anxiety which was felt about the direction of German foreign policy and Germany's place in the world was accompanied by a growing fear about the problems created by urbanization and industrialization. Politicians talked of the necessity of a *Sammlungspolitik*, policies which would produce a solid body of support for the state and the Kaiser and in particular a solid body of opposition to the growing socialist movement. As Johannes Miquel, the Deputy Prime Minister of Prussia, put it in 1897: 'The great task of the present is without prejudice to gather together all the elements which support the state and thereby to prepare for the unavoidable battle against the Social Democratic movement.'[35]

Although Tirpitz himself was primarily concerned with the creation of the navy for its own sake and as a means of achieving a not very clearly defined position as a world power, he was also aware of the role the navy might play in providing a new rallying point for German opinion: 'In the great new national task and the economic gains associated with it lies a strong antidote to educated and uneducated Social Democracy.'[36] Tirpitz's more immediate political aim fitted in with his general suspicions of democracy. This aim was to safeguard the naval programme against disruption by the Reichstag, and much of his planning was intended to ensure that the building and replacement of ships should take place without the necessity of parliamentary approval. He was, in Volker Berghahn's phrase, constructing a fleet 'against parliament and England'[37] and hoped that naval building would favour an authoritarian system of government at home while abroad tipping the world balance of power in Germany's favour.

Yet there were difficulties in the way of using the navy as a focus for a new conservative alliance, the chief of which being that many of the Prussian landowners, the truest conservatives in Germany, were unenthusiastic about the new policy and in some cases actively opposed to it. The situation grew worse as the naval programme increased in scope and cost, since the agrarian conservatives firmly rejected any financial measures such as inheritance or income tax, which would touch their own pockets, so that it was not until 1913, in the face of their opposition and with the support of the socialists, that an income tax was introduced. Although, like Bismarck, Bülow succeeded temporarily in 1903 in patching up a conservative bloc based on a bargain between the economic interests of agrarians and industrialists, it lacked firm foundations and its break-up in 1909 led to Bülow's fall.

On the other hand, Tirpitz's active encouragement of propaganda in favour of his naval programme led to the creation of effective pressure groups, notably the Flottenverein, which themselves became bodies whose views had to be taken seriously by the government and which provided an opportunity for ambitious members of the middle class to achieve positions of influence which had hitherto been the preserve of aristocrats.[38] The growth of the navy and Tirpitz's ambitious programme were signs of the way in which Germany was changing socially and economically, but it can be argued that so far from serving as a rallying point for a divided nation, the navy emphasized the divisions and brought out the contradictory forces in Germany's social and institutional structure while pushing the German government in the direction of a foreign policy which was bound to end in conflict with England and very probably war. The idea of *Weltpolitik* and support for the fleet appealed to circles far wider than the industrialists who stood to gain directly from naval expansion; and even if it never succeeded in winning the working class away from the Social Democratic Party and integrating them into the German *Volksgemeinschaft*, as some of its supporters had hoped it would, the effectiveness of navalist propaganda did not leave the workers untouched: those social democratic politicians who received an invitation to visit a battleship did not conceal their satisfaction, and at least one of them remembered it all his life.[39]

The building of the German navy not only exposed some of the contradictions in German politics and society but also led to the creation of a body of nationalist opinion and the development of an aggressive imperialist rhetoric which contributed to making war seem acceptable and even desirable. The existence of such a body of opinion was one of the factors which the German government between 1911 and 1914 had to take into account. It was not the only problem confronting Theobald von Bethmann Hollweg, who became Chancellor in 1909. His predecessor Bernhard Von Bülow had followed a foreign policy which had resulted in Germany's isolation and in an increasing fear that she was being 'encircled' by hostile powers. This in turn contributed to the pressure to increase the size of the army and navy and consequently increased Germany's financial difficulties. Bülow's fall had been the direct result of a vain attempt to cope with the problem by imposing an inheritance tax; and the situation was to get worse. There were signs that the left-wing liberals and some of the social democrats were looking for an opportunity which would make the Reichstag more powerful and they were also starting to agitate for a reform of the restricted franchise for the Prussian *Landtag*. Any government was going to have to find some way of working either with this new potential grouping of the moderate Left or else with an ever more strident nationalist Right. Although Bülow had been successful in forming a conservative bloc to fight the Reichstag elections of 1907 and inflicting a temporary check on the steady growth of the social democrats, the ground was lost again in the next elections in 1912; and the increased strength of the socialists led to new vociferous demands on the Right for a campaign against them, including calls for a *coup d'état* from above, the abolition of universal suffrage and the introduction of some sort of authoritarian government – ideas which had the active support of the Crown Prince and his circle and with which the Kaiser in his wilder moments expressed some sympathy. Bethmann Hollweg aimed at pursuing what he called 'politics of the diagonal' between these opposing forces. He did not want to alienate the social democrats from the German state still further, especially in view of what he saw as a worsening international situation, and he hoped at the same time to create some sort of new national consensus by providing what in his view would be a government 'above party'. In fact his room for manœuvre was very limited: and certainly this cautious high-minded gloomy conservative bureaucrat was hardly the man to challenge directly the established power of the army leaders and industrialists who denounced as weakness any liberal gesture at home or attempts at compromise abroad.

This became very clear after the Moroccan crisis of 1911, when the various nationalist pressure groups were indignantly attacking Bethmann for failing to get adequate compensation for Germany's acquiescence in the establishment of French control over Morocco and for disappointing the hopes aroused by the despatch of a German warship to Agadir. The nationalists had hoped that this initiative in provoking a major international crisis would be the first step towards establishing a new German empire in Africa and an opportunity to demonstrate Germany's imperial power. As one of their papers wrote on 3 July 1911: 'In Germany the whole nation has breathed a deep sigh of relief as if a bad dream had vanished, as if a nightmare of discontented resignation had been chased away by the rays of the morning sun.'[40] The people who felt that Germany's troubles could only be removed by a dramatic act of national self-assertion even at the risk of war were naturally disappointed when the gains won by Germany's gunboat diplomacy were limited to two small pieces of the French Congo, contemptuously described by the German Secretary of State for the Colonies as 'partly completely worthless, partly almost worthless territory',[41] mostly either swamp or jungle and where the inhabitants were perishing from sleeping sickness. (It was typical of the mood of the time that a French nationalist journalist, complaining about French concessions to Germany, described the same territory as 'marvellous shores frequented by all the beasts of the Garden of Eden, by all the magical beauty with which painters liked to fill their pictures of the creation of the world'.[42]) Moreover, the price for what the Germans considered small gains had been an intensification of anti-German feeling in France and what was regarded as an open expression of British support for France in Lloyd George's Mansion House speech.

Although a new attempt at an agreement with England was made at the time of Haldane's visit to Berlin in March 1912, it was clear that the German Admiralty was not prepared to modify its shipbuilding programme except for an unequivocal promise of British neutrality in a European war. Thus that part of Bethmann's foreign policy which depended on improving relations with England was making no progress, while he was now under increased pressure to win the Reichstag's consent to further naval increases. By the time of the Haldane mission, the Reichstag elections of January 1912 had taken place and had been a defeat for the Right and a triumph for the Social Democrats. Bethmann had deliberately refrained from using Bülow' tactics of 1907 and fighting the elections on nationalist slogans because he did not wish to encourage the Right by appearing to be reacting to their criticisms. As he put it to a friend,

> We must do everything for our defence by sea and land that our finances allow, but not with threatening shouts but as far as possible in quiet silence. Then we can arrange things with England in spite of naval increases so that it doesn't come to a war. That is what I am working for, but the resistance on every side can hardly be overcome.'[43]

In fact he was soon faced with demands for naval increases which he was unable to resist, with the Kaiser declaring that 'My and the German people's patience is at an end'[44] and expressing the greatest contempt for any arguments that financial considerations might limit naval expansion, while the nationalist associations – now joined by a new one, the *Wehrverein*, committed to strengthening the army and preparing all sections of the nation, especially the young, for war – were becoming increasingly strident in their criticisms of the government. By 1913 a new increase of the army was added to that of the navy.

From 1911 until the outbreak of war – and indeed until his fall in 1917 – Bethmann was faced with repeated calls for his resignation; and the punning slogan *Bethmann-soll-Weg* (Bethmann Must Go) was a kind of German parallel to the British Conservative Party's BMG (Balfour Must Go) campaign against their leader Arthur Balfour in the autumn of 1911. Indeed, in March 1912 Bethmann had offered his resignation to the Kaiser because the Kaiser in one of his recurrent fits of anti-English panic had telegraphed direct to the ambassador in London that if the English were to strengthen their North Sea fleet by withdrawing ships from the Mediterranean, this would immediately lead to Germany's mobilization. By the time Bethmann's resignation was offered, the Kaiser had calmed down, but the episode gave the Chancellor the chance of summarizing his policy: any failure in the

ttempt to reach agreement with England must be attributable to the
nglish, otherwise

> not only will our relationship with England significantly deteriorate, but
> also French chauvinism which is already virulent will be encouraged to form
> the wildest hopes. France will become so provocative and overbearing that
> we shall be compelled to attack her. In such a war France will certainly have
> the help of Russia and doubtless also England . . . I cannot take the re-
> sponsibility of working for such a situation. If a war is forced on us, then we
> will fight it and with God's help not be defeated. But for us to provoke a war
> without our honour or vital interests being affected I would regard as a sin
> against Germany's destiny, even if we could hope as far as we can foresee for
> victory.[45]

 was a position which depended on many imponderables, especially
 e meaning to be attached to words like 'honour' and 'vital interests'
nd on how far Bethmann's conception of these coincided basically
 ith that of his nationalist critics; and one sometimes has the impres-
 on that his differences with them were about means rather than ends.
 The difficulty of following a 'policy of the diagonal' was illustrated
 y the row over the Zabern affair (see p.61), when the attempts by a
 ajority of the Reichstag, including the National Liberals and the
 atholic Centre Party as well as the left-wing Liberals and the Social
 emocrats, to censure the army leadership and criticize the Chan-
 ellor's handling of the affair only showed the impotence of the
 eichstag and the difficulties involved in an open confrontation with
 e military authorities. While it would have been unthinkable twenty
 ears earlier for the kind of criticism of the army which the Zabern
 cident provoked to be expressed publicly in the Reichstag and the
 ress, this apparent increase in parliamentary and popular freedom to
 riticize was offset by the demonstration that the Chancellor could still
 nore a parliamentary vote of censure, while the army leaders made
 nly token gestures to discipline the officers responsible for the insults
 nd injustices inflicted on the Alsatian population; and it was charac-
 ristic that the unfortunate Governor of Alsace saw his attempts to
 ssert his authority openly snubbed by the Kaiser, and equally charac-
 ristic, since he was himself a general, that he should have kept silent
 ther than allow the prestige of the army to suffer.
 Bethmann was not the man, as we have seen, to go against the power
 f the army and the prejudices of the Kaiser, partly at least because he
 ared much of their contempt for the professional politicians in the
 eichstag. 'It was a madhouse', he described the Zabern debate. 'By
 eir temper tantrums these people believe they can hide their political
 nocence. The vainglorious Bassermann [National Liberal] arm in
 m with Scheidemann [SPD] and Erzberger [Centre] lack any dig-
 ty . . . Hence I stood in the fiery rain. That is even not so bad. The
 ner revulsion was much too great for me to feel the cinders.'[46] But it

was also partly that, for all his abstract respect for the rule of law, he was also convinced of the special role of the army and navy. 'I shall rather accept a dent in my own reputation than permit the denigration of the army', he said about the Zabern affair;[47] and on the subject of the navy he was even more positive: 'A really Great Power with a seaboard could not be a *Landratte*: she *must* have a fleet, and a strong one . . . not merely for the purpose of defending her commerce but for the general purpose of her greatness.'[48] For all his doubts about the methods and style of the Prussian military class and in spite of his own genuine idealism and culture (he complained to the British ambassador that during the Agadir crisis he had not had time to play his usual Beethoven sonata before going to bed: 'How can I play my beloved old music with the air full of modern discords?')[49], Bethmann Hollweg was limited in his freedom of action both by his own origins and temperament and by the system within which he was operating. His pessimistic, reserved and sensitive nature was susceptible to accusations of cowardliness: Fritz Stern in a perceptive essay has reminded us that in his memoirs Bethmann wrote that for Germany to have followed a different course in 1914 would have amounted to *Selbstentmannung* (self-castration)[50]. His fatalism increasingly led him to believe that there was not much to be done about anything. But even if he had been less fatalistic, there is little he could have done in the face of the entrenched power of the more nationalistic conservatives. His policy of the diagonal was constantly distorted by the pull to the right; and he was powerless to resist.

Between the elections of 1912 and the outbreak of war, much nationalist propaganda was explicitly linking calls for the preparation for war with the hope that a war might put an end to social democracy. The journalists of the Right were not only preparing for a war of Teuton against Slav; they were also making remarks such as 'A fresh and uninhibited war would immediately decimate the 110 Social Democrats in the Reichstag', or, elsewhere, 'War is the only remedy to cure existing ills.'[51] Bethmann did not share this view. Whereas, he said, the conservatives 'expected a war to turn domestic politics in a conservative direction' he himself believed 'that a world war with its unforeseeable consequences will greatly strengthen the power of social democracy since it preaches peace and will topple many a throne'.[52] The consequences of this for German foreign policy were expressed by the Chancellor in November 1913 as follows: 'In a future war which is undertaken without a compelling reason, not only will the crown of the Hohenzollerns be at stake but also the future of Germany. Certainly our policy must be conducted boldly. But to rattle the sword in every diplomatic complication unless the honour, security and future of Germany is threatened, is not only foolhardy but criminal.'[53]

While other members of the German government and high command believed that there was little point in postponing a war which they considered to be inevitable, Bethmann, with his eyes on the internal situation, was concerned that a war if it came should appear to be one in which Germany was attacked by Russia, and also if possible one in which England would remain neutral. He failed in the second part of his policy, but had considerable success in the first, partly because of the attitude of some of the leading social democrats. From the time of Marx and Engels onwards, socialists had always believed that a war against Russia, the most reactionary power in Europe, would be justified, however much they might criticize militarism at home. And although some of the left-wing social democrats, notably Rosa Luxemburg and Karl Liebknecht, in the years immediately before the war had launched a vigorous campaign against militarism and war, the party leadership was more restrained on these issues, pressing for reforms in the system of national defence rather than attacking national defence as such. In spite of the emphasis both by the socialists and by their opponents on the gulf between them – illustrated by the refusal of bourgeois politicians to serve as president or vice-president of the Reichstag when a socialist was elected one of the vice-presidents, and by the refusal of socialist members of parliament to stand and join in the ritual cheers for the Kaiser or to attend court functions – the Chancellor retained contact with some of the right-wing socialists; and the socialists had supported the government by voting for the taxation needed to finance the army increases in 1913. In the July crisis 1914, Bethmann was able to persuade the army leaders not to carry out their intention to arrest the socialist leaders, because he had been assured by his contacts in the Social Democratic Party that, in spite of their demonstrations in favour of peace, the socialists would do nothing to oppose the preparations for war. What has been called the 'negative integration'[54] of the German socialists was demonstrated by the unanimity with which the parliamentary party voted for the emergency war credits on 4 August 1914.

The idea of the primacy of foreign policy (*Primat der Aussenpolitik*) derived from the writings of the great nineteenth-century German historian Leopold von Ranke. He had argued that it was the foreign policy of a state that enabled it to achieve the independence from interference by other powers which would allow it to develop its own national character and institutions, so that its very existence and nature depended on the success of its foreign policy. His ideas were less simple than some later writers believed; and he was too intelligent a historian not to see that, as he put it, 'It is natural and inevitable that external and internal affairs interact with each other.'[55] In Germany many influential historical thinkers were by the beginning of the twentieth century reviving some of Ranke's ideas – about the interplay of the Great Powers and the balance of power and especially about the importance of external relations in determining internal developments, so that domestic policy would have to be subordinate to foreign policy. Such ideas were also expressed by political leaders, as for example by Bernhard von Bülow, the future Chancellor, who wrote in 1890: 'Everything must be subordinated to our unity and our position as a European great power, and even our internal politics must be tailored to this.'[56]

Moreover, Ranke had stressed the importance of maintaining the balance of power and opposing the hegemony of any one state; and his successors in the age of imperialism were pointing to Britain's naval hegemony and the necessity of challenging it so as to restore a balance of power which must now be world-wide and no longer confined to Europe. As one leading historian and publicist, Otto Hintze, put it in an essay published in 1916:

> Our intention was to develop gradually in peaceful competition with England, until the older power would one day be forced to recognize us as an equal competitor in world politics. England is still far from granting any such equality to the continental powers, and the German refusal to admit England's sole supremacy at sea was certainly the main cause that drove the island kingdom into a war with Germany. Our aim in this war can only be to force England to abandon her claim to absolute supremacy at sea, and thus to create a state of equilibrium within the world system of states.[57]

These are ideas which almost exactly coincide with Tirpitz's theories about the aims of the German naval programme.

Unless, therefore, we are to take the view that nobody ever means what they say and that their statements are always mere pretexts to conceal deeper reasons, we must admit that even in the case of Germany it would be wrong to analyse foreign policy solely in terms of a theory of the *Primat der Innenpolitik* or to attribute the decision for war to domestic pressures alone. At the same time there is much evidence to suggest that German politicians, generals and admirals were very conscious of the connection between domestic and foreign policy, not only because at certain moments they believed that foreign ventures might contribute to a mood of national solidarity at home, but also because they feared the strength of socialist opposition to warlike policies. The balance between the awareness of internal problems and dreams of world power was always a delicate one; and if recent historical writing has stressed the importance of the internal contradictions of German society in determining German foreign policy and the decision for war and has thus drawn attention to factors which had been largely overlooked by an older generation of historians, we must not forget that for many leading Germans the positive pursuit of world power or the negative securing of Germany's position in what was regarded as a hostile world was something to be undertaken for its own sake regardless of the domestic profit and loss. The 'politics of the diagonal' was a question not only of balancing between Left and Right but also of balancing between internal and external problems.

The brief examination in this chapter of the relations between internal and external policies in the main belligerent countries suggests that no single explanatory model is applicable to all of them, and that in almost every case the decision for war was the result of contradictory hopes, fears, inherited attitudes and previous plans rather than of cool and rational calculation of profit and loss. In the short term, considerations of domestic policy obviously played their part, but it was an ambiguous one and differed much between one country and another. In Germany the government was under pressure from the Right, in England and France from the Left, so that such estimates as were made about the effects of war on the internal situation were bound to be different. Still, it is true that the war did in fact appear in its first stages to supply a solution to many problems: in England the Irish question could be put in suspense (though only for less than two years); and the suffragette agitation faded out. In France the problem of an income tax and fiscal reform could be postponed, as revenue could be raised by patriotic appeals to invest in government war loans, and the problem of their redemption put off for the duration of the war; at the same time the dispute about the length of military service also disappeared, since every man of military age was mobilized for an indefinite period. Even in Russia, the disruptive effects of war were not immediately confirmed and the hopes that the war might bring out reserves of loyalty to the regime appeared for the time being to be justified. In Germany above all the war seemed to have made Germans forget their differences and produced a temporary mood of solidarity which those who experienced it never forgot.

It is, however, hard to prove that these results were what the leaders of Europe had in mind when they took the decision to go to war. There will for the historian always be a gap between what happened in July 1914 and the general hopes and fears which politicians expressed before that. A detailed examination of the political and strategic decisions taken in the crisis suggests that the motives of statesmen and generals were far less rational and well thought out than the view that they deliberately embarked on war as a way out of their insoluble domestic social and political problems would suggest.

Yet there remain more profound questions about the nature of European society before 1914 and its relation to the outbreak of the First World War. How far were the decisions of July 1914 the inevitable outcome of the structure of industrial and capitalist society? Were there long-term contradictions in the capitalist world such that they were bound sooner or later to lead to armed conflict? And if so, what was the relation of these long-term forces to the actual decisions of July 1914 which led to war at that moment and not sooner or later? This is the next approach to the subject which we must consider.

REFERENCES AND NOTES

1. C. A. Macartney, *The Habsburg Empire 1790–1918* (London 1968) p 768, fn. 1.
2. A. J. P. Taylor, *The Troublemakers* (London 1957).
3. Quoted in Zara S. Steiner, *Britain and the Origins of the First World War* (London 1977) p. 143.
4. Hansard 5th series, Vol. XXXII, cols. 57–8. See also Keith Robbins, *Sir Edward Grey* (London 1971) pp. 252–3.
5. C. E. Callwell, *Field-Marshal Sir Henry Wilson,* Vol. I (London 1927) p 139. For British military thinking about Ireland, see the valuable work of Ann Vorce, 'The role of Ireland in British defence planning 1908–1914' (unpublished MA thesis, University of London 1975).
6. H. H. Asquith, *Letters to Venetia Stanley*, selected and edited by Michael and Eleanor Brock (London 1982) p. 123.
7. J. A. Spender and C. Asquith, *Life of Herbert Henry Asquith, Lord Oxford and Asquith,* Vol. II (London 1932) p. 83.
8. General Sir N. Lyttleton to R. Haldane, PRO London WO32/7081 quoted in Vorce op. cit., p. 4.
9. I am grateful to Mr E. M. Robertson for this information.
10. E. Halévy *A History of the English People in 1905–1918* (London 1934 p. 548, fn. 4.
11. See Wolfgang Hünseler, *Das Deutsche Kaiserreich und die Irische Frage 1900–1914* (Frankfurt-am-Main 1978).
12. G. P. Gooch and Harold Temperley (eds) *British Documents on the Origins of the War 1898–1914*, Vol. X (London 1936) Part II, No. 461, p 675. (Hereinafter referred to as *BD*.)
13. *Die grosse Politik der Europäischen Kabinette*, Vol. XXXIX (Berlin 1926) No. 15674, p. 261. (Hereinafter referred to as *GP*.)
14. See the important work of Gerd Krumeich, *Aufrüsting und Innenpolitik in Frankreich vor dem Ersten Weltkrieg* (Wiesbaden 1980).
15. France, Archives Nationales, Papiers Poincaré, Vol. XXXVI. Note Journalières Mars–Août 1914. Fonds Nouvelles: Acquisition françaises, No. 16027, p. 122. I am most grateful to Professor Arno J Mayer for generously making available to me his transcript of these unpublished notes.
16. *GP* XXXIX, No. 15667, p. 250.
17. Quoted in L. Albertini, *The Origins of the War of 1914* (London 1953 Vol. I, p. 373. See also L. C. F. Turner, 'The edge of the precipice: a comparison between November 1912 and July 1914', *R. M. C. Historical Journal*, **3** (Canberra 1974).
18. Hugh Seton-Watson, *The Russian Empire 1801–1917* (Oxford 1967) p 629; Geoffrey A. Hosking, *The Russian Constitutional Experiment Government and Duma 1907–1914* (Cambridge 1973) pp. 10, 54.
19. Bernard Pares, *The Fall of the Russian Monarchy* (London 1939) p. 157.
20. *Out of my Past: The Memoirs of Count Kokovtsov* (Stanford 1935) p 439.
21. *BD* X, Part II, No. 611, p. 493.
22. Pares, op. cit., p. 157.
23. See Seton-Watson, op. cit., pp. 695–6.

24.   Quoted in I. V. Bestuzhev, 'Russian foreign policy February–June 1914', *Journal of Contemporary History* I, No. 3 (1966) 105.

25.   *BD* IX (2), No. 611, p. 493.

26.   Georges Louis, *Les Carnets* Vol. I (Paris 1926), p. 87, quoted in Erwin Hölzle, *Die Selbstentmachtung Europas* (Göttingen 1975) p. 49.

27.   *BD* IX, Part II, No. 849, p. 690. See also Hölzle, op. cit., p. 54.

28.   Bestuzhev, op. cit., p. 104.

29.   *Mémoires d'Alexandre Isvolsky* (Paris 1923), quoted in Albertini, op. cit., Vol. II, p. 574.

30.   *Die Internationalen Beziehungen im Zeitalter des Imperialismus: Dokumente aus den Archiven der Zarischen und der Provisorischen Regierung* (German edn, ed. O. Hoetsch, Berlin 1931) Vol. I, No. 295, pp. 285–6.

31.   Bestuzhev, op. cit., pp. 100–1.

32.   For an excellent discussion of the arguments see Wolfgang J. Mommsen, 'Domestic factors in German foreign policy before 1914', *Central European History*, VI, No. 1 (March 1973). Also Michael R. Gordon, 'Domestic conflict and the origins of the First World War: the British and German cases', *Journal of Modern History* **46**, 2 (June 1974).

33.   For example by Hans-Ulrich Wehler, esp. in *Bismarck und der Imperialismus* (Cologne 1969) and his article in English, 'Bismarck's Imperialism 1862–1890', *Past and Present*, No. 48 (Aug. 1970). See also H. Pogge von Strandmann, 'Domestic origins of Germany's colonial expansion under Bismarck', *Past and Present*, No. 45 (Feb. 1969).

34.   For example Erich Eyck, *Das persönliche Regiment Wilhelms II* (Zürich 1948). For the Kaiser's methods of government see J. C. G. Röhl, *Germany Without Bismarck* (London 1967).

35.   J. von Miquel, *Reden*, Vol. IV (Halle 1914) pp. 279 ff. See Geoff Eley 'Sammlungspolitik, Social imperialism and the Navy Law of 1898', *Militärgeschichtliche Mitteilungen*, **1** (1974).

36.   Alfred von Tirpitz, *Erinnerungen* (Leipzig 1919) p. 52. For Tirpitz's policies, see esp. Volker R. Berghahn, *Der Tirpitz-Plan* (Düsseldorf 1971); also Berghahn, *Germany and the Approach of War in 1914* (London 1973).

37.   Berghahn, *Tirpitz-Plan*, p. 13 and *passim*.

38.   See Geoff Eley, *Reshaping the German Right: Radical Nationalism and Political Change after Bismarck* (New Haven and London 1980).

39.   Gustav Noske, *Erlebtes auf Aufstieg und Niedergang einer Demokratie* (Offenbach-am-Main 1947) p. 40.

40.   *Kreuzzeitung*, 3 July 1911, quoted in F. Fischer, *Krieg der Illusionen* (Düsseldorf 1969) p. 121.

41.   *GP* XXIX, No. 10770, p. 406.

42.   Quoted in Jean-Claude Allain, *Joseph Caillaux: Le Défi Victorieux 1863–1914* (Paris 1978) p. 415.

43.   Quoted in Fischer, op. cit., pp. 145–6.

44.   *GP* XXXI, No. 11386, p. 155.

45.   A. von Tirpitz, *Politische Dokumente,* Vol. I. *Der Aufbau der Deutschen Weltmacht* (Stuttgart and Berlin 1924) pp. 318 ff. See also Fischer, op. cit., pp. 188–9.

46.   Quoted in Konrad H. Jarausch, *The Enigmatic Chancellor* (New Haven

and London 1973) p. 102.

47. Quoted in Berghahn, *Germany and the Approach of War*, p. 176.

48. *BD* IX (2) No. 47, p. 37. See also Jarausch, op. cit., pp. 141–2.

49. *BD* VII, No. 763, p. 788.

50. Fritz Stern, 'Bethmann Hollweg and the war', in Stern, *The Failure of Illiberalism* (New York 1972) p. 267.

51. Quoted in Berghahn, *Germany and the Approach of War*, p. 185.

52. Quoted in Jarausch, op. cit., pp. 151–2.

53. H. Pogge von Strandmann and Imanuel Geiss, *Die Erforderlichkeit des Unmöglichen* (Hamburger Studien zur neueren Geschichte Band 2: Frankfurt-am-Main 1965) pp. 22–3.

54. For a discussion of German socialist attitudes before 1914 see esp. Dieter Groh, *Negative Integration und revolutionärer Attentismus* (Frankfurt-am-Main 1973).

55. Leopold von Ranke, *Englische Geschichte*, quoted in Friedrich Meinecke, *Zur Theorie und Philosophie der Geschichte* (Stuttgart 1959) pp. 258–9.

56. Quoted in Peter Winzen, 'Prince Bülow's *Weltmachtpolitik*', *Australian Journal of Politics and History*, XXII,2 (Aug. 1976) 230.

57. Quoted in Ludwig Dehio, *Germany and World Politics in the Twentieth Century* (Eng. tr. London 1959) p. 53.

Chapter 6

THE INTERNATIONAL ECONOMY

'Wars are inherent in the nature of capitalism; they will only cease when the capitalist economy is abolished.' By 1914 this had become the orthodox doctrine of the Marxists: and if true it would provide the most comprehensive explanation of the outbreak of the First World War, though it would still leave open the question why this particular war started at that particular moment in the mounting crisis of capitalism. The doctrine had been officially asserted at the International Socialist Congress at Stuttgart in 1907, although the long composite resolution which opened with the declaration about the inevitable links between capitalism and war went on to express a number of contradictory attitudes to a war which might come before the revolution which was to make all wars impossible.[1]

The belief that capitalism made war inevitable has taken several different forms, ranging from the comparatively simple belief that industrialists – and especially armament manufacturers – provoked the war in order to make money or that businessmen encouraged their governments to take military action in order to ruin economic rivals abroad, to more sophisticated theories about the connection between economic imperialism and international conflict. Marxists have continued to maintain that the First World War was the inevitable consequence of imperialist rivalries and that these in turn were the inevitable consequences of the crisis of capitalism. Some of these theories about the connection between capitalism, imperialism and inevitable war had already been developed by radical and socialist thinkers before 1914 – by the Englishman J. A. Hobson (though he thought that capitalism could still be saved), by the Austrian Rudolf Hilferding and by Rosa Luxemburg. The most influential and polemical statement of this view was that of Lenin in his pamphlet *Imperialism – The Highest Stage of Capitalism*, published in 1916 and written in an attempt to prove to those socialists – the majority – who had supported their respective governments in 1914 on the grounds that the war was one of national defence, that it was in fact an imperialist war, the direct consequence of rivalries between states whose capitalist masters were desperately looking for new fields of investment and pushing governments into imperial expansion for this purpose, so that the growing rivalry for control of what was left of the pre-capitalist world had necessarily ended in armed conflict.

Most of the theories that the causes of the First World War were economic have as their basis the belief that imperial rivalries caused the war and that these rivalries in turn were caused by economic pressures, but it is not necessary to accept both assumptions: the psychological effects of imperialism certainly helped, as we shall try to show, to produce the attitude of mind which made war possible, but not all imperialist policies were inspired by direct economic interests. Moreover, other economic factors not directly related to imperialism had an influence on international relations. However, the most thoroughgoing theories of economic imperialism, such as that of Rosa Luxemburg in her *Accumulation of Capital,* attribute almost every development in capitalist society to the underlying influences of an all-pervasive imperialist ethos. Any examination of the suggestion that the causes of the war were primarily economic will certainly involve a discussion of imperialism.

However, we can start by looking at some of the simpler ways in which economic interests have been held responsible for the outbreak of the war. There is, for example, the view that certain industrialists stood to gain by war and that they were able to influence the decisions of their governments. Equally, it can be argued that other groups stood to lose by war, and that their influence was in favour of peace. These are not easy questions to answer, both because it is difficult in the complicated structure of economic life in the early twentieth century to determine where the interests of individual industrialists and businessmen in fact lay; and it is even harder to assess the extent of their influence on governments. It is obvious that the producers of steel welcomed the increased construction of naval vessels; and we know that in Germany the great steel magnates contributed lavishly to the financing of navalist propaganda through the Navy League.[2] Yet this was not the case with the British Navy League – admittedly a smaller-scale affair than its German equivalent – which relied on individual subscriptions and seems to have received only small donations from those industrialists with an interest in the construction of ships for the navy.[3] Moreover, although the steel manufacturers may have welcomed government contracts for naval shipbuilding this does not mean that they necessarily wanted war – especially as many of them were equally involved in the construction of merchant ships and in any case stood to lose money in the event of the interruption through war of international trade, since a substantial part of their production was exported to other countries. At the height of the Anglo-German naval race in 1907 Britain imported some £5m. worth of iron and steel from Germany and Germany imported over £3m. worth from England[4] and there were occasions when it was cheaper for British shipbuilders to buy German steel rather than British, because the high prices which German manufacturers were able to charge at home under a protective tariff enabled them to sell steel abroad at cut prices. Sometimes the foreign demand for German steel made it hard for the manufacturers to satisfy foreign customers as well as their own government: there were long and complex negotiations between the German Admiralty and Krupps, with the government trying to negotiate a lower price of steel in return for steady orders over a long period.[5] Often manufacturers, especially in England, believing that government orders might fluctuate with changes of policy or strategy, were reluctant to sacrifice profits abroad for what might turn out to be short-term gains at home and realized that the stability of their profits depended on the breadth and diversification of their market. Capitalist entrepreneurs in fact wanted the best of both worlds: to maintain their export markets while making large profits from, for example, naval construction; and most of them failed to see that politically the two would in the long run be incompatible.

It is, of course, the great arms firms – Krupp in Germany, Schneider-Creusot in France, Skoda in Austria-Hungary, Armstrong and Vickers in England – who have been popularly regarded as 'Merchants of Death', deliberately provoking wars in order to increase their profits. They were, however, only part of a complicated system of which other parts have attracted less publicity. As the technical complications of weapons and warships increased, so more and more branches of industry were involved: for example the great German electrical firms, AEG and Siemens, played as crucial, if quantitatively not so large, a part as the steel barons in the construction of the German battle fleet. Moreover, firms such as Skoda and Krupp exported many other products besides arms. Skoda for instance had started as a machine-tool business and, although after 1904 the arms trade became the most profitable side of the firm, it was also sending turbines to Niagara and lock-gates to the Suez Canal.[6]

Nevertheless the arms firms were necessarily very closely involved with governments, both because of their interest in defence contracts at home – and even those countries in which state ordnance factories played a major part in the production of munitions needed the private sector in times of rapid expansion of armaments – and because the supply of arms to allies or potential allies became of considerable political importance. Here again, however, the situation was a complicated one. Many profitable markets for arms were provided by countries which were not themselves directly involved in the power calculations of the major states – Spain, for example, who needed arms for her campaigns in Spanish Morocco, or the countries of Latin America who needed arms to use against each other, or China, which gave a large order to Skoda for the modernization of her armed forces after the revolution of 1911. In these areas the arms firms were often demanding government support against their rivals and arguing that national prestige demanded backing for national arms firms. Schneider, for example, pressed the French government hard and with some success to influence the Chileans to place their orders with the French firm. Such pressure did not necessarily correspond to the interests of government foreign policy: the demands by Schneider for diplomatic support were as often directed against English as German competitors.[7] In 1913 Vickers won from their French rivals orders for warships for Russia worth £7m.[8]

Governments did, however, often try to promote or to ban arms sales in support of their policies. The French government urged the arms manufacturers to take advantage of new markets – Rumania, for example, or Turkey during the Balkan wars – in the hope of strengthening their influence in those countries. In the Balkans the rivalry between Krupp and Schneider tended to reflect the rivalry between the French and German governments. In some cases the French were in a stronger position than the Germans because their available capital for foreign loans was greater, so that they were able to make the issue of a loan to a foreign government conditional on their being granted a monopoly of arms sales – tactics which were used repeatedly and successfully in the case of Greece, Bulgaria and Turkey. French financial strength proved stronger than German efforts to use other forms of persuasion such as the family ties between the Kaiser and the kings of Rumania and Greece.

The arms manufacturers sometimes served the foreign policies of their government and they thus came to expect government support even in areas where the government had no direct interests. As with other businessmen of all nationalities there were constant complaints that their own diplomats were doing less for them than those of other governments were doing for their rivals, so that French, German and British arms exporters write in strikingly similar terms. At the same time, diplomats of the old school who believed that trade was none of their business complained about the attention they were expected to give to businessmen and especially the arms merchants: 'French power at every point in the world is placed at the disposition of Le Creusot', the French minister in Belgrade grumbled in 1910.[9]

In general, though, governments needed arms firms more than the arms firms needed governments. The armament manufacturers clearly profited from government orders and had an important interest in maintaining a continuous long-term armament programme, as is especially clear in the case of naval construction. Yet much of their profit came from having a very wide sales network, if possible all over the world: their main rivals were other arms firms rather than foreign governments and they were prepared to spend money on press campaigns aimed at discrediting their competitors' products. In some cases

– the Krupp family, some of the bankers who controlled Skoda, Schneider – they had direct access both officially and socially to some of those responsible for government policy and no doubt they used this both in obtaining government contracts and in their attempts to win government support in their search for export markets. Though this pressure may have had some effect on the technical aspects of governments' defence policy, it seems to have had little influence on the more general aspects of foreign policy; nor do the armaments manufacturers seem to have sought such influence to a greater extent than any other businessmen. For governments, on the other hand, the arms manufacturers were an essential element in the conduct of their foreign policy both in providing them with the naval and military backing for that policy and in influencing their relations with potential allies and neutrals.

The direct export of arms was only a part of a much larger network of international economic relations of which one very important aspect was the role of the big banks. Marxist theory has tended to stress the importance of the banks and their domination over other forms of economic activity in the years before 1914. The growth of 'finance capital' – capital available for investment wherever it would produce the largest returns – meant that the banks held reserves of capital which they were able to use both to establish their control of many branches of economic life at home and to conduct their restless search for new fields of investment abroad. The domestic influence of the banks differed from one country to another, and it has been convincingly argued that the Marxist analysis – especially that of the Austrian socialist economist Rudolf Hilferding whose book *Das Finanzkapital*, published in 1910, particularly emphasizes the role of the banks – is based too exclusively on what was happening in Germany and Austria.[10] However, about the importance of the banks' international role there can be no doubt: nor is there any doubt about the desire of investors in western Europe to find new profitable fields of investment. As Witte, the Russian Finance Minister put it in 1902, discussing Russia's relations with France in terms not unlike those of the Marxist theorists:

> In every country which has reached a high level of industrial and commercial development and where the political horizon is calm and cloudless, a surplus of capital is experienced . . . If in addition, small capitalists possess to a high degree the taste for saving – a taste which for many years has been innate in the French nation – the need for the export of capital becomes an absolute and ineluctable necessity.[11]

In the export of capital the role of the banks was all-important. They invested their own capital directly in enterprises abroad – coal-mines in Russia, gold-mines in South Africa, railways in South America or whatever – but they also acted as agents for foreign governments and industrial undertakings seeking to raise loans abroad. Central and municipal governments in search of foreign loans needed banks to float those loans in the financial centres of the world – London, Paris, Berlin, Frankfurt and, by 1914, New York. The banks would advance the money and then sell to the public shares in the loan at a profit to themselves. The success of the loan depended to a large extent on the bank's own repute and its ability to capture the imagination of small and large holders of capital. Then again, banks would themselves often make short-term loans to foreign governments – an operation which could be profitable when the rate of interest differed from country to country: for example in 1906 the bank rate in Berlin was 5 per cent and in Paris 3 per cent, so that it would pay French banks to borrow at home and to lend to Germany.[12] And in turn, too much reliance on short-term foreign loans made the debtor government vulnerable since the loans were liable to be withdrawn in times of political or economic uncertainty.

These activities of the banks were necessarily closely connected to government policies. In some countries, notably France and Germany but not England, the government could control which foreign securities or government stock could be publicly quoted on the Stock Exchange (a famous example was Bismarck's ban on the Russian loan of 1887: see p. 39), though this did not prevent shares being bought privately outside the Stock Exchange. Such government bans often had a political motive and political consequences. As in the case of the arms manufacturers, bankers needed the assistance and goodwill of governments as much as the governments needed the help of the banks. At the same time, the interests of governments and banks were not always identical. Although bankers individually were as much or as little susceptible to appeals to their patriotism as any other citizen, they were in the business primarily to make money. For example, in 1912–13 the French bankers refused on financial grounds a loan to the Rumanians in the face of pressure by the French government which was hoping to detach Rumania from her alliance with Germany; but in the same year the Banque de Paris et des Pays Bas insisted, in spite of government advice, on lending money to Bulgaria. In the latter case both the government and the banks were constantly shifting their position; and in June 1914 the French government, urged on by their Russian allies, had now decided that it might be possible to bring Bulgaria over to their side with some timely financial help, but by now the Paris bankers, themselves facing a financial recession at home, decided that there was no longer any money to be made from a Bulgarian loan and obstinately refused to back the government's policy.[13]

It is in French foreign policy that the links between government and the banks are clearest, largely because of the size of French investments in other European countries. Although Britain was still the country with the largest total of overseas investment, less than 6 per cent of this was in Europe, whereas in the case of France the figure was about 62 per cent.[14] This did not prevent those French businessmen with an interest in the French colonies or Morocco having an influence out of all proportion to their actual financial importance, but it did mean that, because of the large amount of French money invested in other European countries, the connection between the investment policy of the banks and the foreign policy of the government was bound to be close. However much the German government would have liked to support its diplomacy by financial pressure, Germany was suffering from a permanent shortage of capital after the years of very rapid industrial expansion in the second half of the nineteenth century, whereas the French public – though sometimes criticized by nationalists for investing abroad rather than at home – still had large accumulated savings available. In Britain, the pattern of investment was different, with the largest part of British capital outside the United Kingdom going to the Empire and to North and South America, so that British policy in Europe was to some extent conducted independently of the kind of financial considerations which were important to the French.

More than any other of the international alignments before 1914, the Franco-Russian alliance was held together by financial as well as political and strategic ties. Even if the conclusion of the alliance in 1893 was originally the result of strategic and political pressures on both sides, its negotiation coincided with the launching of the first big series of Russian loans on the French money market. The first loans to the Russian government in 1888, 1889 and 1890 were followed by French investment in other sectors of the Russian economy – municipal loans, railways, mines and industrial enterprises of all kinds – so that by 1914 about a quarter of all French foreign investments were in Russia.[15] Financial ties on this scale were bound to have political consequences, quite apart from the specific conditions, such as the construction of strategic railways or the promise of orders for French firms, attached to some of the loans. The banks which were encouraging their customers to put their money into Russian bonds or mines or railways had everything to gain by projecting an image of Russia as a strong, politically stable and economically expanding country – a worthwhile ally in short. In spite of attacks on Russian autocracy and oppression by the Left in France and in spite of recurrent refusals by the Rothschilds and other Jewish bankers to participate in Russian loans because of Russian ill-treatment of the Jews, confidence in Russia remained surprisingly high right down to the outbreak of war, and indeed right down to 1917.

The clearest example of the inextricable ties between French diplomacy, Russian financial needs and the necessity of creating a certain image of Russia abroad can be found in the negotiations for the loan of

1906, which the Russian Prime Minister, Witte, described as 'the great loan which saved Russia'.[16] The war between Russia and Japan had broken out in January 1904, and in May the Russians had by offering a high rate of interest succeeded in floating a loan in France in spite of the uncertainty of their situation. The French government had also insisted that the Germans should not participate in the loan. By 1905, however, it was clear that Russia was defeated, and this together with growing internal unrest made a further loan very difficult; and by the end of the year, as the revolutionary movement grew in intensity, capital was being withdrawn from Russia at an alarming rate. For the Russian government, trying to recover from the political and economic consequences of the defeat by Japan and revolution at home, a large loan was essential: for the foreign investors the choice appeared to be either to put more money into Russia in the hope of saving their earlier stakes or else to lose everything if Russia were to lapse into revolution, anarchy and bankruptcy. The diplomatic consequences were also complex and important.

In the spring of 1905 the Moroccan crisis had created serious tension and indeed talk of war between France and Germany. In the subsequent negotiations about an international conference on Morocco and at the Conference of Algeciras itself, both the French and the German government were trying to use Russia's urgent need of money as a way of obtaining Russian diplomatic support over Morocco. The German government hoped that the prospect of a German loan might persuade the Russian government to use its influence in Paris to make the French give way on some of the German demands about the future status of Morocco. The French equally made it clear that a loan to Russia would depend on wholehearted Russian support of their position at the Algeciras conference. The French bankers were hesitating on financial grounds about further long-term commitments to Russia, and French government approval was essential if the loan were to stand any chance of success. Thus, although Witte would have preferred an international loan with German as well as French participants, he was forced to choose a loan from France alone. The German government forbade any further financial discussions with Russia; and Russia gave France wholehearted support at Algeciras. It was not therefore surprising that when the Russian representative came to Paris to conclude the final negotiations, Poincaré, at that time Minister of Finance, noted: 'It is the payment of a debt which he has come to claim from France. He talked about the services rendered at Algeciras in a tone which was almost embarrassing for me. He complained of the demands of the French banks which are, it is true, rather avaricious.'[17]

The success of the loan of April 1906 did much to help Russian recovery from the disasters of the previous two years and seemed to be an affirmation of France's confidence in her ally. It was certainly seen as such on the Left: Maxim Gorki complained that France was no longer the mother of Liberty but rather a woman kept by bankers.[18] And when in 1907 the British government made its agreement with Russia, a group of leading intellectuals including Bernard Shaw and John Galsworthy wrote to *The Times* pointing out that

> the proposed agreement will have the effect of strengthening the Russian credit and enabling the Government to appeal successfully to Europe for another loan over which representatives of the Russian people will have no control, and which will be employed only to strengthen the position of the autocracy against them. We also fear that, relying on this improved credit and closer relations between the governments, the English people may be tempted to invest largely in Russian Government stock – an investment likely to influence our political attitude towards Russia and other powers as already seen in the case of France.[19]

Their forebodings about British investments in Russia were perhaps exaggerated (although more British capital was invested in Russia by 1914 than in any other European country), but they were right to recognize the close connections between international credit and the public image of a particular nation.

The French investment in Russia was, as René Girault has pointed out,[20] an investment in the Tsarist regime; and from an economic point of view the decision to put money into Russia in spite of her precarious position in 1906 paid off. Over the next eight years Russian industrial expansion seemed to justify French policy, and with the increasing pace of Russian rearmament after 1909 the need for further loans grew. At the same time French financiers were increasing their hold over other sectors of the Russian economy, such as coal-mining. This close economic relationship was not without difficulties. Russian nationalists were complaining of foreign influence and foreign profiteers in Russia, and one of the points on President Poincaré's agenda when he visited St Petersburg in July 1914 was a court case against the French-directed coal syndicate for breaches of the Russian monopoly laws. Nevertheless, whatever the long-term effect of this nationalist reaction in Russia might have been if war had not come in 1914, the links between finance and strategy were for the moment growing closer. The loan of November 1913 was intended to increase Russia's railway network, including new lines – to be completed by 1918 – required for increasing the speed of Russia's mobilization in the west.

During the negotiations for a further loan, early in 1914, the point was raised again by the French representatives who pressed for an immediate start on building the lines in question, while the Russians tried to avoid being tied too closely to the construction of specific railway lines and stressed the economic importance of strengthening the railway network generally. The French banks at this point were also anxious to invest in a new Russian loan, since for internal political reasons a big French government loan had just been abandoned, so that substantial capital was immediately available. By early 1914, therefore, financial, strategic and political interests had all coincided to make the Franco-Russian alliance closer than ever before. In the interaction of politics and economics which combined to consolidate the alliance, it is hard to point to either factor as more important than the other. Rather, each encouraged the other. Once the political framework of the alliance had been established, both the governments and the businessmen found themselves more and more committed to working within that framework; and the economic desirability of keeping the Germans out of a share in Russian loans or the Russian arms market reinforced the tendency to think in terms of two rival power blocs. The financiers did not make the Franco-Russian alliance, but they were quick to see the advantages, psychological as much as practical, which it provided. The politicians and generals did not initially take the interests of the financiers into consideration when they made the alliance, but they were quick to see how financial links could serve their diplomatic and strategic purposes.

The financial strength of the French made them desirable partners economically. This led, in certain areas and enterprises, notably Morocco and the Baghdad railway project, to some temporary co-operation between Germany and France. After the Moroccan crisis of 1905–6, the German government had come to realize that for the moment not much was to be gained by directly challenging France's position there. During the next few years – generally a period of *détente* between the two countries – both governments were anxious to reach some sort of agreement on their various economic interests in Morocco, for example by encouraging the formation of a Franco-German consortium to exploit the (somewhat exaggerated) mineral wealth of Morocco. This attempt at international co-operation between the Germans Krupp and Thyssen and the French Union des Mines Marocaines broke down, not because of any immediate change in government policy, but because a rival German group, the Mannesmann brothers, were themselves trying to win exclusive control of mining rights in Morocco. They gained the support of one of the important German nationalist pressure groups, the Alldeutscher Verband, and were thus able to present themselves as working for the good of Germany and to claim that the German government was bargaining away Germany's interests to the French. The German government encouraged the banker and industrialist Walther Rathenau to mediate between the two rival groups, but the Mannesmanns turned down his proposals,[21] and the German government decided to give up their support for the Franco-German consortium.

The Agadir crisis in the summer of 1911 had profound effects on the economic relations between the two countries.[22] French national emotions were as strongly aroused as German, and with the renewed fear of war much French short-term capital was withdrawn from Germany, a policy encouraged by the French government. At the same time the French were becoming uncomfortably aware of the extent of German economic penetration of France over the past few years. The German industrialists were worried that their own sources of iron ore were running out and Thyssen and others were accordingly extending their interests in French Lorraine and acquiring control over iron-mines in Normandy. The French government became stricter in its control over the granting of mining concessions to foreigners as well as causing considerable annoyance by the strict application of new customs regulations on imports from Germany. Although many financial, industrial and commercial links remained at the outbreak of war – some of them surreptitiously maintained via Switzerland even during the war – in the mood of enhanced nationalism on both sides of the Rhine these were now subjected to closer scrutiny by the governments and public than ever before. Politics were taking precedence over economics; and profitable economic links were no longer necessarily maintaining peaceful relations between the two countries.

The French government's awareness of the connections between investment policy and foreign policy sometimes raised problems. If, for example, the French government refused to admit an Italian loan to the Paris Stock Exchange, would this make the Italians even more dependent on Germany? Or, if they did allow an Italian loan to be floated in France, could this be used as a means of influencing Italian foreign policy and weakening the alliance with Germany and Austria-Hungary? In 1904–6, when the Italian government needed a foreign loan as a basis for converting earlier government stock, the French ambassador in Rome was constantly reminding both the Italian Finance Minister and his own government of the value of this particular card: 'Italy must reply to the confidence which we would show in facilitating a major financial operation with a final and decisive mark of confidence by supporting France in the political sphere.'[23] Two years later, when the Germans were becoming very doubtful about Italy's loyalty to the alliance with Germany, the German ambassador in Rome was complaining that: 'Our financial weakness compared to the financial power of France is certainly one of the major reasons which explains the Francophilia of many influential circles in Italy.'[24] But it was not always easy for the French to use their financial influence effectively. The Germans directly controlled two major Italian banks, the Banca Commerciale Italiana and the Credito Italiano, which themselves controlled major steel factories, shipyards and electrical firms.[25] Alignments in foreign policy established a certain pattern of relationships in other spheres: when in 1908 the French tried to link a loan to Italy with an undertaking from the Italians to order artillery from French firms, the negotiations broke down because the Italian army could not and would not mix the new

French types of weapons with the old German ones, at a time when anyway there was still confusion about which of Krupp's models should be adopted.[26] In the event, during the struggle between interventionists and neutralists in 1914–15 which ended with Italy's entry into the war on the side of France and Britain, these economic considerations seem to have counted for very little and what carried Italy into the war was an emotional movement (helped it is true by discreet French subsidies to the Italian press) which bore little relation to Italy's economic interests or indeed her economic capacities.

The interaction of French financial strength, German shortage of capital and the respective diplomatic alignments of the two countries can be clearly seen in the case of Austria-Hungary. Twenty-five per cent of Germany's investments in Europe were in Austria-Hungary, and Austrian dependence on Germany increased in the years immediately before the war when money was needed for armaments and for meeting the cost of the military measures taken by the Monarchy during the Balkan wars. Psychologically, many Austrians were unhappy at their country's status as the weaker partner in the alliance with Germany. They were also worried that Germany was making inroads into Austro-Hungarian markets in the Balkans and were annoyed by the fact that Germany had profited by Austria's trade war with Serbia from 1905 to 1909 to take Austria's place as Serbia's principal trading partner. In particular, many Hungarians, ever since the major constitutional crisis of 1905 (see pp.46–7), would have welcomed an opportunity of substituting French financial support for what seemed to them too great a dependence on Berlin and Vienna. This was a prospect which especially alarmed the Germans; and several attempts by Hungarian government and municipal authorities to negotiate loans with French banks were vetoed by the Foreign Ministry in Vienna under German pressure.

On the eve of the war this feeling of helpless dependence was intensified: Austrian financiers were worried whether Germany could produce the finance they required and then resented it when they did. 'Austria has the misfortune', the director of a leading Austrian bank said in 1912, 'to have allies which are no use to her in the financial field.' He himself was, he told the German ambassador, 'a warm and confirmed supporter of the alliance with Germany, but it could not be denied that at the moment Austria was, at least financially, suffering from the alliance'.[27] In practice the Austrians had no choice. In spite of discussions with the French banks about a number of possible loans, the French government, with strong approval from the Russians, refused to allow the Austrian and Hungarian governments and other public bodies to float loans, some of which were intended for military and naval armament, on the Paris stock market. German financiers were not particularly enthusiastic about loans to Austria at a time when capital was extremely short in Germany. However, the German

Foreign Ministry insisted that loans to Austria must go through, even if it meant postponing loans to Turkey and Greece, which would, the bankers thought, have been more profitable from the point of view of bringing in orders for German goods. Jagow, the State Secretary at the German Foreign Ministry, emphasized the political importance of the loan, since a refusal would 'provide a powerful propaganda weapon for the agitation against the Triple Alliance which has recently emerged inspired by our enemies abroad, and would have unfortunate results'.[28] Yet even in July 1914 some Austrian bankers had not given up hope of collaboration with France: on 20 July a representative of the Viennese banks was reporting that Viviani was favourable to the idea of launching an Austrian loan in the autumn. The Austrian Foreign Ministry remained remarkably uninterested in the banks except when pressed by the Germans, while the bankers were more anxious to have advance warning from the Foreign Ministry of possible international crises so as to gauge their effects on the Stock Exchange than to take the initiative in foreign policy. The information they did obtain was not always accurate: in March 1914 the Secretary-General of the Bank of Austria-Hungary could declare: 'Without wishing to play the prophet, I must however note that recently semi-official declarations have succeeded each other, and we also have from well-informed private sources news which allows us to conclude that at least in the near future we need not fear that peace will be disturbed.'[29] Or were some Austrian government circles as surprised by the July crisis as the bankers were?

In the functioning both of the Franco-Russian and the German-Austrian alliances, the investment policy of the banks was serving the foreign policy of the governments. In the case of French financial help to Russia this was by and large a profitable operation. German investment in Austria, however, called for certain financial sacrifices. In other areas where foreign ministries hoped to use financial policy to support their foreign policy – Turkey and the Balkans or Morocco, for example – the financial profit and loss is harder to establish and depended not only on the interest on loans but on the orders for goods which were often a central condition of a loan, and which, since in many cases the banks had a large share in the factories making goods for export, also brought profits to the banks. Bankers were in the business primarily to make money for themselves and their clients, but in the intricate system of international finance which had developed with the growth of industrial capitalism in Europe, the relations between bankers and governments were probably closer than governments' relations with any other interest group. Sometimes bankers pressed for government action – in recovering debts in Egypt, for example, or in enforcing the 'open door' in China. Sometimes governments pressed banks to invest for political reasons in areas where the financial advantages were not immediately apparent.

These relations were made easier by the fact that in most of the major European countries bankers were closer socially to the men who exercised political power than most other businessmen, although the fact that they were in a position to press their views on politicians does not necessarily mean that they in fact did so. Still, they were often part of the same social world: Rouvier, the French Prime Minister at the time of the first Moroccan crisis, was himself a leading banker; and the German government used his financial acquaintances in Germany to reinforce their warnings to the French government in 1905. Lord Rosebery, the British Prime Minister in 1894–95 was married to a Rothschild. Both Kiderlen-Wächter and Bethmann Hollweg came from banking families. Sir Ernest Cassel, a German-born financier living in London, was a prominent member of King Edward VII's circle of friends. Holstein, the most influential figure in the German Foreign Ministry in the decade before 1906 was a close friend of Paul von Schwabach, the head of Bleichröder's bank, whose founder had been Bismarck's personal financial adviser and one of the few Jews to be raised to the Prussian nobility. Tisza, the Hungarian Prime Minister in 1914 was a great friend of the head of one of the leading bankers in Budapest, even if in the rigidly divided social system of Austria, the Vienna bankers, unless they were Rothschilds, were relegated to the 'second society'. The Warburg banking house in Hamburg had close relations with the Foreign Ministry; its head Max Warburg was invited to be a guest of the Kaiser at the Kiel regatta and was shocked, when meeting the Kaiser at a dinner in Hamburg in June 1914 to hear him talking about the possibility of a preventive war against France.[30]

The international bankers were in a paradoxical position, symbolic perhaps of the whole capitalist system in Europe before 1914. On the one hand, through their close collaboration with governments, they encouraged by their investment policy the consolidation of alliances and the growth of colonial rivalries. On the other hand they benefited by the flow of international trade and had an interest in maintaining it uninterrupted by international tension. They had close family and personal ties with foreign banks: the Rothschilds were the most famous of the international dynasties, but the Warburgs of Hamburg, for example, were related by marriage to two of the senior partners of the New York banking house, Kuhn, Loeb and to one of the directors of the Russian firm of Gunzbourg. In the crisis of July 1914, the head of the London Rothschilds was using, although unsuccessfully, all his influence to persuade *The Times* to stop advocating British support for France and Russia; and one of the most powerful factors working against British intervention was the conviction expressed by Grey on 31 July that 'the commercial and financial situation was extremely serious', and that 'there was danger of a complete collapse that would involve everyone in ruin'.[31]

The international links of bankers and businessmen were sometimes

used for confidential diplomatic negotiations. The visit to Berlin of
Lord Haldane in 1912 for talks about naval disarmament had been
preceded by contacts between Albert Ballin, the head of the
Hamburg-Amerika steamship line, and the financier Sir Ernest
Cassel. Ballin was again in London on 24 July 1914 and was invited by
Cassel to meet Churchill and Haldane at dinner, and he sounded out
the British ministers about possible conditions for England's neutrality
in the event of war. Many people believed that the existence of this
network of personal and business contacts all over Europe would in
fact make war impossible since no one stood to gain by a war. 'There
are in Europe at present too many pacifist forces,' the Belgian socialist
leader Emile Vandervelde said when asked about the danger of war in
1911, 'starting with the Jewish capitalists who give financial support to
many governments. . . .'[32] The English publicist, Norman Angell
argued in his best-selling book *The Great Illusion* (1909) that war
would bring economic disaster to victor and vanquished alike and that
'the capitalist has no country, and he knows, if he be of the modern
type, that arms and conquests and jugglery with frontiers serve no ends
of his, and may very well defeat them'.[33]

The nature of economic life at the beginning of the twentieth century
was such that the international trading and financial links often had
ambivalent political effects. While there were still many businessmen
who believed in the classical liberal doctrine that the growth of international trade would inevitably make wars impossible, others, faced
by falling profits and intense competition, were becoming increasingly
nationalistic in outlook and increasingly anxious for governments to
safeguard their interests by imposing protective tariffs or giving them
stronger diplomatic and in some cases, at least in disputed colonial
territories, military support. By the end of the nineteenth century all
the leading European states except Great Britain had adopted protective tariffs. The scale and nature of the tariffs were the subject of bitter
domestic political disputes: the stability of the conservative bloc on
which German governments relied for their parliamentary support
depended on a tough and recurrent bargaining process between
agrarians and industrialists. Protectionist policies were also bound to
have an effect on international relations. Although their effect was
often mitigated by commercial treaties and 'most-favoured-nation'
clauses which automatically accorded to other trading partners concessions negotiated with individual foreign countries, tariffs became
an important diplomatic weapon. The renewal of Italy's adherence to
the Triple Alliance in 1891 for instance was largely dependent on the
simultaneous signature of a commercial treaty acceptable to Italy.[34]

A large state could use a discriminatory tariff to try and impose its
will on a small country, as the Austrians did during their 'pig war' with
Serbia to protest against Serbian proposals for a close economic union
with Bulgaria, and in order to make the Serbs continue to buy arms

from Skoda and not from Schneider-Creusot. In fact this was a total failure for Austria, and her attempt to impose her will by banning Serbian exports only led to Serbia finding markets elsewhere, thus reducing her dependence on Austria and increasing Serb hostility to the Habsburg monarchy. In every country there were special interests which led to complaints that they were particularly harmed by specific items in other states' tariffs, but these anxieties tended to become of international political importance only when the relations between states were strained for other reasons. The French did not take much notice of the new German tariff which came into force in 1906 during the period of comparatively good relations between 1906 and 1910, and only began complaining seriously when those relations deteriorated, while in the hostile atmosphere after the Agadir crisis German complaints about the unfriendly and bureaucratic attitude of French customs officers towards German exporters increased sharply, so that economic disagreements helped to augment the growing ill-feeling between the two nations.

The discussions about renewal of Germany's commercial treaties, signed in 1904–5 and due to end in 1917 not only illustrate some of the serious economic and political problems facing Germany on the eve of the war, but also contributed to the sharply increasing antagonism between Germany and Russia. At the beginning of 1914 a recession was beginning to be felt in Germany, and this increased the internal strains between those manufacturers who wanted access to as wide a market as possible and who were ready to consider lowering tariff barriers in the hope of increasing trade, and the people, largely in the agricultural sector in which the Prussian landowners were the most prominent, who were insisting on the maintenance if not the increase of the existing protective tariffs.

In the spring of 1914 the official policy of the government was that the existing tariff policy was sufficient to safeguard the interests of both German industry and agriculture and that they should try to renew the commercial treaties on the existing terms.[35] This was in fact something which the Russians were not prepared to do. Their industrial progress over the previous few years had increased their confidence in their own economic strength as well as increasing the resentment which Russian nationalists felt at the control of their economy by foreigners. They remembered that the commercial treaty with Germany had been negotiated during the war with Japan at the moment of Russia's greatest weakness and they disliked it for emotional as well as practical reasons. In particular, the Germans had increased their export of rye to Russia and Scandinavia, partly because a concealed government subsidy had enabled them to keep their price down. The Russians wished to reduce the imports of German grain and make their own exports more competitive, and accordingly in June 1914 they introduced a new and heavy duty on the import of foreign grain. Even before the diplomatic crisis of July 1914 there was talk on both sides of the frontier of the 'coming great economic duel between Russia and Germany'.[36]

In England too there had been recurrent anxiety over the past twenty years about an economic duel with Germany.[37] In both countries there had been complaints of unfair competition and fears of discrimination. For the British there were practical reasons for anxiety, but rather on general grounds than because of a particular threat from Germany. The British share of world trade was falling: both the United States and Germany were catching up with British production of iron and steel, while the strength of Britain's older industries had meant that she was slower in developing some of the newer industries and technology. (From the purely economic point of view the United States was at least as dangerous a rival as Germany; yet there was no talk of a growing antagonism between the two countries.) In some areas Anglo-German trade relations were improving, and in fact, as Zara Steiner has pointed out, between 1904 and 1914, Britain became Germany's best customer and Germany was Britain's second-best market.[38] Particular industries in Britain suffered from the German tariff approved in 1902 and introduced in 1906, notably machinery and textiles. Yet German industrialists also complained of British competition, such as the woollen manufacturers worried about 'the deplorable preference shown in certain sections of society for English cloth'.[39] What caused an outcry in England in the 1890s, expressed by a widely read book published in 1896 by E. E. Williams, *Made in Germany*, which argued that, 'On all hands England's industrial supremacy is tottering to its fall, and this result is largely German work',[40] was not so much an objective assessment of England's relative industrial and commercial decline as a fear of the successful penetration by German salesmen into what had been regarded as exclusively British markets, for example in the Middle East. Complaints about the Germans' high-pressure salesmanship were not limited to English businessmen: the French were just as sensitive to German competition, complaining that four or five representatives of French firms in Moscow were competing with 550 Germans,[41] while in 1896 M. Schwab published a book called *Le Danger Allemand*, arguing along the same lines as Williams's book which appeared the same year. Certainly the realization of Germany's extremely high industrial progress and increasing economic strength affected the attitude of foreign countries and especially Britain towards her; but this was for the most part subordinated to other reasons for distrusting Germany. As Sir Edward Grey put it in December 1906,

> The economic rivalry (and all that) do not give much offence to our people, and they admire her steady industry and genius for organization. But they

do resent mischief making. They suspect the Emperor of aggressive plans of *Weltpolitik*, and they see that Germany is forcing the pace in armaments in order to dominate Europe and is thereby laying a horrible burden of wasteful expenditure upon all the other powers.[42]

For the Germans, too, the fear of the campaign in Britain for an end of free trade and the introduction of a protective tariff has to be seen in the wider context of a belief that they were being denied their 'place in the sun' by the grasping British. As one nationalist conservative member of the Reichstag put it, 'In the entire commercial stance of the English I can recognize . . . the clear intention to exclude Germany from the English colonies.'[43] On any utilitarian or statistical balance of profit and loss, there were probably as many businessmen in each country who benefited from trade with each other as were threatened by direct competition or tariff policy. The first group tended to want better relations between England and Germany; the second moved from economic anxiety to political resentment. As Paul Kennedy has put it, 'It surely is significant that neither Prussian agrarians nor Birmingham machine-makers joined the various Anglo-German friendship committees, whereas Lancashire mill-owners and Hamburg bankers did.'[44]

How are we to relate this complicated network of financial and trading relations to the theory that the main causes of the war were economic? Economic considerations were not much to the fore in the minds of the politicians taking decisions in July 1914; and when they were – as when the British government was faced with the possible consequences for the City of London of a complete breakdown of the foreign exchange market and the impossibility of receiving or paying debts where foreign countries were involved – they underlined the disastrous effects of war. Indeed it was taken for granted by nearly everybody in positions of responsibility all over Europe that the threat of economic collapse would be enough to end the war within a few months or even weeks. The Hungarian Minister of Finance thought that the war could not go on for more than three weeks – and Austro-Hungarian war production proved scarcely adequate even for that – so that their dependence on the Germans increased accordingly. The Russian plan in 1914 for expenditure on the army was based on the assumption that 'the present political and economic circumstances of Russia's main neighbours rule out the possibility of a long war'.[45]

Before 1914, governments had worried about the financial and fiscal problems of paying for their huge armament programmes, but they had given little thought to the economic measures that would be required once war had started. Most countries had stocks of gold available to cover the cost of paying their armies on mobilization, but they had made few other preparations for war. The German government had been worried, at least since 1906, about the difficulties of keeping the population fed if imports of food from abroad were cut off.

However, the Minister of the Interior assured them that supplies of domestic rye and potatoes would be sufficient, and nothing was done. An interdepartmental committee was set up in November 1912 – the moment at which the German government decided that war was probable – but it achieved little, mainly because the cost of stockpiling grain was very high on account of the tariff, which the agrarians would not agree to modify.[46] Also in 1912 the General Staff and the Prussian Ministry of War set up a new programme for the production of munitions, partly because they had been impressed by the rate of consumption of ammunition in the Russo-Japanese War. But here again the measures taken proved inadequate and all reserves of ammunition were used up after about two months of war.[47] These preparations have sometimes been used to support the argument that the Germans were deliberately planning to start a war: but all they really show is that from 1912 they were expecting a war and preparing for it, which is not necessarily the same as saying that they were going to provoke it themselves, though it does not exclude this either.[48] The desultory discussions about food and ammunition supply do, however, show clearly that the Germans had little conception of what the war would eventually be like or of its possible length.

Nor had any of the other belligerent states taken into account the economic consequences and needs of a war. The British had made practically no serious economic preparations for war, partly because even the military leaders had very little idea of what a war would involve in the way of supply and manpower policy, and partly because of a deep instinctive refusal among the majority of the Liberal Party to contemplate the prospect of war at all. With the exception of naval building many aspects of the material planning for war were simply ignored, particularly because of the need for economy in view of the competition for resources between naval construction and social welfare. The War Office cut its expenditure on munitions by over a third between 1905/6 and 1912/13.[49] There were some discussions about how food imports could be maintained in war and moments of alarm that Britain's gold reserves might run out, so that 'the growing commercial and banking power of Germany' aroused uneasiness lest the gold reserves of London should be raided just before or at the beginning of a conflict between the two countries'.[50] These alarms passed; and such enquiries as were carried out about stocks of food or munitions or the economic and social consequences of a declaration of war did not really provide a basis for action. On 4 August 1914, Lloyd George declared that government policy was 'to enable the traders of this country to carry on business as usual'.[51] It was only when this proved impossible that the government began gradually to improvise measures for the organization of total war.

The Russians had rifles available for issue on mobilization but had sold off earlier stocks, so that they had no spares. Already in

September 1914 the army command was complaining of the shortage of ammunition, having discovered that the rate of expenditure was three times greater than had been expected, foreshadowing the general crisis in supply and distribution which was to be one of the main causes of the revolution in 1917.[52] In France, while in the two years immediately before the war the government had been concerned to increase the size of the army by introducing the three-year period of conscription and had been worried how to pay for this, very little thought seems to have been given to providing equipment and ammunition for the additional recruits. The army was also short of several types of weapon, notably heavy artillery. As late as 13 July 1914, Senator Charles Humbert was drawing the attention of the Senate to the deficiencies in *matériel*; and after two days of debate it was agreed that the parliamentary committee on the army should make a report on the situation after the summer recess.[53] The state ordnance factories had been unable to satisfy the army's current needs, but private firms tended to charge high prices and not even Schneider-Creusot was yet really equipped for mass production.[54] The automobile manufacturer Louis Renault, one of the most enterprising and successful French industrialists, gave a vivid picture of the situation on the outbreak of war: about 8 or 9 August he was summoned by the War Minister whom he found very upset, walking up and down and repeating, 'We must have shells, we must have shells.' When asked by a senior general if he could make shells, Renault replied that he did not know: he had never seen one. But before he could be put in charge of organizing shell production in the Paris area, the state arsenals and the firms of Schneider-Creusot and Saint-Chamond had to give up their monopoly of shell manufacture, so that it was not until the autumn that the reorganization of the arms industry for war really began.[55]

Governments neglected economic factors in their plans for war, partly because they were certain that the war would be short and partly because they were uncertain what to expect once mobilization was completed and the opening strategic moves made. In some cases perhaps they never really believed that war would actually come at all. Their immediate motives for going to war were not economic, but rather political, emotional or strategic. Trade rivalry had, once attention had been drawn to it by nationalist publicists, served sometimes to increase popular feelings or international distrust and provided one factor, though not by itself a sufficient one, in identifying the enemy. Arms manufacturers made money out of contracts with their own governments, but also out of sales to other governments – a market which they would lose in time of war. Moreover, in many cases they were already producing to their maximum capacity, and it was only because of the reorganization undertaken after several months of war that they were able to meet the additional demands made on them. They certainly made money from the war (one of the main French steel companies, the Aciéries de France, for example, increased its profits fourfold between 1913 and 1915[56]), but so did many other 'hard faced men who looked as though they had done very well out of the war',[57] who had supplied boots or coal or cattle fodder or anything else essential for the war economy. Most of them do not seem to have foreseen the opportunities which war would provide, even if they made the most of them once war had started. There is no evidence that they were prompting governments to start a European war, and the fact that they profited by it is hardly sufficient proof that they were responsible for it.

Certainly there were industrialists and military men who hoped the war once it had begun would end with a peace that would extend their markets or safeguard their strategic position (Field Marshal Hindenburg was to justify his demands for large annexations from Russia with the words, 'I need them for the manœuvring of my left wing in the next war.')[58] There had for several years been talk in German industrial and financial circles, especially among bankers and those involved with some of the newer branches of industry, about the need to increase Germany's economic sphere by the formation of a new *Mitteleuropa*, a vast unified trading area which would provide Germany with markets as well as freeing her from dependence on imported food. Industrialists in the older sectors, the iron and steel producers for instance, had already been trying, as we have seen, to secure their sources of raw materials by acquiring a controlling interest in mines in France and elsewhere. In September 1914, when it still looked as though the Germans were about to win a complete victory over France, there seemed to be a possibility of putting some of these ideas into practice. Bethmann Hollweg approved a programme of extensive annexations in the west to be followed by the pushing back of the Russian frontier and ending of Russian rule over non-Russian peoples. This would have gone far both towards realizing the dreams of a German-dominated *Mitteleuropa* and giving German heavy industry direct control over the mines of Belgium and France. It has been argued by Fritz Fischer that it was deliberately in order to achieve these gains that Germany went to war and that this alone seemed to provide a way out of the economic difficulties and contradictions so widely apparent in the spring of 1914.[59]

Yet some doubts remain as to how far a programme produced after the war had started is necessarily evidence of the immediate reasons for the decision for war two months earlier; and we shall never know just what was in the minds of Bethmann and his colleagues in July 1914 or how they saw the priority among the many considerations which had to be taken into account. Whether they actually declared war in order to achieve these economic and geopolitical goals or for a number of more immediate reasons can never be decided. What is certain is that once war had begun most of the belligerents started to think of the gains they might win if victorious. The British thought of removing

German commercial and industrial competition for many years to come as well as ending the threat from the German navy. The French iron and steel magnates in the Comité des Forges began, like their German counterparts, to think of territorial gains which would ensure for them control of their raw materials. The Russians at once had visions of an advance to Constantinople to win permanent control over the exit from the Black Sea. There is perhaps a distinction to be made between the war aims for which a country goes to war and the peace aims, the terms on which she hopes to make peace once war has begun and victory seems in sight.[60]

Moreover, just as the outbreak of war temporarily relieved several of the governments involved of some of their immediate political problems, so it enabled them to solve for the time being some of their financial difficulties caused by the constant problem of paying for their armament programmes. Taxation at a higher level could be made acceptable on patriotic grounds, as in England, where the income tax was repeatedly increased and an excess profit tax introduced. Special war loans could be floated and the patriotic duty to subscribe to them stressed in well-organized propaganda campaigns, without worrying too much about how the money borrowed was eventually to be repaid (thus producing a major problem for the French and German governments once the war had ended). But here again, it would take a great deal more evidence than we possess to argue convincingly that governments deliberately went to war in order to solve their budgetary problems.

It is hard to find evidence that this particular war at this particular moment was directly the consequence of economic pressures or immediate economic needs. If we are to maintain that the causes of war were economic we shall have to look at longer trends in the development of European society during the decades before the First World War. Jean Jaurès, the most eloquent of the French socialist leaders, declared in 1895: 'Your chaotic and violent society, even when it wants peace, even when it is in a state of apparent repose, carries war within it as the sleeping cloud carries the thunderstorm.' The ethical values of unrestrained capitalist competition, Jaurès maintained, inevitably encouraged man's inhumanity to man. 'For this tormented society, to protect itself against the anxieties which constantly rise from its own depths, is perpetually obliged to thicken its armour plating; in this age of limitless competition and overproduction, there is also competition between armies and military overproduction.' There is, he went on, 'only one way finally to abolish war between people, it is to abolish war between individuals, it is to abolish the economic war, the disorder of present society, it is to substitute for the universal struggle for existence, which ends with the universal struggle on the battlefields, a regime of social peace and unity'.[61] However, right up to his assassination on 31 July 1914, Jaurès continued to hope that war could be averted, in spite of the injustices of the prevailing social and economic system, by measures of disarmament and arbitration, by reforms in the organization of national defence which would make it impossible to wage an aggressive war, by educating men and persuading them to co-operate with each other. Jaurès never worked out in detail just what the exact connections were between the prevailing economic system and war, but limited himself to denouncing militarism and imperialism without analysing them very closely. For all his insistence on the capitalist system as the cause of wars, Jaurès believed that it could be mitigated in such a way that the storm cloud of war would not necessarily burst, a belief which implies that the causes of war and the means of averting it may after all be political rather than economic.

The Marxist theorists who insisted that war was inherent in the nature of capitalism and that the growing crisis of capitalism would lead to war envisaged that this war would result from the imperial rivalries caused by the capitalists' need to maintain their profits by constantly finding new fields for investment, new sources of raw materials and cheap labour and new markets. If war was inherent in capitalism, then we must examine the nature of European imperialism at the beginning of the twentieth century and try to decide how far imperial rivalries were a cause of the war which broke out in 1914.

REFERENCES AND NOTES

1. For the Stuttgart Congress and the resolution on militarism and international conflicts, see e.g. James Joll, *The Second International 1889–1914* (new edn, London 1974) pp. 135–52.
2. See Eckart Kehr, *Schlachtflottenbau und Parteipolitik* (Berlin 1930).
3. For the British Navy League, see W. Mark Hamilton, 'The nation and the navy: methods and organization of British navalist propaganda, 1889–1914' (unpublished Ph.D. thesis, University of London 1978).
4. Paul Kennedy, *The Rise of the Anglo-German Antagonism 1860–1914* (London 1980) p. 299.
5. Volker Berghahn, *Rüstung und Machtpolitik* (Düsseldorf 1973) pp. 55 ff.
6. Bernard Michel, *Banques et Banquiers en Autriche au début du 20e siècle* (Paris 1976) p. 179.
7. Raymond Poidevin, 'Fabricants d'armes et relations internationales au début du XXe siècle', *Relations Internationales* 1, May 1974. Much of what follows is based on this important article.
8. Clive Trebilcock, *The Vickers Brothers: Armaments and Enterprise 1854–1931* (London 1977) pp. 120–1.
9. Poidevin, 'Fabricants d'armes', p. 42.
10. See esp. Bernard Michel, *Banques et Banquiers en Autriche au début du siècle* (Paris 1976) p. 179.
11. René Girault, *Emprunts russes et investissements français en Russie*

1887–1914 (Paris 1973) p. 345, fn. 2. Professor Girault's work is fundamental for an understanding of this whole question.

12. Raymond Poidevin, *Les Relations Economiques et Financières entre la France et l'Allemagne de 1898 à 1914* (Paris 1969) p. 178. Together with the work of Girault mentioned above, this goes a long way to giving a definitive account of the role of economic factors in French and German foreign policy.

13. Girault, op cit., p. 568. Poidevin, *Relations économiques*, p. 678.

14. Herbert Feis, *Europe, The World's Banker 1870–1914* (New York 1965) pp. 23, 51.

15. Girault, op. cit., p. 580; Feis, op. cit., p. 51.

16. Girault, op. cit., p. 430.

17. Girault, op. cit., p. 443.

18. Girault, op. cit., p. 446, n. 77.

19. *The Times*, 11 June 1907.

20. 'Les dirigeants politiques et économiques français de la IIIe République n'ont pas choisi la neutralité vis-à-vis du régime politique de la Russie, ils ont opté pour le tsarisme; ce faisant, ils se sont interdit toute réelle influence sur le cours futur des évènements intérieurs en Russie', Girault, op. cit., p. 447.

21. See Hartmut Pogge von Strandmann, 'Rathenau, die Gebrüder Mannesmann und die Vorgeschichte der Zweiten Marokkokrise', in I. Geiss and Bernd Jürgen Wendt (eds) *Deutschland in der Weltpolitik des 19. und 20. Jahrhunderts* (Düsseldorf 1973) pp. 251–70 and Poidevin, *Relations économiques*, pp. 475–80.

22. Poidevin, *Relations économiques*, pp. 654–819.

23. *Documents diplomatiques français 1871–1914*, 2 série, Vol. IV (Paris 1932) No. 174, p. 245. See also Raymond Poidevin, *Finances et Relations Internationales 1887–1914* (Paris 1970) p. 91.

24. Poidevin, *Finances et Relations Internationales*, p. 92.

25. C. Seton-Watson, *Italy from Liberalism to Fascism* (London 1967) pp. 284 ff.

26. Poidevin, *Relations économiques*, pp. 553–4; John Whittam, *The Politics of the Italian Army* (London 1977) p. 156.

27. F. Fischer, *Krieg der Illusionen*, (Düsseldorf 1969) p. 422.

28. Fischer, *Krieg der Illusionen*, p. 423.

29. Michel, op. cit., p. 366.

30. E. Rosenbaum and A.J. Sherman, *Das Bankhaus M. M. Warburg & Co. 1798–1938* (Hamburg 1976) p. 140.

31. G. P. Gooch and Harold Temperley (eds) *British Documents on the Origins of the War 1898–1914*, Vol. XI (London 1926) No. 367, pp. 226–7.

32. Quoted in Georges Haupt, *Socialism and the Great War: The Collapse of the Second International* (Oxford 1972) pp. 73–4.

33. Norman Angell, *The Great Illusion* (3rd edn, London 1911) p. 269.

34. See Rolf Weitowitz, *Deutsche Politik und Handelspolitik unter Reichskanzler Leo von Caprivi 1890–1894* (Düsseldorf 1978) Ch. 7.

35. See Egmont Zechlin, 'Deutschland zwischen Kabinetts- und Wirtschaftskrieg', *Historische Zeitschrift*, **199** (1964) and Fischer's reply in *Krieg der Illusionen* pp. 529–30.

36. Fischer, *Krieg der Illusionen*, p. 540, quoting the President of the

Russian Duma's committee on agriculture.

37. See the excellent discussions in Zara Steiner, *Britain and the Origins of the First World War* (New York 1977) pp. 59–68, and Kennedy, op. cit., Ch. 15. See also the statistics in Michael Balfour, *The Kaiser and his Times* (London 1964) Appendix I.

38. Steiner, op. cit., p. 41.

39. Kennedy, op. cit., p. 297.

40. Quoted in W. L. Langer, *The Diplomacy of Imperialism* (2nd edn, New York 1951) p. 245.

41. Poidevin, *Relations économiques*, p. 143.

42. G. M. Trevelyan, *Grey of Fallodon* (London 1937) p. 115.

43. Kennedy, op. cit., p. 298.

44. Kennedy, op. cit., p. 305.

45. Norman Stone, *The Eastern Front 1914–1917* (London 1975) p. 145.

46. Fischer, *Krieg der Illusionen*, pp. 286–7.

47. Gerald D. Feldman, *Army, Industry and Labor in Germany, 1914–1918* (Princeton 1966) p. 52.

48. Fischer, *Krieg der Illusionen*, pp. 284–8.

49. David French, *British Economic and Strategic Planning 1905–1915* (London 1982) p. 45.

50. Memorandum on British gold reserves sent to the Chancellor of the Exchequer by Sir G. Paish, January or February 1914. Marcello de Cecco, *Money and Empire: The International Gold Standard 1890–1914* (Oxford 1974) p. 207.

51. French, op. cit., p. 92.

52. Stone, op. cit., p. 146.

53. Georges Bonnefous, *Histoire Politique de la Troisième République*, Vol. II. *La Grande Guerre (1914–1918)* (Paris 1957) pp. 17–18. Douglas Porch, *The March to the Marne: The French Army 1871–1914* (Cambridge 1981) pp. 238–9.

54. Porch, op. cit., pp. 242–3.

55. Patrick Fridenson, *Histoire des Usines Renault*, Vol. I. *Naissance de la grande Entreprise 1898–1939* (Paris 1972) pp. 89–90.

56. Theodore Zeldin, *France 1848–1945*, Vol. II. *Intellect, Taste and Anxiety* (Oxford 1977) p. 1047.

57. The phrase is reported by J. M. Keynes as having been used by the Conservative politician Stanley Baldwin about the members of the British Parliament elected in November 1918. Roy Harrod, *The Life of John Maynard Keynes* (London 1951) p. 266.

58. John Wheeler-Bennett, *Hindenburg, The Wooden Titan* (new edn, London 1967) p. 127.

59. Fischer, *Krieg der Illusionen*, pp. 527 ff; F. Fischer, *Griff nach der Weltmacht* (Düsseldorf 1961) pp. 113 ff.

60. For a discussion of this point see Erwin Hölzle, *Die Selbstentmachtung Europas* (Göttingen 1975) pp. 38–41. Without accepting the premises of Hölzle's attack on Fischer, the distinction seems to me a useful one.

61. Max Bonnefous (ed.) *Oeuvres de Jean Jaurès: Pour la Paix*, Vol. I. *Les Alliances Européennes 1887–1903* (Paris 1931) pp. 75–7.

Chapter 7

IMPERIAL RIVALRIES

Joll thinks: ① this is important. How much? ② How?
③ - specific cause from this to war
④ - what are the weaknesses of this in Jolls argument
1 - mentality
2 - TENSIONS
3 - Actions to WAR

The immediate causes of the First World War lay in Europe; and the imperial rivalries of the late nineteenth and early twentieth centuries sometimes cut across the European alignments of the Great Powers. But nearly a century of imperialist expansion had left its mark on the way in which people looked at international relations and on the language in which they discussed foreign policy. To each of the countries which were engaged in the war, empire meant something different, but, especially in the last two decades of the nineteenth century, nearly all governments were convinced with different degrees of enthusiasm that, in the words of a French statesman, 'to remain a great nation or to become one, you must colonize'.[1]

Each move to acquire new colonies had complex and differing causes; and recently historians have written extensively about the various types of imperialism and have shown that, although in many cases hopes of economic gain were an important element in the initial impetus to colonize, the possession of colonies produced its own dynamism, so that the safeguarding of frontiers or the exclusion of rivals from vacant territory came to be regarded as important for their own sake.[2] The colonies themselves were quick to develop local vested interests which started what have been called 'sub-imperialisms': French officers and proconsuls in Algeria pressed for the acquisition of Morocco so as to make the control of rebel tribesmen easier by stopping them taking refuge across the frontier: the South African businessman Cecil Rhodes, at one time Prime Minister of Cape Colony,was determined to expand British influence in Southern Africa and to win the territory which later bore his name; the Australians by the time of the First World War were anxious to gain possession of the German colonies in the Pacific if only to stop the Japanese from getting them. Moreover, the end of the era of free trade meant that, especially for the British, areas which became the colonies of protectionist countries such as France would no longer automatically be open to British trade; and this provided an additional argument for the acquisition of vacant or disputed territories.

148

Some historians indeed have called British imperialism in the mid-nineteenth century an 'imperialism of free trade' in which British commercial and financial predominance did not necessarily require direct political control;[3] and it is true that the British often preferred to force countries to open their ports to British traders without assuming the responsibility for actual rule, as for example in the two China wars of 1839–42 and 1856–60. However, throughout the nineteenth century both Britain and France had been extending their colonial empires: France conquered Algeria and occupied Tunisia and won large and rich territories in Indo-China. Britain had acquired among other areas Singapore, Hong Kong and Malaya and occupied Egypt as well as consolidating and extending her rule in India and seizing Burma. But in the last two decades of the nineteenth century the pace of imperialist competition increased, especially in Africa and the Far East, and those powers which possessed no colonies, notably Italy and Germany, began to feel that they should have some, on general grounds of prestige and to provide a rallying point for national feelings at home.

The economic motives for colonization had been varied: the protection of the interests of European bond-holders in Egypt or Tunisia, hopes of making a fortune from gold and diamonds in South Africa, the exploitation of local crops – cocoa or coffee or rubber or palm oil – desire for markets for European goods ('The Waganda are clamouring for shoes, stockings and opera glasses and are daily developing fresh wants', Cecil Rhodes's brother wrote hopefully of Uganda in 1893),[4] possibilities of profitable investment in railways or telegraph systems. Many of these could be satisfied without the exercise of direct rule: but often traders found, as in parts of East and West Africa, that they needed government help to deal with the hostility of the inhabitants or to defend their settlements against slave-traders or the representatives of other European powers; and their governments, sometimes reluctantly, felt obliged to take over. The pressure groups able to influence governments were not necessarily those of the greatest economic importance. British trade with China, for example, was only a small percentage of Britain's total overseas trade, but the great China merchants, Jardine Matheson or Butterfield and Swire, possessed an influence with the Foreign Office out of proportion to their commercial importance. In France, where imperialism never became a popular cause to the extent it was in Britain, a comparatively small *groupe colonial* of people with a direct interest – economic, strategic or sentimental – in the French Empire was able largely to determine the policy of successive governments. The German move to obtain colonies in Africa had been started by a few Hamburg merchants hopeful for markets and assisted by explorers and adventurers. This had been taken up by Bismarck in 1884 as a way of winning nationalist votes in the Reichstag elections. In fact Bismarck, who had no long-term interest in the expansion of Germany outside Europe and who looked on colonial activity purely in the light of its effect on European diplomatic alignments or on domestic opinion in Germany, soon gave up the colonialist cause; but an influential pressure group had been started which, after Bismarck's fall in 1890, was able to add its voice to the growing chorus of nationalist organizations pressing for a German *Weltpolitik*.

During the 1890s the main imperial rivalries had been between Britain and France in Africa and Britain and Russia in the Far East. England and France had been close to war in 1898 over their claims to the upper Nile. Anglo-Russian antagonism in Asia had been a continuing factor in international relations at least since the 1830s; and it increased at the end of the century when it was clear that China was becoming the object of a struggle for influence among the European powers. To some extent imperial interests did not always coincide with European alignments. The French did not succeed in persuading their Russian allies to give them active support against the British in Africa, and they were prepared to co-operate with the Germans in China in 1895 in order to weaken Britain's predominant influence there. All the imperialist states, including a newcomer to their number, Japan, were ready to work together in 1901 when the Boxer rising in China appeared to threaten all the foreign powers which had been exploiting Chinese weakness for their own purposes. Within a decade, however, this preoccupation with colonial ambitions and rivalries had ceased to be the main feature of the international scene. In 1904 England reached a colonial settlement with France and in 1907 made an agreement on several outstanding imperial issues with Russia. This was, as we have seen, largely the result of the German decision to embark on naval expansion with a view to becoming a world power, so that Germany now seemed a more immediate threat to Britain's imperial position than France or Russia, while German ambitions in Morocco reinforced the hostility between France and Germany caused by the annexation of Alsace-Lorraine.

The underlying cause of this realignment was still imperialism, but it was an imperialism of a rather different kind from the direct colonial rivalry of the 1890s. The British government had now realized that Britain was an imperial power on the defensive whose resources were not necessarily sufficient to protect her vast possessions. At the same time the Germans had set out to become a *Weltmacht*. For Britain, the euphoria produced by the great imperial pageant in London at the time of Queen Victoria's Diamond Jubilee in 1897 was giving place to doubts – not so much about Britain's right to rule, since most British people, encouraged by the growing popular press, were still convinced that, in Joseph Chamberlain's words, 'the British race is the greatest of governing races that the world has ever seen'[5] – but rather about Britain's ability to maintain her place as the strongest imperial power in the face of other challengers. This change was in part the result of the South African War which brought home to many people the cost of empire in a way no earlier colonial campaigns had done and which had shown clearly the limits of British military strength. But the war in South Africa had also provided a focus for doubts about the methods of British imperial rule and had led, not only to criticism by radicals but also, especially among some of those responsible for carrying out the post-war settlement in South Africa, to the assertion of new ideals for the British Empire which would simultaneously convert it into an association of free peoples, as far as the white colonies were concerned, while admitting that the other colonies might eventually be granted some sort of self-government.

The most grandiose plan for imperial reorganization had been put forward by Joseph Chamberlain, the Colonial Secretary at the time of the Diamond Jubilee. Chamberlain wanted to unite the white-populated colonies in a new imperial federation while also developing an economic union – a *Zollverein* – which would make the whole Empire a free-trade area hedged around by tariffs against the world outside. Chamberlain's proposals were unacceptable both because those dominions such as Australia and Canada which had obtained complete self-government were reluctant to give up any of their sovereignty and were suspicious of a proposal which they thought would involve assuming greater responsibility for the cost of imperial defence, and because the vested interests in free trade were still too strong to permit any protectionist policies. Nevertheless, Chamberlain's suggestions revealed clearly some of the preoccupations of a British Empire faced with new strategic and economic challenges. He told the Colonial Conference of 1897:

If Federation were established, all these questions . . . would be settled by whatever was the representative body of the Federation, and among them, and in the very first rank, must of necessity be the question of Imperial defence. Gentlemen, you have seen something of the military strength of the Empire; you will see on Saturday [at the naval review off Portsmouth] an astonishing representation of its naval strength by which alone a Colonial Empire can be bound together . . . Now these fleets and this military armament are not maintained exclusively or even mainly, for the benefit of the United Kingdom, or for the defence of home interests. They are still more maintained as a necessity of Empire, for the maintenance and protection of Imperial trade all over the world.[6]

Five years later, when the colonial prime ministers were again in London for the coronation of King Edward VII, Chamberlain expressed his beliefs about the economic future of the Empire.

If we chose . . . the Empire might be self-sustaining; it is so wide, its products are so various, its climates so different that there is absolutely nothing which is necessary to our existence, hardly anything which is desirable as a luxury which cannot be produced within the boundaries of the

Empire itself . . . [But] the Empire at the present time . . . derives the greatest part of its necessities from foreign countries, and exports the largest part of its available produce . . . also to foreign countries.[7]

This contrast between the ideals and the reality of the British Empire, between the emotional feeling that the Empire must be preserved and strengthened and the realization of Britain's dependence on world trade and an open economy for its prosperity explains many of the dilemmas in British policy in the years before 1914. The commercial links with the Empire were undoubtedly important – in 1902 they reached their highest point with about 38 per cent of British exports going to British possessions; but these imperial links were only part of the overall pattern of British trade, while many of the colonies, the necessity of retaining which was taken for granted, were in fact economic liabilities rather than economic assets. The idea of the economic advantages of empire was more important than the reality in convincing the British in 1914 that the maintenance of their imperial position was worth the risk of war.

Joseph Chamberlain and the people who were spreading a new concept of empire at the turn of the century saw the British Empire as a means of ensuring British economic prosperity at a time when Britain's industrial supremacy seemed increasingly challenged – by Germany but also by the United States. They stressed the British right to rule and the superiority of the British race over all others. British school-children were brought up on tales of heroic military actions against inferior and barbaric peoples – 'treacherous natives' or members of 'lower races' who 'are greatly influenced by a resolute bearing'.[8] The cruelty and bloodshed of colonial wars were forgotten in the praise given to brave soldiers or disinterested colonial officers who administered impartial justice to vast populations in remote provinces bearing 'the white man's burden', in the famous phrase of Rudyard Kipling, the writer who reflected most accurately the myths and realities of imperial power. But the sense of British superiority which the existence of the Empire had helped to create over many generations was by the beginning of the twentieth century accompanied by an anxiety that the British were losing the martial and administrative gifts which had won the Empire on which it was believed, rightly or wrongly, Britain's prosperity depended. Joseph Chamberlain preached that the Empire could become economically self-contained while at the same time other imperialists were calling for greater efficiency in government, sometimes linking this with the need for a racial policy to encourage the development of the imperial qualities of the British race. The nation, according to Karl Pearson, who had moved from a chair of mathematics at University College, London to a new chair of eugenics specially founded for him, must be 'an organic whole . . . kept up to a high pitch of external efficiency by contest, chiefly by way of war with inferior races, and with equal races by the struggle for trade routes and for the sources of raw materials and food supply'.[9] While demands for increased efficiency, closer links within the Empire and improved preparations for war, including conscription, were taken up by various groups in Britain, and can be regarded as symptoms of the anxiety that the British Empire was now facing unprecedented challenges which could only be met by far-reaching social reforms at home, most of the public took the Empire for granted without question. As the newest of the popular daily papers whose success was based on reinforcing the prejudices of their mass of readers, the *Daily Express*, asserted in its opening editorial in April 1900, 'Our policy is patriotic; our policy is the British Empire.'[19]

The British Empire had entered into the consciousness and the folklore of the British people at many levels, both popular and sophisticated, and the images of empire which they formed were often contradictory. On the one hand there was a community of free nations, with the white colonies sending their young men to help the mother-country in her hour of need in the South African War. On the other hand were the non-European peoples over whom the British assumed the right to rule, and above all India. If one wants to reconstruct a picture of what the Empire seemed like to ordinary people in Britain, one has to think in terms of a whole series of overlapping or super-imposed images. Empire was justified in pseudo-Darwinian language as an essential element in the perpetual struggle for survival: but it was also defended on humanitarian grounds. All the imperial powers would have accepted with a greater or lesser degree of sincerity the doctrine expressed by a Belgian Catholic philosopher and archbishop: 'Colonization seems in the plans of providence to be a collective act of charity which at a given moment a superior nation owes to the dis-inherited races and which is like an obligation resulting necessarily from cultural superiority.'[11] This picture of Europe's cultural mission is overlaid and mixed up, especially for the British, with less pretentious images and sentiments: stories of military life in the colonies, or the brass tray from India and the wooden African stool brought home by a relation who had served as a soldier or administrator. And for the British the fact that many soldiers in the Regular army had served abroad and especially in India meant that these links and souvenirs were not limited to the upper and middle classes alone. How deeply the enthusiasm for empire affected the working classes in Britain – and it certainly hardly touched those in France – is still a matter of contro-versy. One study of public opinion during the South African War[12] has suggested that at least some sections of the urban working class were quite indifferent to the Empire or the war in South Africa and that, as one observer put it, the mere mention of the British Empire 'excites laughter as a subject to which no sincere man would dream of alluding'.[13] Yet the Royal Naval Exhibition in London in 1891 at-tracted nearly 2½ million visitors, and naval recruitment rose substantially after it,[14] while the British Empire Exhibition at Wembley in 1924 – first proposed in 1913, but postponed because of the war and turned into a demonstration of the Empire's strength and resources after the ordeal of war – was visited by nearly 18 million people.[15] The assessment of past public opinion is a historical problem notorious for its difficulty; but the outbreaks of popular enthusiasm during the South African War and that fact that in 1914 opposition to the war was very limited suggest that, even if it was promoted by the government and press, the idea of empire and the necessity for the defence of the Empire was widespread throughout all classes. What criticism there was was directed rather at some of the methods than at the fact of colonial rule.

The conception of the British Empire as an essential element in British life and British prosperity and a central point in British patriotism and the belief that its preservation was literally a matter of life and death account for the widespread fear before 1914 of Germany's vague claims to world power. For Britain in 1914 the threat to the Empire which Germany appeared to represent was not a threat to any particular colony – and indeed, as we shall see, right down to the outbreak of war there was always room for agreement between the two countries on specific colonial questions – but rather a general challenge which the German navy appeared to be making to Britain's strategic lines of communication and her world-wide trade. The old pre-occupation with protecting the routes to India which had dominated much of British foreign policy in the nineteenth century was still a powerful factor in British calculations, only now the threat came from Germany rather than from Russia. The preservation of the 'freedom of the seas' for British trade and British imports of food and the safe-guarding of the sea links with the Empire were an essential part of British imperialism and were stronger motives in the minds of the statesmen of 1914 than the acquisition of further British colonies or even the defence of existing colonial possessions. (The extension of the Empire only became once more a possibility after the outbreak of the war, with the conquest of Germany's African colonies and especially with the plans for the partition of the Ottoman Empire: and in these discussions Britain's main rival was France rather than Germany.) It was because the German challenge to Britain's imperial position was a general one rather than a specific set of territorial demands that it seemed so dangerous.

The Kaiser and his advisers never in fact decided what their goals in embarking on *Weltpolitik* were. Tirpitz's idea was, as we have seen, to make the German fleet so strong that Britain would not risk a war with Germany and would have to give way to German demands, but what these demands would be was never very clear. There was much talk about Germany's need for a 'place in the sun' and a feeling that the German navy was an essential symbol of German power. Even if one of the motives for creating a large German navy was a desire on the part of some of Germany's rulers to create a sense of national unity and provide a means of reinforcing their social control, many intellectuals and publicists saw in Germany's imperialist ambitions a genuinely idealistic task which would transcend the power politics involved. Germany was to liberate the world from the weight of British naval hegemony, and the smaller nations would rally to Germany's side of their own accord as the champion of a new and freer international order.[16] *Weltpolitik* or imperialism in this very general sense — and this was one of the reasons why it could serve as a unifying force for many different groups in German society – seemed to give a new purpose and a new mission to the German state. This is well summed up in two remarks by Max Weber. He said in 1893:

> It is the heavy curse of being the next generation *(Epigonentum)* which burdens the nation from bottom to top. We cannot again bring to life the naive enthusiastic energy which inspired the preceding generation, because we are faced with other tasks. We cannot use them to appeal to grand sentiments common to the entire nation as was the case when it was a question of creating the unity of the nation and a free constitution.[17]

The way out was, as he suggested two years later in his famous Inaugural Lecture at the University of Freiburg:

> We must grasp the fact that the unification of Germany was a juvenile prank *(Jugendstreich)* which the nation committed in its old age and, because of its expense, would have better left undone, if it was to be the conclusion and not the starting point of German world power politics.[18]

The trouble with these general ambitions to be a world power and to challenge Britain's world-wide hegemony was that these were vague aims; and many people refused to face the implications. Some of the more naîve members of the German public thought of the navy in terms similar to the Catholic professor of theology at Bonn who said: 'Peace is indeed the positive and direct will of God, war only a divine affliction and punishment; . . . But God's peace will one day come . . . Until that day may the German fleet ride on the waves of truth, justice and freedom, an escort of patriotic goodness and industry.'[19] Among the leaders of Germany there was a division of opinion about how the new German imperialism could be realized: while some people believed that it was possible to achieve Germany's goals by peaceful means – 'Deutsche Weltpolitik und kein Krieg' as Richard von Kühlmann, the counsellor in the German embassy in London put it in a pamphlet published under a pseudonym in 1913[20] – by means of an agreement with England and some reduction in the pace of German naval building, and some of the industrialists believed that Germany's economic strength would be sufficient to ensure Germany's predominance, at least in Europe ('Let us have yet another three to four years of peaceful development and Germany will be undisputed master of Europe' the industrialist Hugo Stinnes said in 1911[21]), there were many others who believed that Germany's bid for world power would involve war with England and were indeed prepared to welcome this. With the German ambition to be a *Weltmacht* expressed in so many different ways, it is not surprising that foreign assessments of Germany's aims, both at the time and subsequently, have varied. One German imperialist writer summed up the problem clearly in 1912, 'The main reason why our position sometimes makes such an uncertain, even unpleasant, impression when seen from outside Germany lies in the difficulty of presenting any easily comprehensible, as it were tangible, aim for the policies demanded by German ideas.'[22]

Within the general movement in Germany towards *Weltpolitik* there were specific groups and individuals who thought in conventional terms about increasing Germany's colonial possessions and dreamed of a German *Mittel-Afrika* to complement the German *Mitteleuropa* which others hoped to establish. The supporters of this idea included those with a direct interest in the existing German colonies, either because they thought there were profits to be made in Africa or because they themselves were involved in the actual administration of the colonies or because they thought that a deal about Africa might begin a process of *détente* with England, while in the German Foreign Office there were people, notably Paul von Wolf-Metternich, the ambassador in London from 1902 to 1912, and Richard von Kühlmann[23], who insisted that Germany's position as a world power could only be achieved with the support of England and not in opposition to her. The price of this support would have to be some concessions in the naval arms race, but this might, it was hoped, bring in return a political agreement with Britain by which Britain would remain neutral in a European war, and also a deal by which Britain would trade colonial territory in return for an end to the naval rivalry. These indeed were the themes of the discussion when Haldane visited Berlin in February 1912: and the failure of the Haldane mission showed how limited the possibilities of an Anglo-German agreement were. It at once became apparent that the British government was not seriously interested in a political agreement to remain neutral, and that the German Admiralty was determined to press on with the latest proposals for a further naval increase.

The Germans' chief hope of extending their African empire lay either in acquiring part of the Belgian Congo or in implementing the secret agreement made with England in 1898 which allowed for the partition of the Portuguese colonies if the financial situation of Portugal became so bad that she had to dispose of her empire in return for a loan. In the discussions during and after the Haldane mission, the British government indicated that they had no objection to the

Germans gaining territory in the Congo and that they were prepared to revise the 1898 treaty about the Portuguese colonies in such a way that the German share would be increased. It was characteristic of the misunderstandings about what had actually been agreed in the discussions between Haldane and Bethmann Hollweg that the Germans seem to have thought that Haldane had also promised them outright some British colonial territory, the islands of Zanzibar and Pemba off the east coast of Africa, an idea which Grey soon disposed of, declaring that a substantial compensation would be required for such a concession. (Haldane had also said that the Germans could have as part of their share of Portugal's colonial possessions the Portuguese half of the Indonesian island of Timor, and had to be reminded by the Foreign Office that the Portuguese had already promised it to the Dutch.)

Concessions over Belgian and Portuguese territory were not hard for the British to make. The British public, and especially supporters of the Liberal Party had been shocked by recent revelations of misgovernment and cruelty in both the Belgian Congo and the Portuguese colonies, and anyway as far as the Congo was concerned there seemed to be no evidence that the Belgians were thinking of giving it up. Even though the British Foreign and Colonial Offices despised the Portuguese (the editors of the *British Documents on the Origins of the War*, as late as 1938, after quoting a remark of Grey's that 'these colonies are worse than derelict as long as Portugal has them' felt obliged to omit the next few words 'for reasons of international courtesy'[24]), they were somewhat inhibited in their negotiations with the Germans by the fact that immediately after the agreement of 1898, they had formally reaffirmed treaties of alliance with Portugal going back to the seventeenth century which obliged the King of England 'to defend and protect all conquests and colonies belonging to the Crown of Portugal against all their enemies, as well future as present'[25] and in 1912 were still giving the Portuguese the impression that they wanted Portugal to keep her empire. The British ambassador in Berlin expressed the reservations widely felt in the Foreign Office when he wrote: 'It rather makes my blood run cold when we talk to Germany about the shortcomings of our Portuguese allies. Is it *quite* playing the game? Of course it is quite true what we say about them – but is it quite right or even politic to say it to the Germans?'[26] Although eventually an agreement was reached revising the 1898 partition scheme in Germany's favour, its status remained in doubt since the British insisted that both the Anglo-German treaty and the Anglo-Portuguese agreements should be published – a proposal to which the Germans had not agreed by the time war broke out. The question of an agreement to divide the Portuguese colonies, though actively pursued by the two colonial offices[27] was only central to German policy if it could be coupled with a British pledge of neutrality in Europe. This was something which the British were not prepared to give, especially as the French government, encouraged by the British ambassador in Paris, were making their suspicions and distrust of any Anglo-German *détente* quite clear. For once the Kaiser was perhaps right when he summed up the results of the Haldane mission: the English, he wrote, 'have conceded nothing at all in Europe . . . On the other hand they have referred us to African colonies belonging to other powers and they naturally don't know whether these powers will voluntarily give them up: but they certainly won't risk their good relations with them for our sake.'[28]

The idea that a colonial agreement between England and Germany might lead to a general improvement in their relations with each other – as in the case of the Anglo-French and Anglo-Russian agreements – did not come to anything because their imperial rivalry was wider and more intangible than could be resolved by bargaining over specific colonial and territorial questions. The conversations were kept going as long as they were because the two colonial offices were interested in agreement, and the members of the British colonial service had a genuine respect for the Germans as colonial administrators and certainly preferred them to the French as possible neighbours in Africa. There were also members of the British government, notably Haldane and Harcourt, the Colonial Secretary, who still believed that an agreement with Germany was both possible and desirable, while, on the German side, some influential politicians and officials, including Bethmann himself, thought that his survival as Chancellor depended on his achieving some sort of political agreement with England. The colonial negotiations confirmed that there was no direct territorial rivalry between the two countries, but they also revealed that neither side was prepared to give up its pretensions to world power in a broader sense.

The Anglo-German negotiations about the partition of the Portuguese colonies were conducted at the same time as discussions about British participation in the construction of the Baghdad Railway, discussions in which Britain's local aims of establishing economic control and political influence in Mesopotamia were by 1914 increasingly subordinated to her wider diplomatic and strategic needs.[29] The story of the project to construct a railway from Constantinople to the Persian Gulf is a complex one which brings out many aspects of imperialism at the beginning of the twentieth century: the interaction of economic and strategic interests with diplomacy, the way in which a weak state – Turkey – could play stronger powers off against each other, the extent to which imperial interests cut across European alignments. In 1889 a German group, headed by the Deutsche Bank, had won a concession to build the first section of a railway across Anatolia; and in 1899 they had obtained from the Ottoman government approval for the next stage. In 1903 the German promoters were backed by the German government and the Kaiser who, ever since his visit to Constantinople in 1898, posed as the friend and protector of Turkey and the Islamic world, but they were short of capital for such a large and expensive project and tried to raise money in London and Paris. The result has been well summarized by A.J.P. Taylor: 'In France the financial forces favoured participation, political motives were against it; and the politicians won. In England, the politicians were favourable, the financiers hostile; and the financiers won.'[30] The French government, that is to say, were doubtful about co-operation with the Germans, partly because the Russians were strongly opposed to the idea, partly because they believed that the Baghdad Railway might damage existing French railway interests in Syria, partly because they were conscious of the intense rivalry for Turkish orders between Krupp and the French armament firms, and so were determined to oppose any extension of German economic influence. Consequently the French government did all they could to stop those French bankers who thought there might be money to be made out of participation in the railway.

In England, on the other hand, the Conservative government, and especially the Foreign Secretary, Lord Lansdowne, believed that involvement in the extension of the railway would improve communications with India and strengthen Britain's position in the Persian Gulf. The fundamental division, however, was between those people in England who were hoping to improve relations with Russia and those who hoped that co-operation with Germany would help to check Russian ambitions in the Middle East. Both groups were aware that the balance of power was changing, but there was as yet uncertainty about how Britain should react. The influential publicists who were already worried about German *Weltpolitik* were supported in the cabinet by Joseph Chamberlain – partly perhaps from personal pique as he had been away in South Africa and resented decisions taken in his absence – also by many members of the public who were still upset by the anti-English campaign in the German press during the Boer War. 'We are still suffering', Lansdowne wrote, 'from an insensate hatred and suspicion of anything which can be described as of German origin and these feelings will not die out in a hurry – it is ridiculous and to my mind humiliating.'[31] As a result of the anti-German campaign in the conservative press supported by influential political figures, the British financiers at this point withdrew from the Baghdad Railway project, while the government limited themselves to a formal declaration of their determination to keep the Persian Gulf as a British sphere of interest.

In the agreement of 1907 the British and Russian governments settled their respective spheres of influence in Persia, so that any direct Russian threat to the Gulf seemed to have been removed. However, the internal situation in Turkey changed as a result of the Young Turk revolution in 1908 and Turkey's defeat in the First Balkan War, and both the British and the Germans were uneasily afraid that they might be losing their influence on the Turkish government whose own future was uncertain. By now, too, plans were being made and capital sought for the final stretch of the railway, from Baghdad to the Persian Gulf. There was now a basis for an Anglo-German bargain: the German promoters of the railway needed more money; they also needed British approval on the international board which controlled the Turkish customs dues, since the Turks were going to have to raise additional revenue by raising the tariff if they were to be able to pay the sums which they were obliged to guarantee to the Baghdad Railway Company for every kilometre of track completed.

Moreover, the original agreement between Britain, France and Russia to maintain a joint opposition to the Baghdad Railway scheme seemed to be breaking down. In 1910, when the Tsar visited Potsdam and there was a brief improvement in Germany's relations with Russia, the Russians had withdrawn their objections to the completion of the railway to Baghdad and had their own plans for linking it to Tehran and a new railway in north Persia. In these circumstances, the British government decided that by taking part in an international scheme for the completion of the railway they would preserve their own interests in Turkey and prevent either the Germans or the Russians having too much influence, even if it meant giving up their claims to an exclusive economic position in Mesopotamia. The Germans accepted the fact that without British co-operation they would neither find the capital to build the railway nor overcome the long-established British vested interests in Mesopotamia. The German Chancellor and Foreign Office – though not always the Kaiser or those German businessmen who thought that foreign competition in Turkey could be eliminated – realized the limitations on their freedom of action in the Middle East and were prepared to do a deal with the British. The British made it clear that their main aim in the area was the securing of the Persian Gulf and the maintenance of British influence in the south of Persia. On this basis protracted and complex negotiations could be carried out about British participation in the Baghdad Railway and the question could be treated on its own without reference to the wider rivalries between the two countries.

One other factor provided a basis for agreement – a factor which a few years later would have made agreement improbable if not impossible: the growing realization of the importance of the oil deposits in Mesopotamia and southern Persia. In 1914 this was still a comparatively new development, and it had taken decades to develop the technology required for extracting, refining and transporting the oil. But in 1912 the British Admiralty decided to start converting some of the fleet from coal to oil fuel and to construct new oil-fired Dreadnoughts; and already by 1914 25,000 tons of oil a month were being imported from south Persia.[32] Oil was about to become a strategic as well as a commercial product, though the implications were only just beginning to be realized. The British, after negotiations between the Turkish government and the various international groups which held concessions to drill for oil, succeeded in winning a controlling share in the oil companies operating in Mesopotamia and Persia. Although the German financial groups involved finally failed to win more than a 25 per cent share of the exploitation of oil deposits in Turkey, this was less because of a failure of the two governments to agree than because of the chronic German shortage of capital. The Turkish government was also able to exploit the fact that the American Standard Oil Company was now offering to pay cash for a transfer to them of the oil concessions – whose legal status was undoubtedly confused, if not dubious – so that the British and German governments and financiers quickly settled their differences in the face of this new threat.

Although the British and Germans succeeded in reaching agreement over their economic and strategic interests in Turkey in spite of their wider imperial rivalry, it remains uncertain who got the better bargain, because, however these agreements might have worked out in peacetime, war broke out within two months of the initialling of the Baghdad Railway agreement (and the railway itself was still hundreds of miles from Baghdad). The Turkish government were increasingly concerned that their obvious weakness, after their defeats in the Tripoli and Balkan wars and the loss of nearly all their European territory, made them vulnerable to a threat of partition, and they became convinced that they had more to fear from Russia than from Germany. On 2 August, the day after the German declaration of war on Russia, they signed a hastily negotiated secret treaty of alliance with Germany in return for a guarantee of their territorial integrity against Russia; and in November they came into the war on Germany's side.

The Anglo-German negotiations about the Baghdad Railway showed, like the bargaining about the Portuguese colonies, that it was still possible to find a basis for specific agreements even within the framework of the wider rivalry between the two countries; and in any case ordinary diplomatic and economic relations continued right up to the outbreak of war, and it was only at the last minute – and not always even then – that they were subordinated to preparations for war. Nevertheless the case of Turkey – like that of China a decade earlier – and the complex story of Anglo-German co-operation and rivalry there suggests that here was an area in which imperialist rivalries among the European Great Powers were contributing to the instability which made the outbreak of war possible. The existence of a large but fragile state tempted stronger powers to stake a claim for spheres of influence and economic control, while the Ottoman Empire was the object not only of encroachment by the European Great Powers but also of the aspirations of national independence among its non-

Turkish subjects. The result was a continuous crisis from 1908 onwards. The Turkish officers who made the Young Turk revolution of 1908 because they hoped to modernize the Ottoman state and prevent its disintegration inadvertently inaugurated the process which was to lead to the final collapse of the Empire in 1918. The immediate consequences were the annexation by Austria-Hungary of Bosnia and Herzegovina in 1908 before the new Turkish government could assert its formal suzerainty over the provinces which Austria had occupied since 1878. Similarly, the last formal ties between Bulgaria and Turkey were broken and the union of Crete with Greece finally achieved. These developments increased Turkish suspicions of the subject nationalities they still controlled – Arabs and Armenians as well as the Balkan Christians; and the hopes that the revolution might lead to the conversion of the Ottoman Empire into a genuinely multinational state in which non-Muslims and non-Turks would have equal rights were quickly disappointed, as the new regime, after a series of military coups and counter-coups, developed into an increasingly repressive military dictatorship. At the same time, the political instability of the years 1908–13 not only encouraged the Balkan states to combine to drive Turkey out of Europe; it also made the Great Powers, especially Russia (though even the Austro-Hungarian government, as if it did not have enough to worry about, played with the idea of acquiring a colony in Asia Minor),[33] think about the partition of Turkey.

The first step which was to lead to the general crisis in the Balkans was the Italian attack on the Turkish provinces of Tripoli and Cyrenaica – perhaps the most direct and open act of imperialist expansion in the years immediately before the war. Ever since the unification of Italy, some Italian nationalists had dreamed of an empire in North Africa which would show that the new Italian state was the true heir to the Roman Empire. They had been disappointed when France won the protectorate over Tunisia in 1881; they had been bitterly humiliated when the Italian army was defeated by the Ethiopians at Adua in 1896. As French ambitions in Morocco became apparent, so successive Italian governments thought that Italy might claim the only remaining territory in North Africa not yet controlled by a European state – the Turkish provinces of Tripoli and Cyrenaica, which the Italians took to calling by the Roman name of Libya as though to stress a bogus historical claim. The French government, as part of their policy of trying to weaken Italy's links with the Triple Alliance (see pp.51, 133–4) had indicated in 1900 and reiterated in 1902 that they would have no objection to Italy acquiring Turkish territory in North Africa. At the same time, Italian economic interest in Tripoli was increasing: from 1907 onwards the Banco di Roma was investing heavily in various enterprises there; and through its links with politicians as well as with the Roman Catholic Church it was able to exercise considerable political pressure. Moreover, the leading exponents of an extreme nationalism were now organizing themselves effectively in pressure groups such as the Associazione Nazionalista Italiana and the Dante Alighieri Society, reinforcing the views of many Italians that Italy had too long been regarded as a museum for tourists living on its past and must now assert itself as a modern Great Power. The nationalists and the members of the Istituto Coloniale also exaggerated the attractions of Libya as a colony: 'Tripoli opens her arms and is waiting, the land is the same as that of Tunis, if not more fertile: the climatic conditions are the same; minerals there must be . . . What is needed is a government which acts or is willing to assist action.'[34] Italy was, it was claimed by Corradini, one of the most rhetorical of the nationalist spokesmen, 'the proletarian nation', an underprivileged country confronting the rich and powerful imperial states; and her pressing social problems and the economic backwardness of the south could only be solved by the acquisition of colonies.

In this atmosphere, the Agadir crisis and the French claim to Morocco provided an opportunity for the Italian nationalists and those with economic interests in Tripoli to press the government to act – especially as a few weeks earlier the inauguration in Rome of the vast and pompous monument to King Victor Emmanuel II had seemed to symbolize Italy's new international pretensions. The government somewhat reluctantly – it was less than a year since the Foreign Minister had declared, 'The Turks have still not succeeded in understanding one thing, although it is very clear. Italy does not wish to take Tripoli and desires that it remains Ottoman'[35] – under pressure from parliament, nationalists and the Banco di Roma was by July talking of military action. At the end of September an ultimatum was sent to Turkey and improvised plans made to send an Italian force to Tripoli. This arrived in the first half of October and quickly occupied Tripoli and other towns on the coast, using for the first time in a war an aeroplane for reconnaissance and to drop grenades on the enemy.[36] However, an epidemic of cholera quickly reminded the soldiers of the realities of a colonial campaign, while the Arabs in the interior maintained a resistance which was to last for more than ten years. But the war was not just a colonial campaign: it was a war against the Ottoman Empire, which, however decrepit, was not prepared to acknowledge defeat immediately. To the alarm of the other European powers, the naval war spread to the eastern Mediterranean. The Italian fleet bombarded the forts at the entrance to the Dardanelles and seized the Dodecanese Islands. In July 1912 negotiations between Italian and Turkish representatives began in Switzerland; but it was only the mobilization of the states of the Balkan League at the end of September, taking advantage of Turkey's predicament, which finally forced the Turks to sign a treaty accepting Italy's gains before turning to face the even greater strains of the First Balkan War. It was not only Turkey and the Balkan states which were directly affected by the

Italian actions. During the war with Italy the Turks had closed the Straits; and the result was a substantial fall in Russia's foreign trade during the latter part of 1911, so that those Russians who believed that control of the Straits must be the main aim of their foreign policy had fresh evidence to support their view.

Giolitti, the Italian Prime Minister, had not been enthusiastic about the Libyan campaign and only accepted it as what he called 'historical fatality'.[37] He had foreseen that the consequences would go far beyond the gaining of a colony for Italy. He had said in April 1911:

> Tripolitania is a province of the Ottoman Empire, and the Ottoman Empire is a European great power. The integrity of what remains of the Ottoman Empire is one of the principles on which the equilibrium and peace of Europe is based . . . Can it be in the interests of Italy to shatter one of the cornerstones of the old edifice? And what if after we have attacked Turkey, the Balkans begin to stir? And what if a Balkan war provokes a clash between the two power blocs and a European war? Can it be that we can shoulder the responsibility of putting a match to the powder?[38]

Certainly Italy's imperialist war was one of the sparks lighting what one historian has called 'the long fuse'[39] linking the outbreak of the First World War to remote origins in the Balkans.

The outbreak of war in 1914 was not caused by immediate imperialist rivalries; and Germany's aspirations for colonial territory might well have been achieved by agreement with Britain if the Germans had been prepared to abate their claims to naval hegemony and world power. Nevertheless weak independent states such as Morocco and the Ottoman Empire itself were a constant temptation to imperialist or would-be imperialist powers, so that Franco-German rivalry in Morocco and Italian ambitions in Tripoli could produce crises in 1911 which added to the instability of the international system. By 1914, however, specifically colonial conflicts in North Africa or the Middle East were subordinated to a wider pattern of international ambitions and apprehensions. The crisis over Morocco was solved by a compromise colonial agreement between France and Germany which left neither side wholly satisfied, but the importance of the crisis lay less in the specific redistribution of African territory than in the general exacerbation of mutual suspicion between France and Germany and the intensification of the arms race, supported by a new wave of nationalist propaganda on both sides of the frontier. By 1914 the psychological consequences of a generation of imperialism were more important than the actual territorial gains or losses.

The older imperial rivalries had not disappeared, but they had been pushed into second place by the new alignment caused especially by German ambitions to take a place among the world powers. A mass of detailed disagreements still troubled relations between Britain and France in spite of the *Entente Cordiale* – arguments, for example, over the international status of Tangier or economic interests in Syria; and these were to become worse once the war had started and the possibility of a partition of the Ottoman Empire revived old suspicions and aroused new ambitions. Yet again and again both in London and Paris the need for mutual support against Germany led, if not to a solution of these differences, at least to an agreement to overlook them temporarily. British relations with Russia were more difficult. Although the Anglo-Russian agreement of 1907 appeared to resolve the conflicting claims on the borders of the two empires – in Afghanistan and Tibet and Persia – local rivalries and old distrust that went back for generations still caused problems. The agreement had been criticized in both countries, particularly because the recognition of British and Russian spheres of influence in Persia coincided with a revolution there in which both sides tried to win British or Russian support.[40] Both Russian and British military men felt that too many concessions had been made in the interests of a diplomatic agreement, while in England many of Grey's Liberal supporters – and also the British minister in Tehran – were outraged by what they regarded as a betrayal of the liberal movement in Persia when the British government acquiesced in a Russian-backed counter-revolution. Yet in spite of moments of tension, as when in 1908 the Russian commander of the Shah's Cossack Brigade ordered his troops to surround the British legation in Tehran, Grey and the Foreign Office consistently sacrificed local interests in Persia and the Far East to a wider cause of maintaining the *entente* with Russia. Yet British attitudes to Russia remained ambiguous: Russia was an essential ally against Germany, but some senior Foreign Office officials also feared that Russia, once she had recovered completely from the disasters of 1905, might again become England's main imperial rival. 'The Russians could be exceedingly awkward in the Mid and Far East and could seriously shake the British position in India', Sir Arthur Nicolson, the Permanent Under-Secretary at the Foreign Office, wrote in April 1913. 'This is to me such a nightmare that I would at almost any cost keep Russian friendship.'[41] There was in Nicolson's mind always a lurking fear that unless Britain were prepared to appease Russia over what he regarded as minor matters, Russia might do a deal with Germany and confront the British Empire with a threat which it might be too weak to survive. Other advisers of the British government, while recognizing a potential threat from a revived Russia, thought that the agreement with Russia should be renegotiated so as to safeguard Britain's interests, especially in Persia. The argument between those who in the spring of 1914 thought that now was the time to stand up to Russia's claims and those who, like Nicolson, believed that friendship with Russia must be preserved at all costs to enable Britain to confront the Germans, was never resolved since it was overtaken by the events of July 1914, but it perhaps suggests that the leaders of the British Empire, overstretched as they believed it to be, had still in 1914 not all made up their minds where the threat to it was ultimately coming from.

Britain's relationship with India was central to the idea of empire and had been the key to British foreign policy for more than a century. The fact of British rule over this vast empire was often taken for granted and not often subjected to calculations about profit and loss, but India was still one of Britain's main markets and still a fruitful field for the investment of capital as well as a direct source of government revenue. At the same time, the Liberal government was having to face the fact that at a time when there was talk, at least with respect to the older white colonies, of the Empire eventually being transformed into an association of self-governing dominions, the system of government in India was becoming more and more anomalous, while the nationalist movement was growing, even if it was not yet the threat it was to become ten years later. Nevertheless, the construction of a grandiose new capital at New Delhi and the spectacular Durbar held by the new King-Emperor George V in 1911 suggested that British rule was as firmly based as ever, and it was still widely taken as axiomatic that, as Lord Curzon wrote in 1901: 'If we lose [India] we shall drop straight away to a third-rate power.'[42]

With the agreement with Russia in 1907, one of the main threats to India's external security seemed to have been removed – even if the government of India and the soldiers were rather reluctant to recognize the fact. Germany could never threaten India in the way in which Russia could, though there were fears that the Baghdad Railway, if Britain could not exercise some control over it, might become a vehicle for the expansion of German influence. When in 1911 the Russians withdrew their objections to the Baghdad Railway in return for a link between the main line and Tehran, the old British anxieties revived in a new form: 'It would be a very serious matter', Grey wrote, 'if Germany obtained any control of this branch. For in times of Pan-Islamic excitement, it might be used to mobilize German-trained Mussulman forces. Germany, who held no Mussulman subjects, was not embarrassed by Pan-Islamism, but it might be very serious to Russia and England.'[43] The Kaiser, in his role as self-appointed protector of Islam, had indeed hinted from time to time that a war with Germany could lead to the loss of India, and on 30 July 1914, in a blind outburst of hatred against England, he wrote: 'Our consuls and agents in Turkey and India must inflame the whole Mohammedan world into a wild rebellion against this hated, lying, unscrupulous nation of shopkeepers; for even if we must bleed to death, then at least England shall lose India.'[44] Although the British were not unaware of this danger, a direct German threat to India was never taken very seriously; and even after the war had started, German plans to inflame the world of Islam against Britain did not have much success. On the other hand, the danger of a revival of the Russian threat to India was very much in the mind of British officials, many of whom believed that just for this reason Russian friendship must be retained at all costs; and indeed the Russians in their proposals in June and July 1914 for a strengthening of the ties between the two countries and especially for a naval agreement, were hinting that a more formal alliance might include a Russian guarantee of the security of India. Here once again the discussions were overtaken by the July crisis and the outbreak of war, so we do not know how Anglo-Russian relations might have developed. It has indeed been suggested[45] that it was anxiety about India which brought England into the war on Russia's side as the only way of preventing a renewed Russian threat to India should Russia win a war in which Britain had remained neutral. This is attributing too much consistency and foresight to a divided British government and a Foreign Office which was by no means unanimously clear where the main danger to the British Empire lay, but it reminds us how often British governments were thinking of their European policy in imperial terms.

The immediate motives which led governments to decide to go to war in 1914 were not directly imperialist and the crisis they faced was a crisis in Europe, but earlier imperialist policies had contributed to the frame of mind in which decisions were taken. For Russia the lure of Constantinople and the Straits was a main motive in her Balkan policy, to which Asian ambitions were temporarily subordinated. For Germany vague aspirations to world hegemony had contributed to the decision to construct a navy which was inevitably seen by Britain as a challenge. England who, as the German ambassador in London remarked, 'has the best colonies and doesn't need a war with us to acquire more',[46] had nevertheless come to accept the British Empire as something that had to be preserved at any cost. The French, by accepting the need urged by the *parti colonial* to gain control of Morocco had added a colonial dimension to their resentment against Germany in Europe, while the Germans by deliberately provoking the Agadir crisis contributed to the growth of nationalist agitation in both countries and the acceleration of the arms race, and thus added to the growing international tension in 1912–14, tension in the growth of which the collapse of Ottoman rule in Europe under the impact of Italian imperialism and Balkan nationalism had also played a major part.

Imperialist thinking had always accepted the risk of war and regarded armed struggle as an essential part of imperial expansion, even though in fact imperialist wars had hitherto for the most part been limited in scope. By 1914 this intensified the crisis in which German ambitions, French grievances, Russian expansionism, British anxieties and Austrian fears led to the decision that war was inevitable if vital national interests were to be preserved. That decision could not have been possible if the prevailing mood in Europe had not been ready to accept and even welcome war; and to the creation of that mood the rhetoric even more than the reality of imperialism had contributed much.

REFERENCES AND NOTES

1. Léon Gambetta, quoted in Léon Brunschvig, *Mythes et Réalités de l'Impérialisme colonial français* (Paris 1960) p. 9. See also James Joll, *Europe since 1870* (New edn, London 1983) Ch. 4.

2. See esp. Wolfgang J. Mommsen, *Theories of Imperialism* (London 1980); D. K. Fieldhouse, *Economics and Empire 1830–1914* (London 1973); R. Robinson and J. Gallagher, *Africa and the Victorians: the Official Mind of Imperialism* (London 1968).

3. See D. C. M. Platt, *Finance, Trade and Politics in British Foreign Policy 1815–1914* (Oxford 1968); R. Robinson and J. Gallagher, 'The imperialism of free trade', *Economic History Review*, **6** (1953); D. C. M. Platt, 'The imperialism of free trade: some reservations', *Economic History Review*, **21** (1968); 'Further objections to an "imperialism of free trade" ', *Economic History Review*, **26** (1973).

4. Quoted in W. L. Langer, *The Diplomacy of Imperialism* (New York 1951) p. 123.

5. 11 November 1895, quoted in J. L. Garvin, *The Life of Joseph Chamberlain*, Vol. III (London 1934) p. 27.

6. Garvin, op. cit., pp. 187–8.

7. Julian Amery, *The Life of Joseph Chamberlain*, Vol. IV (London 1951) p. 436. For an account of the movement for tariff reform and imperial federation, see Wolfgang Mock, *Imperiale Herrschaft und Nationales Interesse* (Stuttgart 1982).

8. Quoted in V. G. Kiernan, *European Empires from Conquest to Collapse, 1815–1960* (London 1982) pp. 156, 158.

9. Quoted in Bernard Semmel, *Imperialism and Social Reform: English Social and Imperial Thought, 1895–1914* (London 1960) p. 41.

10. Quoted in Semmel, op. cit., p. 57.

11. Quoted in Paul Mus, *Le Destin de l'Union française* (Paris 1954) p. 18.

12. Richard Price, *An Imperial War and the British Working Class: Working Class Attitudes and Reaction to the Boer War 1899–1902* (London and Toronto 1972).

13. Quoted in Price, op. cit., p. 73.

14. W. Mark Hamilton, 'The nation and the navy: methods and organization of British navalist propaganda 1889–1914' (unpublished Ph.D. thesis, University of London 1978) pp. 92 ff.

15. *The Times*, 1 Nov. 1924.

16. See Ludwig Dehio, 'Thoughts on Germany's mission 1900–1918', in Dehio, *Germany and World Politics in the Twentieth Century* (Eng. tr. London 1959).

17. Marianne Weber, *Max Weber: ein Lebensbild* (Tübingen 1926) p. 138.

See Wolfgang J. Mommsen, *Max Weber und die Deutsche Politik* (Tübingen 1958) p. 35; also Arthur Mitzman, *The Iron Cage: An Historical Interpretation of Max Weber* (New York 1970) pp. 106–7.

18. Max Weber, *Gesammelte Politische Schriften* (Munich 1921) p. 29. See also Mommsen, *Max Weber*, p. 78 and Mitzman, op. cit., pp. 137–47.

19. Winfried Philipp Englert, *Das Flottenproblem im Lichte der Sozialpolitik* (Paderborn 1900), quoted in Eckart Kehr, *Schlachtflottenbau und Parteipolitik* (Berlin 1930) pp. 369–70.

20. F. Fischer, *Krieg der Illusionen*, (Düsseldorf 1969) p. 378. See also Wolfgang J. Mommsen, 'Nationalism, imperialism and official press policy in Wilhelmine Germany' in Philippe Levillain and Brunello Vigezzi (eds) *Opinion Publique et Politique Extérieure 1870–1915* (Rome 1981) p. 380.

21. Heinrich Class, *Wider den Strom* (1932) p. 217, quoted in Egmont Zechlin, 'Motive und Taktik der Reichsleitung 1914' in Wolfgang Schieder (ed.) *Erster Weltkrieg: Ursachen, Entstehung und Kriegsziele* (Cologne 1969) p. 197.

22. P. Rohrbach, *Der Deutsche Gedanke in der Welt* (1912) p. 202, quoted in Dehio, op. cit., p. 78, n. 1.

23. See Gregor Schollgen, 'Richard von Kühlmann und das Deutsch-Englische Verhältnis 1912–14', Historische Zeitschrift, **230** (1980).

24. G. P. Gooch and Harold Temperley (eds) *British Documents on the Origin of the War 1989–1914*, Vol. X (London 1936) Part II, No. 226, p. 224. (Hereinafter referred to as *BD*).

25. *BD* I, No. 119, p. 85.

26. *BD* VI, No. 579, pp. 750–1.

27. See P. H. S. Hatton, 'Harcourt and Solf: the search for an Anglo-German understanding through Africa 1912–14', *European Studies Review* I, No. 2 (1971).

28. *Die grosse Politik der Europäischen Kabinette*, Vol. XXXI (Berlin 1936) No. 11474, p. 210.

29. See Stuart A. Cohen, *British Policy in Mesopotamia 1903–1914* (London 1976).

30. A. J. P. Taylor, *The Struggle for Mastery in Europe 1848–1918* (Oxford 1954) pp. 410–11, fn. 2.

31. Quoted in George Monger, *The End of Isolation: British Foreign Policy 1900–1907* (London 1963) p. 122.

32. Elizabeth Monroe, *Britain's Moment in the Middle East 1914–1956* (London 1963) p. 122.

33. See F. R. Bridge, '*Tarde venientibus ossa:* Austro-Hungarian colonial aspirations in Asia Minor', *Middle East Studies*, Oct. 1970.

34. Quoted in Richard Bosworth, *Italy, the Least of the Great Powers: Italian Foreign Policy before the First World War* (Cambridge 1979) p. 138.

35. Quoted in Bosworth, op. cit., p. 134.

36. Kiernan, op. cit., p. 128.

37. Quoted in Bosworth, op. cit., p. 163.

38. F. Malgeri, *La Guerra di Libia 1911–12* (Rome 1970) pp. 98–9, quoted in S. M. O. Jones, 'Domestic factors in Italian intervention in the First World War' (unpublished Ph.D. thesis, University of London 1982) p. 61. See also Bosworth, op. cit., p. 148.

39. Laurence Lafore, *The Long Fuse* (London 1966).
40. See Firuz Kazemzadeh, *Russia and Britain in Persia 1864–1914: A Study in Imperialism* (New Haven and London 1968).
41. Quoted in Zara S. Steiner, *The Foreign Office and Foreign Policy 1898–1914* (Cambridge 1969) p. 137.
42. Quoted in Max Beloff, *Britain's Liberal Empire 1897–1921* (London 1969) p. 91, fn. 4.
43. *BD* X, I, No. 653, p. 623.
44. Karl Kautsky, Graf Max Monteglas and Prof. Walter Schücking (eds) *Die deutschen Dokumente zum Kriegsausbruch, Vol. II (Berlin 1919) No. 401, p.133.*
45. For example by Erwin Hölzle, *Die Selbstentmachtung Europas* (Göttingen 1975) esp. pp. 85–95, 216 ff.
46. Prince Karl Max Lichnowsky, 'Wahn oder Wille' (Jan. 1915), in John C. G. Röhl (ed.) *Zwei deutsche Fürsten zur Kriegsschuldfrage: Lichnowsky und Eulenburg und der Ausbruch des Ersten Weltkriegs. Eine Dokumentation* (Düsseldorf 1971) p. 55.

Chapter 8

THE MOOD OF 1914

Any government, even the most dictatorial, needs to be sure of popular support before starting a war. For this reason, as we have seen, each of the governments which declared war in 1914 was concerned to present its decision in such a way as to win the maximum public approval: the French were fighting to defend the soil of France against a new German invasion; the Germans were fighting to defend the soil of Germany against the Cossack hordes, and so on. But the mood in which the peoples of Europe accepted and in some cases even welcomed the idea of war and temporarily forgot their social and political differences was not just the result of the way in which their governments had justified their immediate political decisions. It was founded on an accumulation of national traditions and attitudes which had formed beliefs about the nature of the state and its authority, reinforced by the curriculum in the schools over the past decades and the kind of language in which politicians and journalists had discussed international relations. The analysis of this complex of beliefs and attitudes and of the accumulated mentality of a nation is a very difficult task. To establish anything which can be called the 'mood' of Europe in 1914 is probably impossible. We lack the detailed study of opinion for most countries, even where the material for it exists and is accessible, although Jean-Jacques Becker's work *1914 − Comment les Français sont entrés dans la guerre*[1] has told us much about the attitude of French people at the moment of mobilization and also taught us much about the methodology as well as the limitations of such a study.

Still, the evidence which we do have and the studies of attitudes, both popular and governmental, suggest that there are certain factors in all the belligerent countries which contributed to the mood which made war possible. Although there had been, as we have seen, a series of international crises which, at least since 1905, had caused talk of war, and although some writers and most generals and admirals believed in the inevitablity of international conflict, the crisis of July 1914 when it came was a shock to many people who were given little time to reflect on what was actually happening. Indeed, observers of

the state of international relations had found the situation in the early
months of 1914 more encouraging than for several years: the effects of
the Balkan wars had been more or less contained without conflict
between the Great Powers: the Zabern affair, which might have been
expected to increase tension between France and Germany had been
received comparatively calmly in France: although the naval rivalry
between England and Germany still provoked rhetorical phrases on
both sides, there were some signs that the pace of naval building might
be about to slacken, and the two countries were negotiating amicably
about the Portuguese colonies and the Baghdad Railway. True, there
was in March an outbreak of mutual attacks in the German and
Russian press, while there was some anxiety that the failing health of
the aged Emperor Franz Joseph might have international repercussions, but there did not seem in the summer of 1914 any immediate
danger of a major international crisis. The foreign offices of Europe
were preoccupied with routine work: as the Permanent Under-
Secretary in the British Foreign Office wrote to the ambassador in
Berlin in May: 'You will see from the print that there is very little of
interest taking place at this moment in Europe, and were it not for the
troubles in Mexico we should be in comparative calm here.'[2]

In fact both in Britain and France much more attention was being
paid to the internal political situation than to foreign affairs. When *The
Times* headed its leading article on 3 July, 'Efforts for peace' and said,
'The public in England and Scotland do not realize how near the nation
is to disaster', it was to the crisis over Ulster that it was referring; and
Ulster dominated British politics right down to the moment when on
24 July, as Winston Churchill later recalled with his characteristic
sense of historical drama, after the Cabinet had 'toiled round the
muddy byways of Fermanagh and Tyrone', they heard 'the quiet grave
tones of Sir Edward Grey's voice . . . reading a document which had
just been brought to him from the Foreign Office. It was the Austrian
note to Serbia.'[3] In France, the elections and the controversy over the
introduction of an income tax were themselves thrown into the background by the sensational case of Madame Caillaux, wife of the
Finance Minister and leader of the Radical Party, who had murdered
the editor of *Le Figaro* on 16 March and whose trial opened on 20 July.
Even at the height of the crisis on 29 July, the trial took up 30 per cent
of the columns of *Le Petit Parisien* and 45 per cent of those of *Le Temps*
compared with 15 per cent and 19 per cent respectively on the international situation.[4] Although the Germans were not confronted by an
immediate crisis as grave as that in Ulster or by a scandal as sensational
as that of Mme Caillaux, for most of them in the first half of 1914 the
economic recession and the growing domestic tension between the
social democrats and the conservatives were of greater concern than
international problems. The murder of the Archduke Franz
Ferdinand, in an age when the assassination of royal personages had

not been uncommon, did not arouse many serious forebodings: the German trade union leader Carl Legien was in a minority when he warned that the 'Austrian warmongers' might make a 'world conflagration' unavoidable.[5] Once the immediate shock of the news had passed, the civilian and military leaders proceeded to go on their summer holidays as usual; indeed some of the military and naval leaders in Germany and Austria were encouraged to take their normal summer leave so as to avoid giving the impression that anything out of the ordinary might be going to happen.

Accordingly, the short period between the news of the Austrian ultimatum to Serbia and the outbreak of war did not allow for much considered reflection about the implications of the crisis. 'It has only needed a week to bring Europe to the eve of a catastrophe unique in history', the French business weekly *La Semaine Financière* commented on 1 August;[6] and a young Austrian socialist wrote a few months later: 'The outbreak of the war surprised and depressed us all. We may well have been previously convinced that the anarchy of the capitalist world would eventually lead to a bloody clash between the European powers, but the moment of catastrophe found us completely unprepared.'[7] Just as in studying the actions of the politicians and diplomats we have the impression that they were repeatedly being overtaken by events, so too the public had little time or opportunity to grasp what was happening. This is one of the reasons for the collapse of the movement against war which had been a prominent feature of pre-war politics and which had been taken very seriously by the governments of those countries such as Germany and France where it appeared to be strongest.

The movement against war took two forms. There was a body of respectable middle-class liberal opinion which believed, as the English Utilitarians had done, that, in Bentham's words, 'between the interests of nations there is nowhere any real conflict. If they appear repugnant anywhere it is only in proportion as they are misunderstood.'[8] At the same time, however, there was a growing movement among the working-class parties of Europe which emphasized that, 'Wars are inherent in the nature of capitalism; they will only cease when the capitalist economy is abolished.'[9] The threat of war would be met by the threat of revolution; and the international solidarity of the proletariat would make war impossible. By the beginning of the twentieth century the middle-class organizations in favour of international arbitration, disarmament and the development of a code of international behaviour which, even if it did not abolish war, would do something to limit and mitigate its effects, were becoming increasingly active. This movement was strongest in Britain and the United States, but it was able to win an influential body of support in France and a smaller number of intellectuals and professional people in Germany, but, especially in Britain and France, it had sufficient connections with the ruling groups for governments to feel, or at least pretend to feel, that they had to pay some attention to it. Some of the older humanitarian organizations, notably the International Red Cross, founded in 1864, were also already recognized international forces.

The support for these peace movements came both from those who believed that a rational organization of international society could limit the causes of war and from those, like the famous Austrian peace propagandist Baroness Bertha von Suttner, who believed in the need for moral reform if war was to be abolished. 'War continues to exist', the Baroness wrote in 1912, 'not because there is evil in the world but because people still hold war to be a good thing.'[10] In addition to those who placed their hopes for peace in institutions and legal codes and in a reform of moral values, there was also in the years before 1914 a growing belief that war was now becoming so costly and so deadly that it would in fact become impossible. The rich Warsaw banker Ivan Bloch in a six-volume work published in 1898 and widely translated and discussed, studied the technical development of weapons and tactics and argued that no offensive could succeed in the face of the fire-power of modern weapons, so that an offensive war was unlikely ever to be launched, while Norman Angell in *The Great Illusion* (1910) argued that the economic cost of war was so great that no one could possibly hope to gain by starting a war the consequences of which could be disastrous.

The greatest apparent success, even if a hollow one, for these peace movements was the holding of two international conferences at The Hague in 1899 and 1907. The first was the result of a proposal by the Tsar Nicholas II, received with sceptical surprise by the diplomats of Europe, that there should be a conference to discuss ways of reducing armaments and of providing for the peaceful settlement of international disputes. The initiative seems to have come from the Russian Foreign Minister and also from the Tsar himself – partly no doubt from a genuine if unfocused idealism not unlike that of his great-grandfather Alexander I – and there is some evidence that he was temporarily impressed by the ideas of Ivan Bloch. Most observers, however, took a more cynical view of the Tsar's proposals and pointed out how anxious the Russian government must be to find ways of making economies in expenditure on arms at a time when they were in some financial difficulty. In any event, while the states invited accepted so as not to hurt the Tsar's feelings, few of their representatives went to The Hague in either an optimistic or a constructive mood. The Kaiser declared: 'Die Conferenzkomödie mache ich mit, aber den Degen behalte ich zum Walzer an der Seite' ('I'll go along with the conference comedy but I'll keep my dagger at my side during the waltz')[11], while later he went even further: 'I agree to the stupid idea so that [the Tsar] doesn't look a fool in front of Europe! But I will in practice in future only rely on and trust God and my sharp sword! And sh[it] on all the resolutions!'[12] The British War Office said much the same thing in more diplomatic language: 'It is not desirable to agree to any restrictions upon the employment of further developments in destructive agencies . . . It is not desirable to assent to an international code on the laws and customs of war.'[13] In these circumstances it was surprising that the conference achieved anything at all: but the liberal advocates of reform of the conduct of international relations could at least take some comfort from the establishing of machinery for voluntary arbitration and of new conventions about the conduct of war. How little the conference had contributed to resolving the immediate problems of keeping peace was shown within three months when war broke out between the British and the Boer republics in South Africa.

The idea of a second Hague Conference was originally proposed in 1904 at a meeting at Saint Louis of the Inter-Parliamentary Union, a body established to promote better international relations. It was taken up enthusiastically by President Theodore Roosevelt and marked the first of many attempts in the twentieth century by successive US governments to reorganize the international order. In fact, largely because the Russian government rightly considered that, since they were at war with Japan, it was hardly the moment to discuss such subjects as arbitration and disarmament, the conference did not meet until the summer of 1907. By this time the Liberals were in power in England and some of them were sufficiently committed to the reduction of expenditure on armaments to insist, against the wishes of several members of the government as well as of the opposition, the Admiralty and King Edward VII, that this should be proposed by the British delegates to the conference. However, again, as in 1899, the cynicism of most of the delegates was complete: the head of the British delegation, a high-minded Quaker jurist, complained of 'the evident wish of some of the Great Powers that the results of the Conference should be as small as possible',[14] while the Foreign Office representative on the delegation talked of 'perpetual flurry and tedious and invariably useless work'.[15] When the German delegate made a long speech opposing the whole idea of an international court of arbitration he was congratulated by the Cuban delegate with the words, 'You are quite right. That is all American humbug.'[16] As in 1899, the work of the conference in fact only resulted in a revision of the rules of war intended to limit the effects of war on international business rather than in doing much to prevent war as such; and, as at so many subsequent disarmament conferences, each country made it clear that any reduction in armaments should apply to other states and not to themselves, so that the question of limitation of armaments was soon excluded from the discussions. Yet no government was prepared to be the first to break up the conference and each accused the others of obstructing progress. This is perhaps at least evidence that the various movements for peace, arbitration and disarmament were sufficiently

175

strong for some governments to feel that they had to take notice of them.

Both the optimism and the limitations of the peace movements were demonstrated in the spring of 1913 when a meeting of members of the French and German parliaments was organized in Berne to discuss disarmament and the peaceful settlement of disputes between the two countries. The meeting was regarded as a success by the two bodies mainly responsible for it, the German Verband für internationale Verständigung and the French organization Conciliation Internationale; of those attenting 121 were from France and thirty-four from Germany; and all but six of the Germans were socialists, whereas eighty-three of the French delegates were from non-socialist parties. Although serious and respectable and not without a certain influence, these were groups which in practice represented only a comparatively small section of the political world. Most of the members of the peace movements were anxious to stress that their attempts to reform the system of international relations and to reduce armaments did not mean that they lacked patriotism, and they welcomed official recognition by governments, as when the delegates to the Inter-Parliamentary Union's London conference in 1906 were received by the King and later taken on a visit to the naval dockyard at Portsmouth. It is therefore not surprising that in 1914 nearly all of them supported the war rather than opposed it: 'There can be no doubt about the duties of the pacifist during the war', the German Peace Association announced in August 1914, 'We German pacifists have always recognized the right and obligation of national self-defence. Each pacifist must fulfil his common responsibilities to the Fatherland just like any other German.'[17] And while a few of the British pacifists remained true to their professed beliefs throughout the war, they were only a small minority in a movement of which most members held, as one of them put it, that 'We cannot continue criticism of the policy which has led to this war as we did in the case of South Africa, for our safety is at stake. We can none of us now think of anything but this one object.'[18]

The movement against war among the socialists of Europe appeared stronger than that among middle-class liberals; and governments were more alarmed by it and its implications, even though in the event it was no more successful and collapsed for some of the same reasons. 'The working man has no country', the *Communist Manifesto* had proclaimed in 1848, 'National differences and antagonisms are daily more and more vanishing owing to the development of the bourgeoisie, the freedom of commerce, the world market, the uniformity in the mode of production and the conditions of life corresponding thereto.' Thus the struggle between nations would eventually give way to the international class struggle: and in the meantime the proletariat must develop its international links in order, as Marx's inaugural address to the First International put it, 'to obtain unity of purpose and unity of action'. Marx and Engels were not against war as such; and they were full of contempt for the liberal pacifists of the mid-nineteenth century: 'hypocritical phrasemongers, squint-eyed set of Manchester humbugs', as Marx called them, who spoke peace abroad while using the police to control their workers at home.[19] Each war, Marx believed, must be judged according to whether it was likely to hasten or delay the historical developments which were inevitably leading to revolution. On this criterion, the main obstacle to revolution in Europe was the reactionary power of Tsarist Russia; and any war against Russia was deserving of support. The internal regime of a state which was opposing Russia was of little importance: Turkey, for example, in the Crimean War was on the side of history because, as Engels put it a few years later: 'A subjectively reactionary force can in foreign policy fulfil an objectively revolutionary mission.'[20]

Thus the Second International – the body founded in 1889 to link the growing socialist parties of the world – found itself in a situation in which the leaders of the mass socialist movements in the advanced industrialized countries of western Europe might have to decide whether a war should be supported or not, since not all wars were necessarily reactionary. Indeed the possibility of a contradiction between the claims of internationalism and support for war had already been demonstrated in 1870. 'The French need a thrashing', Marx had written at the start of the war. 'If the Prussians win, the centralization of state power will be useful for the centralization of the German working class'; and he also added characteristically, 'German preponderance will besides move the centre of gravity of the European working class from France to Germany. The preponderance of the German proletariat will mean at the same time the preponderance of our theory over that of Proudhon.'[21] Some German social democrats supported the war for less sophisticated reasons, and were as susceptible to the wave of German nationalism as members of other classes. But others consistently opposed the war; and on the day after Marx had designated the Prussians as, so to speak, the vehicle of history, the two socialist members of the parliament of the North German Confederation, Wilhelm Liebknecht and August Bebel made their famous declaration of abstention from voting the war credits: 'As opponents in principle of all wars, as social republicans and members of the International which opposes all oppressors and aims to unite all the oppressed into a great league of brotherhood, we cannot declare ourselves either directly or indirectly in favour of the present war, and therefore abstain from voting.'[22] It was a precedent which was to be recalled in August 1914, when the German socialists were torn between the same considerations of ideological correctness, humanitarian dislike of war and the appeal of patriotism.

After Marx's death, Engels was developing new ideas about the nature of modern war and the problems which it posed for socialists, and he realized that the next war would be more destructive and more disastrous than any previous one. He wrote in a well-known prophetic passage in 1887:

> Eight to ten million soldiers will swallow each other up and in so doing eat all Europe more bare than any swarm of locusts. The devastation of the Thirty Years War compressed into the space of three or four years and extending over the whole continent; famine, sickness, want, brutalizing the army and the mass of the population; irrevocable confusion of our artificial structure of trade, industry and credit, ending in general bankruptcy; collapse of the old states and their traditional statescraft, so that crowns will roll by dozens in the gutter and no one be found to pick them up; it is absolutely impossible to predict where it will all end and who will emerge from the struggle as victor. Only *one* result is absolutely certain: general exhaustion and the establishment of the conditions for the final victory of the working class.[23]

This analysis of the effects of war suggested a new dilemma from which the international socialist movement never escaped. On the one hand it seemed as if war was bound to weaken the structure of capitalist society and prepare the way for revolution, but on the other hand it was the working class, the workers and peasants who provided the majority of soldiers in the conscript armies of the European continent, who would be the first to suffer the horrors of modern war. Thus the problem whether to welcome war as an accelerator of revolution or whether to try and prevent war because of the suffering and devastation it would cause was never resolved; and this accounts for some of the ambiguities and contradictions in the attitude of socialists to the threat of war in the years before 1914.

The international socialist movement appeared to be confident that it could prevent war and that the very strength of the organized socialist parties would be sufficient to deter governments from making war. 'Let the governments remember', the International Socialist Congress which met at Basle during the Balkan War of 1912 declared, 'that, with the present condition of Europe and the mood of the working class, they cannot unleash a war without danger to themselves.'[24] However, in the years before the war, however confident some socialists might be that capitalism was now entering its last phase and that this would soon be followed by war and revolution, there were still immediate problems about their short-term attitudes to the question of national defence. The socialists were particularly concerned to ensure that the army would not be used against the workers themselves. This was clearly a danger in Germany, where the Kaiser, with his usual flair for saying the wrong thing, had told recruits in 1891: 'In the present social confusion it may come about that I order you to shoot down your own relatives, brothers or parents but even then you must follow my orders without a murmur.'[25] But even in democratic France the great rail strike of 1910 was broken by mobilizing the railwaymen into the army; and in Switzerland, where the militia system provided a model to which socialists elsewhere looked with envy, the army had been used against strikers. The easiest solution seemed to be to do what the German social democrats did. They regularly voted against the military budget in the Reichstag – 'Not a man and not a penny to this system' was their slogan; they protested against ill-treatment of soldiers and against high living – gambling and 'other orgies' – in the officers' messes. But what they really hoped was that the pressure of socialist numbers would eventually deal with this as with all other problems. As Engels put it in 1891: 'Today we reckon to have one socialist soldier in five, in a few years we will have one in three and around 1900 the army . . . will have a majority of socialists.'[26] But things did not work out quite that way.

It was in France, where the Marxist influence on the working-class movement was much less strong than in Germany, that criticism of the military establishment as well as direct opposition to war was most vigorously expressed. On the one hand the socialist leader Jean Jaurès produced in his study *L'Armée Nouvelle* (published in 1910) the fullest scheme attempted by a socialist for a complete reform of the system of national defence. On the other hand, some of the revolutionary syndicalists and some socialists on the left of the party were calling for a general strike against mobilization and an insurrection on the outbreak of war. The latter threat was taken more seriously by the French government than Jaurès's proposals for reform, in spite of his substantial parliamentary following. The prefects of the *départements* were busy, right down to July 1914, revising the notorious *Carnet B*, the list of people who were to be arrested in the event of mobilization as being likely to sabotage the preparations for war. The list included a wide, though sometimes arbitrary, range of names of committed syndicalists and established trade unionists who were believed to be active in anti-militarist propaganda.[27] Actually, even before the experience of July 1914 showed that these official fears were without foundation, it appears that the activity in which these suspects were engaged was almost exclusively verbal, and that, however much the revolutionary syndicalists and some socialists reiterated their intention to carry out a general strike against war, they had made no actual preparations to do so.

The French example illustrates two of the difficulties which socialists everywhere were experiencing in maintaining a consistent attitude not only to war but also towards the society in which they were living. The militant anti-militarists did not have any practical plans or organization to carry out their threats. At the same time those socialists such as Jaurès who were concerned to reform the system of national defence wanted to make it more efficient and more democratic; they certainly did not want to abolish it altogether. *L'Armée Nouvelle* is as much an eloquent appeal to French patriotic feelings as it is an attack on the system, and while it calls for means to defend an ideal and reformed republic, it nevertheless implies that the existing Third Republic may well still be worth defending. Representatives of both the revolutionary and the reformist attitudes to war and national defence could be found within the same party, and the contradiction between their two attitudes was often obscured by the need for the party leaders to make gestures towards their own left wing. There has, for example, been much controversy about the attitude of Jean Jaurès in July 1914.[28] At the conference of the French Socialist Party on 15 and 16 July – held before the international crisis became acute and intended to prepare for the proposed congress of the Second International to be held in Vienna in September – Jaurès supported a motion stating that of all ways to prevent war a general strike was likely to be the most effective. This was not in fact taken very seriously by the government. Was it just a tactical move on Jaurès's part to maintain contact with the Left? For it is hardly credible that he really believed that the general strike against war was practicable; and it is certain that within ten days, when war seemed imminent, he was pledging support to the government. Was it a move to impress the German social democrats with the seriousness of French intentions, aimed at suggesting that they should call a general strike against the German government if Germany were to attack France? As Jaurès was murdered on 31 July and as speculation about what his actions during the war would have been has gone on ever since, we can never be sure. All we do know, as the police agent reporting on the Socialist Party conference put it, is that 'On ne peut s'empêcher de constater que la motion de Jaurès est d'une obscurité et d'un vague qui frisent le verbiage' ('One can't help remarking that Jaurès's motion is of an obscurity and vagueness that borders on mere verbiage').[29]

There is a sense in which the leadership of the German Social Democratic Party was more realistic. They repeatedly rejected the idea of a general strike against war, or indeed for any other purpose, declaring that 'Generalstreik ist Generalunsinn' ('General strike is general nonsense'). If the party were strong enough to carry out a general strike, it would be strong enough to do a great deal more, or, as Wilhelm Liebknecht had put it in 1891, 'If the military strike and the economic strike were more than a pious wish, if the social democratic parties of Europe possessed the power to carry through these strikes, then there would be a situation which would make every war impossible.'[30] The German socialist leaders were also convinced – and in this they were true followers of Marx – that a war against Russia was one which they were bound to support, as they repeated again and again. August Bebel had declared:

> The soil of Germany, the German fatherland belongs to us the masses as much and more than to the others. If Russia, the champion of terror and barbarism, were to attack Germany to break and destroy it . . . we are as

much concerned as those who stand at the head of Germany and we would resist Russia, for a Russian victory means the defeat of social democracy.[31]

It was an attitude which those who stood at the head of Germany knew how to exploit in 1914.

But if Bebel and the other German socialist leaders were afraid of Russia, they were even more afraid of the power of the German state. They never forgot the twelve years under Bismarck's anti-socialist law which had made very many of the usual activities of a political party impossible and they were terrified that similar restrictions might be imposed again; and indeed there were many conservatives calling for just this. The socialist leaders were thus embarrassed by the violence of the anti-militarist activity of Karl Liebknecht – son of the famous Wilhelm and a man whom Bebel had once hoped to see among the party leaders of the next generation – because of the unwelcome attention such agitation must arouse from the Prussian authorities. Bebel in fact accepted the socialists' impotence in the face of the German state and the Prussian military caste in conversations which he had with the British consul-general in Zurich between 1910 and 1912. Bebel admitted – and the message was passed on to Sir Edward Grey with Bebel's permission – that even if his party were to have a majority in the Reichstag they would still not be in a position to prevent war and that the only hope of defeating Prussian militarism lay in a determined effort by Britain to maintain her naval superiority so as to be able to inflict a decisive defeat on Germany.[32] Even allowing for the fact that Bebel was old – he died in 1913 – and depressed by a series of family bereavements, he perhaps understood the nature of the Prussian–German state more clearly than some of his more optimistic colleagues. In these circumstances, it is not surprising that, at the first reports of mobilization, the German social democratic leadership ensured that their funds were transferred to Switzerland in case the party was about to be outlawed as in Bismarck's day. It was, as it turned out, an unnecessary move which was soon revoked when it became clear that Bethmann Hollweg was anxious to ensure the co-operation of the socialists and that they were willing to support the war when it came.

Within a few weeks, or even days, the vaunted international solidarity of the working class was shown to be as ineffectual as the efforts of the liberal peace movements. When the Bureau of the Second International met in Brussels on 29 July, it could do little more than register its impotence, although the meeting also showed how slowly its members had come to realize the gravity of the crisis, since much of the discussion was devoted to making arrangements for the removal of the forthcoming international conference from Vienna to Paris and bringing forward the date from September to 9 August, on the assumption that it would still be possible to hold it then. The reasons for this failure of what was widely believed to be an effective opposition which would make war impossible lie in the degree to which, in spite of their revolutionary rhetoric, even the most radical socialists were integrated into their respective national societies.

In the short term, governments were very successful in convincing their citizens that they were the victims of aggression and in appealing to immediate feelings of patriotism and self-preservation which proved stronger than any internationalist convictions. This was particularly true of the German movement; as we have seen, much of Bethmann's diplomacy ever since 1912 had been aimed at ensuring that, if war came, Russia could be accused of starting it. The fact, too, that mobilization in each country proceeded without a hitch showed how strong the sense of discipline and patriotism was which the conscripts had acquired during their period of military service. Although in the areas of France studied by J-J. Becker the announcement of mobilization was received with tears and consternation,[33] only a very small number of men thought of disobeying their call-up orders. In Germany the declaration of war was accepted almost unanimously. Although in the last week of July there were a number of well-attended and effective demonstrations against war organized by local social democrats, these were directed more against the policy of Germany's ally Austria-Hungary than against the German government, which had succeeded in convincing even some of the left-wing socialists of its peaceful intentions. Bethmann Hollweg kept in touch with some of the socialist leaders throughout the final crisis, and, like the French government, instructed the authorities not to take any measures against the social democrats. More important still, the government had by 2 August secured the co-operation of the trade union leaders for measures needed to overcome the dislocation and unemployment which mobilization was likely to cause, while the unions decided to suspend all strikes and wage claims for the duration of the war. In an atmosphere in which hatred and fear of Russia were rapidly spreading, the appeal of national solidarity was strong; and the social democratic members of the Reichstag decided after long and painful discussions to vote in favour of the war credits demanded by the government on 4 August. Once mobilization had been declared and men had actually left for the front, any agitation against war could easily seem an act of betrayal not of an abstract fatherland but of one's own party comrades. One socialist member of the Reichstag remembered that just before leaving for Berlin and the vote on the war credits, a reservist said to him, 'You are going to Berlin, to the Reichstag: think of us there: see to it that we have all we need: don't be stingy in voting money.'[34]

The Austrian socialist politicians had much the same experience, faced with the popular mood in Vienna which, as the British ambassador noted, on receipt of the news of the breach of relations with Serbia 'burst into a frenzy of delight, vast crowds parading the streets and singing patriotic songs till the small hours of the morning'.[35] Victor

Adler, the internationally respected leader of the Social Democratic Party, shocked his colleagues at the meeting of the International Socialist Bureau by declaring: 'The party is defenceless . . . Demonstrations in support of the war are taking place in the streets . . . Our whole organization and our press are at risk. We run the risk of destroying thirty years' work without any political result.'[36] In these circumstances, the Austrian party had already given up all hope of resistance to the war. In Hungary, although the socialist press had criticized the despatch of the ultimatum to Serbia, the party was too small to effect events; and in the parliament at Budapest all other parties were agreed on sinking their differences and unanimous in their enthusiastic support for the war.

The experiences in the other capitals of Europe were similar. In Russia the five Bolshevik members of the Duma did indeed vote against the war credits (and were later arrested) while the other socialists abstained. But these at the time appeared very small gestures compared with the enthusiasm for war expressed at least by the articulate members of Russian society; and there were people on the Left ready to support the war. The old anarchist leader, Prince Peter Kropotkin, in exile in London, in the hope that war on the side of Britain and France would have a liberalizing effect on Russia, was soon urging the Russians to 'defend themselves like wild beasts' against the Germans 'fighting like devils and trampling on all the rules of humanity'.[37]

In Britain, a country without conscription, the immediate effects of mobilization were less dramatic and widespread than in the continental countries, and we still lack detailed studies of the reactions to the declaration of war in different places and among different classes. But the opposition to war dwindled fast and those few radicals in Parliament who on 3 August criticized the government's decision for war were dismissed by Balfour with the words, 'What we have been hearing tonight are the very dregs and lees of the debate.'[38] Reports on the mood of the English varied: 'There is strained solemnity on every face', Beatrice Webb noted in London on 5 August.[39] But others felt enthusiasm themselves and observed it in others. 'I may possibly live to think differently; but at the present moment, assuming that this war had to come, I feel nothing but gratitude to the gods for sending it in my time. Whatever war itself may be like, preparing to fight in time of war is the greatest game and the finest work in the world', one radical reformer wrote shortly after volunteering for the army,[40] while Bertrand Russell, looking back on August 1914 and perhaps conscious of the courage which it had taken to swim against the stream in wartime, remembered: 'I spent the evening [of 3 August] walking round the streets, especially in the neighbourhood of Trafalgar Square, noticing cheering crowds, and making myself sensitive to the emotions of passers-by. During this and the following days I discovered to my amazement that average men and women were delighted at the prospect of war.'[41] While not everyone used the high-flown language of the poets who asserted that 'Honour has come back, as a king, to earth' or 'And life is Colour and Warmth and Light / And a striving evermore for these; / And he is dead who will not fight, / And who dies fighting has increase',[42] yet the number of volunteers for the army was very large and by no means limited to the middle and upper classes, since the recruits included sufficient coal-miners and industrial workers to cause fears of a manpower shortage.

For all the misgivings and anxiety which many in all countries of Europe must have felt, there is enough evidence of widespread enthusiasm especially among the more articulate members of society to suggest that the mood with which war was received was often one of excitement and relief. More detailed research may show that the enthusiasm for what the German Crown Prince called a *frischfröhliche Krieg* (a phrase used in conservative circles at least since the 1850s and echoing perhaps a popular hunting song 'Auf auf zum fröhlichen Jagen, frisch auf ins freie Feld'[43] suggesting the extent to which many Europeans still considered war a kind of sport) needs modification. But it is certain that for a brief period in August 1914, to which some men were always to look back as one of the great moments of their lives, war made people forget their differences and created a sense of national unity in each country, so that in French villages the curé and the schoolteacher spoke to each other for the first time and in the Reichstag in Berlin socialist deputies attended the Kaiser's reception. In Britain, even if Ulster Unionists would not appear at patriotic meetings on the same platform as supporters of Home Rule for Ireland, the issue which had looked like leading to civil war was at least shelved for the time being.

This mood of simple patriotism and national solidarity showed how far the socialists and other opponents of war had overestimated the strength of internationalist feeling and underestimated the instinctive emotions of nationalism to which the governments of Europe were able to appeal. It was not just that the socialists had often mistaken words for reality or that the militants who called for a general strike against war had not made any practical preparations for it. The acceptance of war when it came was the result of decades in which patriotism had been inculcated at many levels of national life all over Europe. It was also the result of years in which international relations had been discussed in the neo-Darwinian language of the struggle for survival and the survival of the fittest, and in which ideas of liberation through violence, whether for personal or national emancipation, had become common. The mood of 1914 must be seen partly as the product of a widespread revolt against the liberal values of peace and rational solutions of all problems which had been taken for granted by many people for much of the nineteenth century.

The liberals of the mid-nineteenth century had envisioned a world in which, as Herbert Spencer had put it, 'Progress . . . is not an accident but a necessity . . . Surely must the things we call evil and immorality disappear; so surely must men become perfect.'[44] This progress included the breaking down of national barriers by means of free trade, and the solution of international disputes by rational negotiation, since, on this view, there were no problems without solutions. In domestic politics, self-government in one form or another would be extended, so that each national group would eventually achieve autonomy, while some form of democratic government would become the usual constitutional system everywhere. But even before experiences of the First World War shattered many of the assumptions of nineteenth-century liberalism, those assumptions were under attack from many directions. In particular, in the last two decades of the nineteenth century, a new type of strident nationalism, often but not always associated with the new popularity of imperialist expansion, had found expression in the writings of publicists and nationalist pressure groups in many countries in Europe. Some of these groups were formed in order to advocate specific measures of preparation for war, such as the Navy Leagues in Britain and Germany. Some, but not all, of them were anti-democratic in tone, whether on general ideological grounds or because they were convinced that the delays and compromises of parliamentary life made for national inefficiency.

In a more general way, the new nationalism was thought of as being a matter of instinct rather than of reason, based on the fundamental ties between men and the soil of their country and the links with, in the phrase of the influential French nationalist writer Maurice Barrès, 'la terre et les morts'. Such ideas were closely associated with racialist theories about the necessity of maintaining the purity of the national stock and avoiding the corruption caused by the assimilation of alien elements, so that, for many writers, the idea of fostering a healthy national spirit was inextricably involved with that of preserving it from contamination by what were regarded as corrupting cosmopolitan forces, notably, of course, the Jews. Most important of all in creating the intellectual climate in which the new nationalism flourished was the influence of the ideas derived from a misunderstanding of Darwin's theories, which, as we have seen, had a profound influence on the ideology of imperialism. If the world of states, like the natural world, was one in which everything was subordinated to the struggle for survival, then preparation for that struggle was the first duty of governments. The belief in the necessity and even the desirability of war as the form in which the international struggle for survival would be carried on was not limited to the Right. It was taken for granted in widely different circles of society. Thus a conservative general, Conrad von Hötzendorf, the Austro-Hungarian Chief of Staff, and the great French novelist Emile Zola, a man committed to a rational and scientific view of the world and to radical republican politics, expressed themselves in not dissimilar terms. Conrad wrote after the war:

> Philanthropic religions, moral teachings and philosophical doctrines may certainly sometimes serve to weaken mankind's struggle for existence in its crudest form, but they will *never* succeed in removing it as a driving motive in the world . . . It is in accordance with this great principle that the catastrophe of the world war came about inevitably and irresistibly as the result of the motive forces in the lives of states and peoples, like a thunderstorm which must by nature discharge itself.[45]

And some thirty years earlier, in 1891, Emile Zola had written even more positively:

> Would not the end of war be the end of humanity? War is life itself. Nothing exists in nature, is born, grows or multiplies except by combat. We must eat and be eaten so that the world may live. It is only warlike nations which have prospered: a nation dies as soon as it disarms. War is the school of discipline, sacrifice and courage.[46]

There was indeed a widespread belief that war was not only inevitable but desirable: the virtues of discipline and obedience, which the Fascists were to stress after the war when they emphasized the importance of the war experience, were already being proclaimed before war broke out. Italian nationalists in particular were constantly expressing sentiments such as: 'While mean-minded democrats cry out against war as a barbarous advance of out-dated savagery, we think of it as the strongest stimulus for those who have grown feeble, a rapid and heroic means to power and riches. A people not only needs deep feelings, but another virtue which is becoming more and more despised and less understood – obedience.'[47] War was seen as an experience which would bring both personal and national well-being, an idea summed up by the leader of the Italian Futurist writers and artists, F. T. Marinetti, in his notorious phrase, 'Guerra, sola igieia del mondo'. A well-known English publicist, Sidney Low, had made much the same point at the time of the first Hague Peace Conference: 'A righteous and necessary war is no more brutal than a surgical operation. Better give the patient some pain, and make your own fingers unpleasantly red, than allow the disease to grow upon him until he becomes an offence to himself and the world, and dies in lingering agony.'[48] In France, members of the nationalist Right said much the same: the writer Abel Bonnard wrote of war in 1912: 'We must embrace it in all its wild poetry. When a man throws himself into it, it is not just his own instincts that he is rediscovering, but virtues which he is recovering . . . It is in war that all is made new.'[49]

When the war broke out, the British at least were encouraged by their newspapers, propagandists and religious leaders to attribute the war specifically to the influence of two German writers, the philosopher Friedrich Nietzsche and the historian Heinrich von Treitschke ('pronounced respectively Neets-shay and Tritsh-kay', as one pamphlet obligingly if misleadingly informed its readers).[50] While this was mainly the result of the hysterical Germanophobia of the first months of the war, the choice of Treitschke and Nietzsche was not without significance. Again and again members of the German ruling class, including Moltke and Tirpitz, paid tribute to the effect which Treitschke's lectures in the University of Berlin had had on them in their youth, with the lesson that war was 'the peoples' tribunal through which the existing balance of power will find general recognition'.[51] Throughout his historical writings and the lectures on politics delivered in the last years of his life between 1874 and 1895 to enthusiastic audiences in Berlin, Treitschke stressed that the state was bound by different standards than the individual. Much of what Treitschke wrote was similar to ideas widely accepted throughout Europe, and it was not only Germans who believed that, 'If the flag of the State is insulted, it is the duty of the State to demand satisfaction, and if satisfaction is not forthcoming, to declare war, however trivial the occasion may appear, for the State must strain every nerve to preserve for itself the respect which it enjoys in the state system.'[52] In this state system, the defence of national values, material and spiritual, is paramount, and a prime duty of the state is to organize that defence: 'The moment that the State proclaims "Your State and the existence of your State are now at stake", selfishness disappears and party hatred is silenced . . . In this consists the grandeur of war, that trivial things are entirely lost sight of in the great ideal of the State.'[53] Treitschke's vision of Prussia and Germany was of a state which had become great because of its army, and which had succeeded in the face of attempts by the French or the English or the Jews or the Roman Catholics to prevent it; and he reflected a certain paranoid strain in German nationalism which can be seen again in 1914, as the German fear of encirclement grew.

If Treitschke was using widely accepted concepts of the nation state and the necessity of war to secure its survival but giving these ideas a specific frame of reference arising out of his conception of the course of German history, Nietzsche's message had been a broader one. The assumption by the English, including the editor of *The Times*, in 1914, that Nietzsche was somehow responsible for the war was perhaps characteristic of a nation which had not bothered to read his work. Nietzsche was nevertheless the most influential thinker of his age, and his works, especially *Thus Spake Zarathustra*, were best-sellers in most of the other countries of Europe apart from Britain. And even if later attempts to make Nietzsche responsible not only for the First World War but also for National Socialism involve a one-sided interpretation of his complex and contradictory message, there is much in his work which aroused a response in the generation of 1914 and contributed to the intellectual climate in which war broke out. It was not only Nietzsche's calls for action and violence or the necessity of toughness and ruthlessness and the 'Will to Power' or his notorious concepts of the Superman and the Blonde Beast which made him popular, or even beliefs such as 'War and courage have done more great things than love of one's neighbour' which appealed to those militarists who bothered to read him, but rather his attack on so many of the values of contemporary bourgeois society, its hypocritical moral values, its stuffiness, its Philistinism. To young people all over Europe in the twenty years before the war Nietzsche preached a gospel of liberation both personal and political; and to some of them, like the assassins of the Archduke Franz Ferdinand quoting Nietzsche to each other in the cafés of Zagreb, it was liberation through violence. Copies of the popular edition of *Thus Spake Zarathustra* were to be found in the knapsacks of thousands of soldiers in 1914, and not just in Germany, since in Russia too, as *The Times* correspondent reported, 'Almost all the noble spirits of modern Russia have drunk deep of the wells of Nietzsche.'[54] While Nietzsche's gospel of personal liberation ('Werde was du bist' – 'Become what you are') did not necessarily involve war, his constant references to the necessity of a brutal cure for the sickness of contemporary European society found many echoes among those who accepted and welcomed war when it came.

It can be argued that the writers whom we have been discussing did not have a large popular audience, since their readers were only to be found among the educated. Even leaving aside the question of how far some of these ideas, at least in those countries with a high rate of literacy, filtered down through a growing popular press, the people who responded to the new radical nationalism were people in a position to influence the decisions of the rulers of Europe in 1914. Certainly the young men who went off with such enthusiasm to fight in the first campaigns of the war were full of ideas of the desirability of war as a liberating experience and as the means of achieving a new national solidarity. In France, for example, in 1912 two writers using the pseudonym 'Agathon' carried out for a Paris newspaper an opinion survey among students in Paris. Although this was by no means an impartial survey, since the authors were concerned to attack the positivist republican academic establishment, nevertheless it contains interesting evidence about the state of mind of a group of students who belonged to the faculties and schools traditionally associated with the French political élite. At least these few hundred young men (nothing is said of the views of young women) were much more warlike than the previous generation and were prepared to subscribe to sentiments such as 'it is in the life of camps and under fire that we shall experience the supreme expansion of the French force that lies within us'.[55] This is certainly evidence of the extent to which the ideas of, especially, Maurice Barrès had influenced the students in the Law Faculty and the Ecole Libre des Sciences Politiques, though there is some evidence that students of other disciplines did not share these views and were, or example, opposed to the law extending national service to three ears. In any case, this particular group of the French élite were not iven much chance to exercise their influence, since within two years of Agathon's enquiry many of them were dead on the battlefields.

The fact that the theorists and rhetoricians of the new nationalism in Europe before 1914 necessarily influenced only a comparatively small, even if politically and socially important, group of people, suggests hat we must also look elsewhere for the origins of the patriotic instincts which produced the acceptance, often with enthusiasm, of the all to arms in 1914. However one evaluates the influence of the new radical nationalist, racialist and pseudo-Darwinian writers and publicists, the reactions of ordinary people in the crisis of 1914 were the esult of the history they had learnt at school, the stories about the national past which they had been told as children and an instinctive ense of loyalty and solidarity with their neighbours and workmates. In each country children were taught the duties of patriotism and the glory of past national achievements, even if, especially in countries like France which had experienced several changes of regime within living memory, the problem of which aspect of the national tradition each successive government should emphasize sometimes caused difficulties. Yet a passage from a popular manual of French history for schools, republished and revised in 1912, is surely not very different in sentiment from similar textbooks in use in Germany or Britain: 'War is not probable, but it is possible. It is for that reason that France remains armed and always ready to defend itself . . . In defending France we are defending the land where we were born, the most beautiful and the most bountiful country in the world . . . ' This simple patriotic pride was accompanied by the sense that each country had its own specific virtues which were worth fighting for and preserving. 'France', the same passage continues, 'since the Revolution has spread ideas of justice and humanity throughout the world. France is the most just, the freest and most humane of fatherlands.'[56]

In each country of Europe children were being taught to take pride in their historical tradition and to respect what were regarded as characteristic national virtues. The Prussian Ministry of Education in 1901 stressed the importance of the study of German so that 'the hearts of our young people may be elevated with enthusiasm for the German *Volkstum* and the greatness of the German mind'.[57] The government of the Third Republic stressed for example in 1881 that teachers 'must above all be told . . . that their first duty is to make [their charges] love and understand the fatherland'.[58] Although in each country educational reformers or socialist politicians tried to inculcate different values, the reactions in 1914 showed that they had made little headway, and the patriotic language with which the war was greeted reflected the sentiments of a national tradition absorbed over many years. Léon Jouhaux, the General Secretary of the French Trade

Union Confederation and a man closely linked with the anti-militaris'
movement, in his speech at Jaurès's funeral reluctantly accepted a war
'to repel an invader, to safeguard the inheritance of the civilized and
generous ideology which history has bequeathed to us', and, looking
back later, wrote: 'There are at certain moments in the life of a man
thoughts which seem foreign to him and which nevertheless are the
sum of the traditions which he carries in him and which circumstances
make him recall with more or less force.'[59]

However, the intensification of national and imperialist feeling in
the twenty years before the war had in many cases been helped by a
number of pressure groups or ideological movements formed both to
promote specific objectives and to encourage patriotic feelings in a
general way. The Navy Leagues in Britain and Germany, founded in
the 1890s, were both intended to foster political and popular support
for the navy: in Germany a *Wehrverein* was started in 1912 'to press for
an increase in the size of the army' – a sign of the rivalry between the
two services and of the dilemma faced by a country which seemed to be
preparing simultaneously for a continental war against France and
Russia and a maritime war against England. In France the organized
pressure groups were less important, partly because, as we have seen
questions such as the extension of the period of conscription were at
the centre of political discussion in parliament and the efforts of the
politicians and their followers were directly focused on them. The
right-wing organizations such as the Ligue des Patriotes and the
monarchist Action Française, while claiming to be the repository of
the true nationalist traditions, found themselves outflanked as more
and more members of the republican establishment became political
spokesmen for the patriotic cause, with a radical politician opposing
the introduction of drab-coloured uniforms for the army (following the
introduction of khaki and field grey in the British and German armies
because red trousers 'have something national about them',[60] and the
ex-socialist Millerand when Minister of War introducing *Retraites
Militaires* – evening parades with bands – in provincial cities. The
Action Française and its youth movement the Camelots du Roi could
mobilize several hundred young men at short notice for patriotic
demonstrations, at least in Paris, but the main pressures for military
reform and military efficiency came from within the army and the
republican parties rather than from any external pressure group.

The aims and methods of such pressure groups necessarily varied
with the political institutions of each country. The British Navy
League, for example, was mainly concerned with the maintenance of
the strength of the British navy and its technical equipment. Its
members, therefore, tended to be retired officers, journalists and
professional people with a somewhat specialized interest in naval
matters, and it saw itself as a ginger group keeping the Admiralty up to
the mark rather than a direct instrument of Admiralty policy. I

encouraged popular interest in the navy by means of lectures and exhibitions, but it was working within a tradition going back for centuries in which the navy had always been a popular cause, whereas the German Navy League was supporting a largely new creation intended not only to serve the aims of German foreign policy but also to provide a symbolic rallying point which would unite a divided nation. Both organizations, however, show how alongside the more traditional 'militarism' associated with the cult of the army, which in the popular view was linked with conservatism and the old order, a new 'navalism' could appeal to wider sections of society.

The organizations in Edwardian England which expressed the new national feeling combined pride in Britain's imperial achievement with anxieties about the future. Thus, particularly after the South African War had revealed the weaknesses in Britain's army, there was a growing demand for increased 'national efficiency' and for better training of young people to prepare them to defend the Empire. One form in which this anxiety about Britain's preparedness for war expressed itself was in the movement for the introduction of compulsory military service, and especially the National Service League, presided over by Lord Roberts, the commander popularly supposed by the British to have been responsible for the ultimate victory over the Boers in South Africa. The failure of this energetically promoted cause was due to the refusal of the Liberals to consider conscription, which indeed they only finally and reluctantly accepted in 1916 after nearly two years of war. Other movements to promote physical fitness and encourage patriotic enthusiasm by providing military-type training for boys or encourage the celebration of an annual Empire Day were the result of a similar mixture of pride and anxiety. The organization which achieved the greatest practical success was the Boy Scouts, founded by one of the heroes of the South African War, Robert Baden-Powell.

Earlier movements associated with one or other of the churches, such as the Boys' Brigade or the Church Lads' Brigade, had attempted to cope with the problem of providing physical and moral training and healthy leisure activities for boys from the industrial cities. The popularity of the Boy Scouts was due to the way in which they combined national and imperialist appeal with a social purpose, while at the same time offering the attractions of outdoor activities and the study of nature without the overtly military discipline of some of the other youth movements. Above all, though, Baden-Powell saw the movement as a way of enabling the Empire to survive in the Darwinian struggle: 'We must all be bricks in the wall of that great enterprise – the British Empire – and we must be careful that we do not let our differences of opinion on politics and other questions grow so strong as to divide us. We must still stick shoulder to shoulder as Britons if we want to keep our present position among the nations.'[61] And – with a characteristic appeal to both patriotic and sporting instincts though perhaps a shaky knowledge of ancient history – 'Don't be disgraced like the young Romans who lost the Empire of their forefathers by being wishy-washy slackers without any go or patriotism in them. Play up! Play up! Each man in his place and play the game!'[62]

The absence of conscription in England gave a particular flavour to British youth movements which was absent on the Continent, where two or three years of compulsory military service were an experience which nearly every young man had to undergo. In Germany, indeed, there was a paradoxical situation. On the one hand many students were anxious to conform to the military values of the old ruling class: they joined the reactionary student fraternities, with their emphasis on a brutal nationalism and an insensitive toughness exemplified by their practice of duelling: many took the option open to university students of volunteering for twelve months' service instead of serving the full period of conscription, thereby increasing their chances of achieving the coveted status of reserve officer. On the other hand, in the decade before the war, the new youth movements became increasingly popular among the children of the middle classes. Their creed was based mainly on ideas derived ultimately from Nietzsche and represented a rebellion against the stuffy respectability of the Wilhelmine bourgeoisie. They stressed their roots in the soil of the fatherland, in the forests and mountains of Germany, and they preached a new sense of community, instinctive, spontaneous and free from the hypocrisies and conventions of contemporary German society and the hollowness of German politics. They disassociated themselves from the brash and formal patriotism of imperial Germany and believed that they were contributing to a new awareness of the national *Volksgemeinschaft:* 'They who if need be are ready at any moment to sacrifice their lives for the rights of their people, also want to dedicate their fresh pure blood to the fatherland in the struggle and peace of everyday life',[63] the invitation to the great youth festival in 1913 proclaimed. (The year 1913 was one full of contradictory memories for the Germans, since the youth festival was part of the commemoration of the upsurge of patriotic liberal feeling against Napoleon, while for the conservatives the year was the anniversary of a triumph of German arms, so that it was a centenary which could be held to enshrine both conservative and liberal nationalist values.)

The Wandervögel and the other youth movements emphasized their opposition to conventional German patriotism, and it was partly for this reason, as well as because the Social Democratic Party had started its own youth movement, that the authorities were increasingly concerned about the need to indoctrinate boys leaving school with values which would both immunize them against the infection of social democracy and encourage positive patriotic feelings and enthusiasm for the army which they would within a few years be joining as conscripts. In spite of interdepartmental rivalries and the usual difficulties of creating a national organization in a country with a strong federal element in its constitution, as well as opposition from some of the existing youth organizations, a number of voluntary associations had been created in the first years of the century, in the belief that, as one of such groups in Munich put it, 'A quiet and prudent appeal to the warlike spirit of the nation can provide the counterweight to the increasingly successful fantasies about "perpetual peace".'[64] In 1910 the Kaiser issued orders for the formation of 'a kind of youth army (Jugendwehr) similar to the British Boy Scouts';[65] and, after long discussions, finally in August 1911 the Jungdeutschlandbund was founded in the hope of providing some sort of central organization for the nationalist youth associations. There seems to have been some disappointment at the result: and the success of the Social Democratic Party in the Reichstag elections of 1912 seemed to emphasize the need for ever more vigorous action to counter socialist influence and foster patriotism, while the extension of the period of military service in France alarmed the Prussian War Minister and convinced him that 'the increase in the intrinsic value of the army' could only be attained by 'the preparation of young men for military service and especially by influencing them to a very wide extent between leaving school and entering the army'.[66] Accordingly, shortly before war broke out, measures were being prepared to make some sort of training compulsory – 'gymnastics, sport, games, hikes and other physical exercise' – together with the teaching of 'fear of God, sense of the homeland (*Heimatsinn*) and love of the Fatherland'.[67] The internal enemies – the social democrats – had become inextricably linked with the external foe, and a single organization would fight them both.

The Jungdeutschlandbund combined the insistence on physical fitness and patriotic values such as was to be found indeed in the British Boy Scouts with more emotional sentiments: 'War is beautiful . . . We must wait for it with the manly knowledge that when it strikes, it will be more beautiful and more wonderful to live for ever among the heroes on a war memorial in a church than to die an empty death in bed, nameless.'[68] The Nietzschean rhetoric, the craving for release and for new forms of action which were characteristic of the German youth movements led them, for all their differences, to an emotional attitude not so very different from that of the nationalists whom they criticized; and the feelings of excitement in 1914, the temporary upsurge of a new sense of the German unity, seemed to the Wandervogel, as to the members of the rival militaristic and patriotic youth movement, to be the expression of much they had been working and waiting for.

Few of the people who talked of war had a very clear picture of what the war would be like; and very few indeed foresaw anything like what the war actually became. Some of those who praised the beneficial effects of war, including the Italian Futurist leader F. T. Marinetti, hurried to the siege of Adrianople in the First Balkan War to get a taste of the sights and sounds of modern war, and some specialists observed the effects of artillery there, though not all of them drew the right lessons from what they saw. But for most of the public a war was seen rather incoherently in the terms of recent wars which had been very different from each other – the South African War, the Russo-Japanese War and the Balkan wars. Memories of colonial campaigns, in the case of England, and of the war of 1870, in the case of France and Germany, were still strong but they had been modified in Britain and Germany by the picture, encouraged by the widely read works on the nature of sea power by Alfred Thayer Mahan, of a decisive clash between great battle fleets. In England there were recurrent panics about 'a bolt from the blue', a sudden attack by the German fleet on the coast of Britain as a preliminary to an invasion; and in Germany the blustering and indiscreet language of the British First Sea Lord, Admiral Sir John Fisher, contributed to a fear that the British navy might make a sudden strike at a German navy base – a fear sufficient in 1907 to make parents in Kiel keep their children away from school for two days because 'Der Fischer kommt'.[69]

These fears, as always in times of a growing arms race and protracted international tension, led to the construction of fictional and speculative scenarios about war. Many historians, following the work of I. F. Clarke,[70] have noted the popularity of novels about invasions and wars and have drawn attention to a whole new school of science-fiction writers drawing fantastic pictures of the war of the future. But at least from the 1890s on, novels describing war in a plausible political setting were reflecting some of the anxieties and expectations of the public. British readers had been alarmed by the translation in 1904 of a novel by August Niemann, *Der Weltkrieg: Deutsche Träume*, under the title *The Coming Conquest of England*, which sketched a frightening picture of a continental league against Britain, with a German landing in Scotland and a Russian landing in England. During the next years British and French novelists concentrated on the German threat and gave up the theme of an Anglo-French war which had attracted writers on both sides of the Channel in the 1880s and 1890s. The French writer 'Capitaine Danrit' who in his earlier novels had depicted France at war with Germany and England indiscriminately, by 1905 was drawing attention to the Far East and the 'Yellow Peril' (which was also one of the Kaiser's obsessions) and then concentrating on the coming war with Germany. In England, the bad but popular novelist William Le Queux, who in 1899 had been obsessed with French espionage in London (*England's Peril*) was, in his most successful novel *The Invasion of 1910*, published in 1906 with a letter of commendation by Field Mashal Earl Roberts, reflecting the popular fear of Germany and frightening his readers with an account, full of topographical detail, of a successful German invasion resulting from Britain's neglect of military training. These novels provided for their readers, English,

French and German, not only a mirror of their own anxieties but also an assurance of final triumph. In I. F. Clarke's words: 'During the last two decades of the nineteenth century the epic had moved out of the legendary past; it became a popular and prospective myth projected into a near and seemingly realizable future.'[71]

The spread of the invasion novel was accompanied by the spread of the spy story; and this both reflected and promoted the paranoid fear of spies in real life. In *The Invasion of 1910*, German action was prepared by an army of spies; in *Spies of the Kaiser* (1910) Le Queux encouraged the belief that almost any foreigner was a spy, and this was even taken up by the military authorities.[72] In France, too, Léon Daudet of the Action Française was active in denouncing a mythical network of German Jewish spies in France, in a book published in 1913 which sold 11,500 copies by the outbreak of war[73] and which may well have contributed to the violent outbreak of spy-mania (*espionnite*) in the first days of August 1914, when the placards advertising the well-known soup concentrate *Bouillons Kub* were believed to carry secret indicators for the Germans. In Britain, too, in the first days of the war every German was a spy and many harmless waiters and hairdressers were denounced by vigilant citizens and the government was under heavy pressure to introduce a policy of wholesale internment.

By 1914 the idea, if not the reality, of war was familiar. Each international crisis from 1905 on seemed to bring it nearer, although each time war was avoided there were always optimists who thought this would always happen. Jean Jaurès, for example, was still saying on 30 July 1914 'It will be like Agadir. There will be ups and downs, mais les choses ne peuvent ne pas s'arranger.'[74] Yet for many people war was not considered as a wholly undesirable experience: some saw it as a solution to social and political problems, a necessary surgery to make the body politic whole: others saw it as an opportunity to escape from the routine and tedium of their ordinary lives, a great adventure or a sporting challenge. A few saw it as an opportunity for revolution, as, to use Lenin's later phrase, a 'great accelerator'. According to one report of Victor Adler's remarks at the meeting of the International Socialist Bureau in Brussels on 29 July 1914 the Austrian socialist leader said regretfully, 'In the nationalist struggles war appears as a kind of deliverance, a hope that something different will come.'[75] This ambiguous hope was indeed shared both by the Austro-Hungarian leaders who regarded war with Serbia as a necessity if the Monarchy were to survive and by the Serbian nationalists who believed, as an American diplomatic observer put it, 'that it will be much more consoling to risk a desperate war than to die slowly from the strangulation which unfortunate circumstances impose upon them'.[76]

For many Southern Slavs, including the group which assassinated the Archduke Franz Ferdinand, the national cause transcended all considerations of prudence and utilitarian calculation. But this all-demanding, all-excusing nationalism was not limited to small nations striving for independence and unity. By the end of the nineteenth century these ideas had become linked to the belief that the state was a living organism which was more than the sum of its citizens who could only fulfil themselves completely within it, so that it had an overriding claim on their loyalty and obedience. Although liberals continued to insist on the right of the individual to resist the state in certain circumstances – and in Britain during the war the right to object to military service on grounds of conscience became an important issue – and although socialists had preached that the international solidarity of the working class would replace national loyalties, the attitude to the outbreak of war in 1914 showed that the claims of the nation state and the values it had inculcated remained for most people stronger than any other loyalty.

Those political leaders who took the decision to go to war had a sense of the overriding importance of preserving what were regarded as vital national interests. These national interests were partly defined in traditional territorial or strategic terms – the recovery by France of Alsace-Lorraine, the securing for Russia of Constantinople and the Straits, the British concern that the coast of Belgium should not be occupied by a hostile power – but also in more general terms which implied a whole *Weltanschauung*, a view of the nature of things and of the course of history. This included ideas about the necessity of maintaining or changing the balance of power, about the international struggle for survival and the inevitability of war, about the role of empire as the prerequisite for victory. When the decision to go to war was taken, governments were able to fight the war because their subjects accepted the necessity for it. To most people war appeared, or was presented, as an inescapable necessity if they were to preserve their country and their homes from foreign invasion; and they did not question what they had heard for generations about the glories and superior qualities of their own nation.

The mood of 1914 can only be assessed approximately and impressionistically. The more we study it in detail, the more we see how it differed from country to country or from class to class. Yet at each level there was a willingness to risk or to accept war as a solution to a whole range of problems, political, social, international, to say nothing of war as apparently the only way of resisting a direct physical threat. It is these attitudes which made war possible; and it is still in an investigation of the mentalities of the rulers of Europe and their subjects that the explanation of the causes of the war will ultimately lie.

REFERENCES AND NOTES

1. Jean-Jacques Becker, *1914—Comment les Français sont entrés dans la Guerre* (Paris 1977).
2. G. P. Gooch and Harold Temperley (eds) *British Documents on the Origins of the War 1898—1914*, Vol. X (London 1932) Part II, No. 510, p. 746. (Hereinafter referred to as *BD*.)
3. Winston Churchill, *The World Crisis* (one vol. paperback edn, London 1964) pp. 113–4.
4. Becker, *1914*, p. 133.
5. Dieter Groh, *Negative Integration und revolutionärer Attentismus: die deutsche Sozialdemokratie am Vorabend des Ersten Weltkrieges* (Frankfurt-am-Main 1973) p. 611.
6. Quoted in Becker, *1914*, p. 127.
7. J. Deutsch, *Der Kampf*, Dec. 1914, quoted in N. Leser, *Zwischen Reformismus und Bolschewismus* (Vienna 1968) p. 265. See also S. Müller, *Burgfrieden und Klassenkampf* (Düsseldorf 1974) p. 36.
8. Jeremy Bentham, *Plan for a Universal and Perpetual Peace* (1786–89; published posthumously 1843), quoted in F. H. Hinsley, *Power and the Pursuit of Peace* (pb. edn, Cambridge 1967) p. 302.
9. Resolution passed at the International Socialist Congress, Stuttgart 1907, quoted in J. Joll, *The Second International 1889—1914* (2nd edn, London 1974) pp. 206–8.
10. Quoted in Roger Chickering, *Imperial Germany and a World Without War: The Peace Movement in German Society 1892—1914* (Princeton 1975) p. 91.
11. *Die Grosse Politik der Europäischen Kabinette*, Vol. XV (Berlin 1924) No. 4257, p. 306. (Hereinafter referred to as *GP*.) For the Hague Conferences, see Jost Dülfer, *Regeln gegae den Krieg? Die Haager Friedenskonferenzen von 1899 und 1907 in der internationalen Politik* (Frankfurt-am-Main 1981).
12. *GP* XV, No. 4320, p. 306.
13. *BD* I, No. 276, p. 226.
14. *BD* VIII, No. 256, p. 295.
15. *BD* VIII, No. 254, p. 287.
16. *GP* XXIII, 1, No. 7963, p. 275.
17. *Nach Ausbruch des Europäischen Krieges*, Aug. 1914, quoted in Chickering, op. cit., p. 322.
18. L. T. Hobhouse to John Burns 6 Aug. 1914, quoted in Keith Robbins, *The Abolition of War: The 'Peace Movement' in Britain 1914—1919* (Cardiff 1976) p. 39.
19. Karl Marx, 'The war', *New York Daily Tribune* 15 Nov. 1853 in Eleanor Marx (ed) *The Eastern Question* (London 1897) p. 151.
20. Quoted in E. Molnàr, *La Politique d'Alliances du Marxisme 1848—1889* (Budapest 1967) p. 152.
21. Quoted in Gustav Maier, *Friedrich Engels* (The Hague 1934) Vol. II, p. 186.
22. Maier, op. cit., p. 187.

23. F. Engels, Introduction to S. Borkheim, *Zur Erinnerung für die deutschen Mordspatrioten 1806–12* (1887), quoted in Karl Kautsky, *Sozialisten und Krieg* (Prague 1937) pp. 250–1.

24. Quoted in V. I. Lenin, *The War and the Second International* (London 1936) p. 57. For a further discussion of these questions see James Joll, 'Socialism between peace, war and revolution' in S. Bertelli (ed.) *Per Federico Chabod (1901–1960)*, Vol. II. *Equilibrio Europeo ed Espansione Coloniale 1870–1914* (Perugia 1982).

25. Quoted in Erich Eyck, *Das persönliche Regiment Wilhelms II* (Zurich 1948) p. 62.

26. Quoted in Kautsky, op. cit., p. 274.

27. See Jean-Jacques Becker, *Le Carnet B* (Paris 1973).

28. See e.g. Becker, 1914, pp. 106–17; J.J. Becker and Annie Kriegel, 1914: *la guerre et le mouvement ouvrier français* (Paris 1964); Georges Haupt, *Socialism and the Great War: The Collapse of the Second International* (Oxford 1972) pp. 171–80; Annie Kriegel, *Le Pain et les Roses* (Paris 1968) pp. 107–24.

29. Quoted in Annie Kriegel, 'Jaurès en 1914' in *Le Pain et les Roses*, p. 115.

30. Quoted in Maier, op. cit., Vol. II, p. 519.

31. Bebel at SPD Congress 1891, *Protokoll über die Verhandlungen des Parteitages der Sozialdemokratischen Partei Deutschlands* (Berlin 1891) p. 285.

32. See R. J. Crampton, 'August Bebel and the British Foreign Office', *History*, **58** (June 1973) and Helmut Bley, *Bebel und die Strategie der Kriegsverhütung 1904–1913* (Göttingen 1975).

33. See the tables in Becker, *1914*, pp. 286–91.

34. *Vossische Zeitung* 5 May 1916, quoted in Edwyn Bevan, *German Social Democracy during the War* (London 1918) p. 15. See also Joll, *Second International*, p. 179.

35. *BD* XI, No. 676, p. 356.

36. Quoted in Georges Haupt, *Socialism and the Great War: The Collapse of the Second International* (Oxford 1972) pp. 251–2.

37. Quoted in George Woodcock and Ivan Avakumović, *The Anarchist Prince* (London 1950) p. 379.

38. Hansard, 5th series, Vol. LXV, col. 1881.

39. Margaret I. Cole (ed.) *Beatrice Webb's Diaries 1912–1924* (London 1952) p. 26.

40. 'In Kitchener's Army', *New Statesman*, 5 Dec. 1914; F. H. Keeling, *Keeling Letters and Reminiscences* (London 1918) p. 209, see Arthur Marwick, *The Deluge* (London 1965) pp. 35–6.

41. *The Autobiography of Bertrand Russell 1914–1944* (London 1968) p. 16.

42. Rupert Brooke, 'The dead', *1914 and other Poems* (London 1915) p. 13; Julian Grenfell, 'Into battle', Nicholas Mosley, *Julian Grenfell: His Life and the Times of his Death* (London 1976) p. 256.

43. The phrase was used by the conservative historian Heinrich Leo in 1853 so had presumably been familiar for some decades. See Christoph Freiherr von Maltzan, *Heinrich Leo* (Göttingen 1979) p. 213. I am grateful to Lord Dacre of Glenton and Mr Daniel Johnson for this reference. The suggestion of the folk-song echo is made by Maurice Pearton, *The Knowledgeable State: Diplomacy War and Technology since 1830* (London 1982) p. 32.

44. Herbert Spencer, *Social Statics* (London 1868) p. 80.

45. Franz Baron Conrad von Hötzendorf, *Aus meiner Dienstzeit* (Vienna 1923) Vol. IV, pp. 128–9.

46. *Le Figaro*, 1 Sept. 1891, quoted in Claude Digeon, *La Crise allemande de la Pensée française* (Paris 1959) p. 278.

47. G. Papini and G. Prezzolini, *Vecchio e nuovo Nazionalismo*, quoted in Mario Isnenghi, *Il Mito della Grande Guerra da Marinetti a Malaparte* (Bari 1970) p. 77.

48. Quoted in W. L. Langer, *The Diplomacy of Imperialism* (New York 1951) p. 90.

49. *Le Figaro*, 29 Oct. 1912, quoted in Becker, *1914*, p. 40.

50. Canon E. McLure, *Germany's War-Inspirers Nietzsche and Treitschke* (London 1914) p. 5. For a further discussion of this topic, see James Joll, 'The English, Friedrich Nietzsche and the First World War' in Imanuel Geiss and Bernd Jürgen Wendt (eds) *Deutschland in der Weltpolitik des 19. und 20. Jahrhunderts* (Düsseldorf 1973).

51. Quoted in Peter Winzen, 'Treitschke's influence on the rise of anti-British and imperialist nationalism in Germany' in Paul Kennedy and Anthony Nicholls (eds) *Nationalist and Racialist Movements in Britain and Germany before 1914* (London 1981) p. 164.

52. Heinrich von Treitschke, *Politik: Vorlesungen von Heinrich von Treitschke* (ed. Max Cornicelius) (Leipzig 1899–1900) Vol. II, p. 550, English tr. in H. W. C. Davis, *The Political Thought of Heinrich von Treitschke* (London 1914) p. 177.

53. Treitschke, op. cit., Vol. I, p. 74; Davis, op. cit., p. 152.

54. *The Times*, 31 Oct. 1914.

55. 'Agathon' (Henri Massis and Alfred de Tarde), *Les Jeunes Gens d'Aujourd'hui* (Paris 1913) pp. 32–3. See Robert Wohl, *The Generation of 1914* (Cambridge, Mass. 1979) Ch. I.

56. E. Lavisse, *Manuel d'Histoire de France* (Cours moyen 1912), quoted in Pierre Nora, 'Ernest Lavisse: son role dans la formation du sentiment national', *Revue Historique*, **228** (1962) 104.

57. R. H. Samuel and R. Hinton Thomas, *Education and Society in Modern Germany* (London 1949) p. 71.

58. Quoted in Eugen Weber, *Peasants into Frenchmen: The Modernization of Rural France 1870–1914* (London 1977) pp. 334–5.

59. Quoted in Becker and Kriegel, op. cit., pp. 141, 138.

60. Douglas Porch, *The March to the Marne: The French Army 1871–1914* (Cambridge 1981) p. 184. See also David B. Ralston, *The Army of the Republic* (Cambridge, Mass. 1967) p. 324.

61. Robert Baden-Powell, *Scouting for Boys* (London 1908) p. 282. See John Springhall, *Youth, Empire and Society: British Youth Movements 1883–1940* (London 1977) pp. 15–16.

62. Baden-Powell, op. cit., p. 267.

63. Freideutsche Jugend, *Festschrift zur Jahrhundertfeier auf dem Hohen Meissner* (Jena 1913) pp. 4–5, quoted in Gerhard A. Ritter (ed.) *Historisches Lesebuch 2. 1871–1914* (Frankfurt-am-Main 1967) p. 363. On the German youth movements see Walter Laqueur, *Young Germany: A History of the German Youth Movements* (London 1962).

64. Klaus Saul, 'Der Kampf um die Jugend zwischen Volksschule und Kaserne: ein Beitrag zur "Jugendpflege" im Wilhelminischen Reich

1890–1914', *Militärgeschichtliche Mitteilungen*, Vol. I (1971) pp. 116–7.

65. Saul, op. cit., p. 118.
66. Saul, op. cit., p. 137.
67. Saul, op. cit., p. 125.
68. Quoted in Martin Kitchin, *The German Officer Corps 1890–1914* (Oxford 1968) p. 141.
69. A. J. Marder, *From the Dreadnought to Scapa Flow*, Vol. I. *The Road to War 1904–14* (London 1961) p. 114.
70. I. F. Clarke, *Voices Prophesying War 1763–1914* (London 1966).
71. Clarke, op. cit., p. 126.
72. See David French, 'Spy fever in Britain 1900–1915', *Historical Journal* **21**, No. 2 (1978) 355–70.
73. Becker, *1914*, p. 510.
74. Emile Vandervelde, *Jaurès* (Paris 1919) p. 6.
75. Haupt, op. cit., (Oxford 1972) p. 252.
76. Norman Hutchinson, US Chargé d'Affaires in Bucharest and Belgrade, to State Dept. 27 Feb. 1909, quoted in Vladimir Dedijer, *The Road to Sarajevo* (London 1967) p. 320.

Chapter 9

CONCLUSION

Each of the factors which we have been considering as possible causes of the First World War seems to have contributed something to the decisions in the final crisis of July 1914. The individuals who took those decisions were, often to a greater extent than they realized, limited in their choice of action not only by their own nature but by a multitude of earlier decisions taken by themselves and by their predecessors in office.[1] War had been avoided in the immediately preceding crises – 1908, 1911, 1913 – and yet was not avoided in 1914; and each previous crisis had contributed to the decisions of 1914. The Russians in 1913 had failed to give Serbia the backing she needed in order to secure an Adriatic port; and in 1914 their choices were limited by the feeling that failure to support Serbia again would lead to a complete loss of Russian credibility and influence in the Balkans. The Austro-Hungarian government believed that, having been unable to prevent the Serbs from winning substantial territorial gains, even if they did not get the port they wanted, they must crush Serbia this time if they were to withstand the internal threat to the Monarchy caused by the Southern Slavs. The Germans believed that Austria-Hungary was their only reliable ally who should be supported at all costs if she were not to collapse or seek help elsewhere; and they too felt they were bound to stand by her in 1914 after what had seemed half-hearted support in the crisis of the previous year. Sir Edward Grey initially hoped to repeat the success as a mediator which had he believed prevented war in 1912–13, and this conditioned his diplomacy in the early stages of the 1914 crisis, but when mediation clearly had become impossible, the British government believed that they too would lose their international influence and standing if they stayed out of a European war, as well as fearing that their *entente* with Russia might break down and face them with a renewed Russian threat in the Middle East and India.

The continuing international tension had created a feeling, especially in Germany, that since war was inevitable sooner or later the important thing was to choose the right moment, before the Russian rearmament programme was complete, for example, or the French

had carried out their military reorganization or the British and Ru
sians made an effective naval agreement. Once war was accepted
inevitable by the German leaders, as it was by December 191
whether because they thought that what would now be called a pr
emptive strike was the only way of defending themselves again
encirclement by hostile powers or because they thought a war was t
only way to achieve the world power at which some of them we
aiming, then, as the development of the July crisis showed, the
strategic plans became all-important and these had more immedia
military consequences than those of any other power.

The arms race in which all the major powers were involved h
contributed to the sense that war was bound to come, and soon
rather than later. It caused serious financial difficulties for all t
governments involved in it; and yet they were convinced that there w
no way of stopping it. Although publicly it was justified as having
deterrent effect which would make for peace rather than for war, r
government had in fact been deterred from arming by the arms pr
grammes of their rivals, but rather had increased the pace of their ov
armament production. By 1914 Tirpitz, who had hoped that tl
German fleet would be so strong that no British government wou
risk going to war, had to face the fact that the British refused to play tl
role assigned to them and were determined to maintain their nav
superiority whatever the financial and political cost. The continui
international tension and the strains of the armaments race ea
contributed to a mood in which war was accepted almost as a relief. A
a French observer in 1912 put it, 'How many times in the last two yea
have we heard people repeat "Better war than this perpetual waiting
In this wish there is no bitterness, but a secret hope.'² 'Il faut en fini
the slogan which had a certain popularity in 1939, expressed equal
what many people felt in 1914.

The immediately preceding international crises, the military ar
naval increases which had accompanied them and the mood which the
produced all helped to determine that this particular war broke out
that particular moment. These crises were themselves the result
long-term developments which have to be followed back at least f
decades. In particular, previous wars, especially that of 1870 which ha
established German military predominance in Europe and left tl
French with a permanent grievance over the loss of Alsace ar
Lorraine, had set the framework within which the internation
relations of the first years of the twentieth century were to be co
ducted. Added to this, the imperialism of the 1880s and 1890s ha
produced, especially in Britain and Germany, a new language in whi
international relations were discussed and a new sort of nationalis
different from that which had inspired the movements for nation
unity and national self-determination earlier in the nineteen
century. At the same time, however, the nationalism of those peopl

hich still, wholly or in part, lived under alien rule – a creed which
aintained that the cause of national independence was more impor-
nt than anything else – was a continuous factor threatening the
xistence of the Habsburg and Ottoman empires and so contributing to
e instability of the international system.

Even in the short term we have an enormous range of possible
auses' of the First World War from which to choose our explanation;
d the choice is, if not an arbitrary one, one which is conditioned by
ur own political and psychological interests and preconceptions.
ome political scientists have found the acceptance of such a plurality
individual explanations intolerable and have attempted to quantify
e factors in the pre-1914 situation so as to be able to measure their
lative importance, and by assessing the balance of power in objective
rms, show precisely what circumstances led to the war. While this
eo-positivist approach can be helpful to historians in suggesting
gnificant factors which they might otherwise underestimate, it neces-
rily has limitations when it comes to assessing the significance of
hat are by their nature unquantifiable variables such as states of mind
d questions of what is loosely called 'morale', even if it is possible to
ork out – though this is by no means certain – an accurate estimate of
e economic and strategic factors which cause international insta-
lity.[3]

Nevertheless, the protagonists in 1914 often themselves felt that
ey were the victims of objective forces which they could not control,
that they were part of some ineluctable historical process.
ethmann Hollweg, who, as we have seen, discovered at the height of
e crisis that 'es sei die Direktion verloren'[4] had already ten days
efore seen 'a doom greater than human power hanging over Europe
d our own people'.[5] Lloyd George, partly no doubt to obscure the
gnificance of his own switch from being the spokesman of the peace
arty in the British Cabinet to his realizing that his future lay in being
e man who would win the war, wrote later that the nations 'slithered
ver the brink into the boiling cauldron of war'.[6] Such a sense of the
elplessness of man in the face of the inexorable processes of history
rovided a relief from the overwhelming sense of personal respon-
bility which some politicians certainly felt. But the picture of history
s a great river or a mighty wind could also make men aware of the
verwhelming importance of action at the right moment if they were
ot 'to miss the bus', as the phrase went. This view was vividly ex-
ressed by Bismarck:

> World history with its great events does not pass by like a railway train at a
> constant speed. No, it goes forward by fits and starts, but then with irresis-
> tible force. We must always make sure that we see God striding through
> world history, then jump and cling to the hem of his garment so that we are
> carried along with it as far as we must go.[7]

Lenin also stressed, again using the simile of a railway train, th importance of decisive action at the right moment, and he despised a those who 'would be ready to recognize the social revolution if histor led up to it as peacefully, tranquilly, smoothly and accurately as German express train approaches a station'[8] instead of being able t seize the opportunity when the speed of history could be accelerated In the crisis of 1914 we often have the feeling that none of the leadin European statesmen possessed the sense of timing of a Bismarck or Lenin which might have enabled them to control events, and that the were swept away towards a goal which they could not see along a roa for which they lacked the maps.

But even without necessarily accepting the familiar metaphor which suggest that history is a river or a gale or a railway or a runawa horse ('History is galloping like a frightened horse' the communis Karl Radek once remarked) we nevertheless feel the need to place ou explanations for the outbreak of war in 1914 within a wider perspec tive. Each of the crucial decisions was taken within a specific insti tutional and social framework. They were conditioned by a wide rang of assumptions about the behaviour of individuals and government and by values resulting from long cultural and political traditions a well as from the social and economic structure of each country. Th problem of these ever-widening circles of causation is that the attemp to find a general explanation for the outbreak of war is likely to get los in a vast number of possible causes so that it is difficult to know wher to stop if one is not to be left with explanations of such remoteness an generality that one still finds oneself without an adequate under standing of why this particular war broke out at that particula moment.

The attraction of a Marxist theory of history is that it appears to offe an explanation for a very wide range of phenomena in terms of comparatively small number of basic factors. The importance o Marxism for non-Marxist historians is obvious; and it has changed fundamentally and irreversibly the kind of questions which historian ask. What it does not always do is to supply the answers. When, fo example, we look at which economic groups stood to gain from wa and which to lose, we are struck not only by the difficulty of deter mining the exact points at which these groups actually influence governments but also by the complexity and divergence of interest within the capitalist world, a divergence which by no means corre sponded to the divisions between national states. Even if it wer accepted that war is inherent in the nature of capitalism, becaus capitalism developed the spirit of competition and the conditions fo an armed struggle for the maintenance of profits by a few financier and other capitalists, there is still a gap between this type of expla nation and the analysis of July 1914 in terms of specific decisions by particular individuals. While Rosa Luxemburg's argument that im

erialism colours the whole range of moral as well as economic values
f a society draws attention to the connections between imperialism,
rotectionism and militarism, it still leaves many stages to be filled in
efore one can decide in what precise way Wilhelmine Germany or
Edwardian England were imperialist societies and how this explains
he actual decisions of 1914.

One solution of this particular historiographical dilemma is to reject
ll attempts at any long-term, wide-ranging explanation in terms of
eneral social, economic or intellectual factors. Some historians,
specially in England, believe that all they can hope to find out are the
mmediate short-term actions of politicians and the immediate short-
erm reasons for them. To look for anything else is to try to impose a
attern on events for which there is no evidence. But many of us are
ufficiently Hegelian, if not Marxist, to want to try to bring into our
xplanations the moral values of a society, the *Zeitgeist*, as well as the
conomic interests of the participants both as individuals and as
nembers of a class. Perhaps this means resigning ourselves to a kind of
wo-tier history. On the one hand there are the broad lines of social
nd economic development, of demographic change or of the even
onger-term effects of differences in the climate and other aspects of
he environment. Some of these can be analysed in terms of scientific
aws and so form the basis for predictions about the future. In changes
f this kind even so revolutionary a development as the First World
War is only a minor episode, a small irregularity on the graph. On the
ther hand there is the world in which the decisions of individual
eaders, whatever their origins, can affect the lives and happiness of
nillions and change the course of history for decades.

For this reason the question whether war was inevitable, or at least
hat particular war at that particular date, is not one which can be
nswered except in terms of individual responsibility. In spite of all the
orces making for war and in spite of all the evidence we now have
bout the will to war of certain sections of the European, and
specially the German, ruling class and about the domestic pressures
o which they were subjected, we still feel that a war a few years later
night have taken a different form and had a different result. More-
ver, a study of the individual decisions of 1914 and the limits within
vhich they were made shows that the consequences were not those
vhich were expected. If some of the belligerents achieved the goals for
vhich they went to war – the French recovered Alsace-Lorraine and
he British ended the German naval challenge – the price turned out to
e much higher than almost anyone in 1914 had dreamed. And those
countries with even more ambitious aims – the German drive for
nternational hegemony, the Russian drive to Constantinople, the
Austro-Hungarians' desperate bid to keep their decrepit empire intact
- found that their ambitions turned to defeat and ruin, while those
nembers of the governing classes who had believed that war might

consolidate the state and end the fear of revolution had to face the fa
that war only produced the result it was intended to prevent.

It used to be said that a maxim impressed on young members of th
British foreign service ran: 'All actions have consequences: cons
quences are unpredictable: therefore take no action.' The tragedy
political decisions derives from the fact that again and again politicia
find themselves in situations in which they are constrained to act
ignorance of the consequences and without being able to assess calm
the probable results, the profit or loss which action may bring. (Nor
one more optimistic that the results will be any more predictable wh
some of these calculations are left to computers.) Men are not mo
vated by a clear view of their own interests; their minds are filled wi
the cloudy residues of discarded beliefs; their motives are not alwa
clear even to themselves.

This makes the historian's task a difficult one. Each generatic
tends to approach the problem of the responsibility for the First Wor
War in the light not only of its own political preoccupations but also
changing views of human nature and the springs of human action.
the 1980s we perhaps find it easier to conceive of foreign policy
being motivated by domestic preoccupations and by economic i
terests than by abstract concepts of the balance of power or the prop
status of a *Weltmacht*, let alone by considerations of national presti
and glory. It does not necessarily follow that the men of 1914 thoug
in the same way as we do. While it is no doubt true, as Elie Halé
pointed out many years ago, that 'the wisdom or folly of our statesm
is merely the reflection of our own wisdom or folly',[8] the wisdom
folly of one generation is not necessarily that of the next. To unde
stand the men of 1914 we have to understand the values of 1914; and
is by these values that their actions must be measured.

REFERENCES AND NOTES

1. Some of what follows is based on James Joll, 'Politicians and the freedo
    to choose: the case of July 1914' in Alan Ryan (ed.) *The Idea of Freedor
    Essays in Honour of Isaiah Berlin* (Oxford 1979).
2. 'Agathon' (Henri Massis and Alfred de Tarde) *Les Jeunes Ge
    d'Aujourd'hui,* (Paris 1913) p. 31.
3. See e.g. the special issue of 'Quantitive international history:
    exchange', *The Journal of Conflict Resolution* XXI, No. i (March 1977
    also e.g. George H. Questor, 'Six causes of war', *The Jerusalem Journ
    of International Relations*, **6**, No. 1 (1982).
4. See p. 21 above.
5. See p. 31 above.
6. David Lloyd George, *War Memoirs* (new edn, London 1938) Vol. I,
    32.

Quoted in Lothar Gall, *Bismarck, der weisse Revolutionär* (Frankfurt-am-Main 1980).

V. I. Lenin, 'Can the Bolsheviki hold state power?' Oct. 1917, quoted in William Henry Chamberlain, *The Russian Revolution 1917–1921* (New York 1935) Vol. I, p. 290.

Elie Halévy, *The World Crisis of 1914–1918: A Reinterpretation* (Rhodes Memorial Lecture, University of Oxford 1929) reprinted in E. Halévy, *The Era of Tyrannies* (tr. by R. K. Webb with a note by Fritz Stern) (Garden City, NY 1965) p.245.

FURTHER READING

This is only a small selection from the very large literature and i
restricted to works of direct relevance to some of the topics discusse
in this book.

See also the books and articles referred to in the notes at the end o
each chapter.

There are fuller bibliographies in e.g.:

F. H. Hinsley (ed.) *The Foreign Policy of Sir Edward Grey.* Cam
bridge 1977.

V. R. Berghahn, *Germany and the Approach of War in 1914.* Londo
1973.

Zara S. Steiner, *Britain and the Origins of the First World War.* Londo
1977.

1. GENERAL ACCOUNTS OF THE DIPLOMATIC BACKGROUND AND THE OUTBREAK OF WAR

A. J. P. Taylor, *The Struggle for Mastery in Europe 1848–1918*
Oxford 1954.

Luigi Albertini, *The Origins of the War of 1914* (3 vols). Eng. tr
Oxford 1952–57.

Imanuel Geiss, *July 1914: Selected Documents.* London 1972.

Paul Kennedy, *The Rise of the Anglo-German Antagonism
1860–1914.* London 1980.

H. W. Koch (ed.) *The Origins of the First World War: Great Powe
Rivalry and War Aims.* London 1972.

Laurence Lafore, *The Long Fuse: an Interpretation of the Origins o
World War I.* London 1966.

Joachim Remak, *The Origins of World War I.* New York 1967.
L. C. F. Turner, *Origins of the First World War*, New York 1967.

Michael R. Gordon, 'Domestic conflict and the origins of the First
    World War: the British and German cases', *Journal of Modern
    History*, **46**, No. 2, June 1974.
Arno J. Mayer, 'Domestic causes of the First World War' in L. Krieger
    and F. Stern (eds) *The Responsibility of Power: Historical Essays
    in Honor of Hajo Holborn*. New York 1967.

2. THE POLICY OF INDIVIDUAL STATES

AUSTRIA-HUNGARY

F. R. Bridge, *From Sadowa to Sarajevo: the Foreign Policy of Austria-
    Hungary 1866 – 1914.* London 1972.
F. R. Bridge, *Great Britain and Austria-Hungary 1906 – 1914*: London
    1972.

ENGLAND

F. H. Hinsley (ed.) *The Foreign Policy of Sir Edward Grey.* Cam-
    bridge 1977.
C. J. Lowe and M. L. Dockrill, *The Mirage of Power: British Foreign
    Policy 1902 – 22* (3 vols). London 1972.
George Monger, *The End of Isolation: British Foreign Policy
    1900 – 1907.* London 1963.
Keith Robbins, *Sir Edward Grey.* London 1971
Zara S. Steiner, *Britain and the Origins of the First World War.* London
    1977.
Zara S. Steiner, *The Foreign Office and Foreign Policy 1895 – 1914.*
    Cambridge 1969.

FRANCE

Christopher Andrew, *Théophile Delcassé and the Making of the
    Entente Cordiale: A Reappraisal of French Foreign Policy
    1898 – 1905.* London 1968.
Geoffrey Barraclough, *From Agadir to Armageddon: Anatomy of a
    Crisis.* London 1982.

Eugene Weber, *The Nationalist Revival in France 1905–1914*. Berkeley 1959.

GERMANY

Michael Balfour, *The Kaiser and his Times* (1964).

V. R. Berghahn, *Germany and the Approach of War in 1914*. London 1973.

Lamar Cecil, *The German Diplomatic Service 1871–1914*. Princeton 1976.

Ludwig Dehio, *Germany and World Politics in the Twentieth Century*. Eng. tr. London 1959.

Lancelot L. Farrar Jr, *Arrogance and Anxiety: the Ambivalence of German Power 1848–1914*. Iowa City 1981.

Fritz Fischer, *Germany's Aims in the First World War*. Eng. tr. London 1967.

Fritz Fischer, *War of Illusions*. Eng. tr. London 1975.

Fritz Fischer, *World Power or Decline: the Controversy over Germany's Aims in the First World War*. Eng. tr. New York 1974.

Imanuel Geiss, *German Foreign Policy 1871–1914*. London 1976.

Konrad H. Jarausch, *The Enigmatic Chancellor: Bethmann Hollweg and the Hubris of Imperial Germany*. New Haven and London 1973.

Wolfgang J. Mommsen, 'Domestic factors in German foreign policy before 1914', *Central European History* VI, No. 1 (March 1973).

John A. Moses, *The Politics of Illusion: The Fischer Controversy in German Historiography*. London 1975.

John C. G. Röhl, *1914: Delusion or Design*. London 1973.

Fritz Stern, 'Bethmann Hollweg and the war: the limits of responsibility' in L. Krieger and F. Stern (eds) *The Responsibility of Power: Historical Essays in Honor of Hans Holborn*. New York 1967.

ITALY

Richard Bosworth, *Italy, the Least of the Great Powers: Italian Foreign Policy before the First World War*. Cambridge 1979.

Richard Bosworth, *Italy and the Approach of the First World War*. London 1983.

RUSSIA

Dietrich Geyer, *Der Russische Imperialismus: Studien über den*

Zusammenhang von innerer und auswärtiger Politik 1860–1914. Göttingen 1977.
G. A. Hosking, *The Russian Constitutional Experiment: Government and Duma 1906–1914.* Oxford 1973.

SERBIA AND THE BALKANS

R. J. Crampton, *The Hollow Détente: Anglo-German Relations in the Balkans 1911–1914.* London 1979.
Vladimir Dedijer, *The Road to Sarajevo.* London 1967.
Joachim Remak, *Sarajevo.* London 1959.

3. ARMIES, NAVIES, STRATEGIC PLANNING, ETC.

P. M. Kennedy (ed.) *The War Plans of the Great Powers 1880–1914.* London 1979.
A. J. P. Taylor, *War by Timetable: How the First World War Began.* London 1969.
Barbara Tuchman, *The Guns of August.* New York 1962.

AUSTRIA-HUNGARY

Norman Stone, 'Army and society in the Habsburg Monarchy 1900–1914', *Past and Present* No. 33 (April 1966).
Norman Stone, *The Eastern Front 1914–1917.* London 1975.

ENGLAND

Nicholas D'Ombrain, *War Machinery and High Policy: Defence Administration in Peacetime Britain 1902–14.* Oxford 1973.
David French, *British Economic and Strategic Planning 1905–1915.* London 1982.
J. Gooch, *The Plans of War: The General Staff and British Military Strategy 1900–1916.* London 1974.
A. J. Marder, *From the Dreadnought to Scapa Flow: the Royal Navy in the Fisher Era 1904–1919.* Vol. 1. *The Road to War 1904–1914.* London 1961.
Samuel R. Williamson Jr, *The Politics of Grand Strategy: Britain and France prepare for War 1904–1914.* Cambridge, Mass. 1969.
E. L. Woodward, *Great Britain and the German Navy.* London 1935.

FRANCE

Richard D. Challener, *The French Theory of the Nation in Arms 1866–1914*. New York 1955.

Gerd Krumeich, *Aufrüstung und Innenpolitik in Frankreich vor dem Ersten Weltkrieg: die Einführung der dreijährigen Dienstpflicht 1913–1914*. Wiesbaden 1980.

Douglas Porch, *The March to the Marne: The French Army 1871–1914*. Cambridge 1981.

David B. Ralston, *The Army of the Republic: The Place of the Military in the Political Evolution of France 1871–1914*. Cambridge, Mass. 1967.

GERMANY

Gordon Craig, *The Politics of the Prussian Army 1640–1945*. New York 1964.

Martin Kitchin, *The German Officer Corps 1890–1914*. Oxford 1968.

Gerhard Ritter, *The Schlieffen Plan*. Eng. tr. London 1958.

Gerhard Ritter, *The Sword and the Sceptre: The Problem of Militarism in Germany*, 4 vols. Eng. tr. London 1972–73.

David Schoenbaum, *Zabern 1913: Consensus Politics in Imperial Germany*. London 1982.

Jonathan Steinberg, *Yesterday's Deterrent: Tirpitz and the Birth of the German Battle Fleet*. London 1965.

ITALY

John Whittam, *The Politics of the Italian Army 1861–1918*. London 1977.

RUSSIA

Norman Stone, *The Eastern Front 1914–1917*. London 1975.

4. IMPERIALISM

Max Beloff, *Imperial Sunset: Britain's Liberal Empire 1897–1921*. London 1969.

Leon Brunschvig, *French Colonialism 1871–1914: Myths and Realities*. Eng. *tr* London 1966.

Stuart A. Cohen, *British Policy in Mesopotamia 1903–1914*. London 1976.

D. K. Fieldhouse, *Economics and Empire 1830–1914*. London 1973.

Firuz Kazemzadeh, *Russia and Britain in Persia 1864–1914: A Study in Imperialism*. New Haven and London 1968.

V. G. Kiernan, *European Empires from Conquest to Collapse 1815–1960*. London 1982.

W. L. Langer, *The Diplomacy of Imperialism 1890–1902*. New York 1951.

Wolfgang J. Mommsen, *Theories of Imperialism*. Eng. tr. London 1980.

R. Robinson and J. Gallagher, *Africa and the Victorians: The Official Mind of Imperialism*. London 1968.

5. ECONOMIC FACTORS

J. H. Clapham, *The Economic Development of France and Germany 1815–1914*. Cambridge 1936; reprinted 1968.

Marcello de Cecco, *Money and Empire: the International Gold Standard 1890–1914*. Oxford 1974.

Herbert Feis, *Europe, the World's Banker 1870–1914*. 1930; reprinted New York 1965.

René Girault, *Emprunts russes et investissements français en Russie 1887–1914*. Paris 1973.

R. J. S. Hoffman, *Great Britain and the German Trade Rivalry 1875–1914*. Reprinted New York 1964.

Raymond Poidevin, *Les Relations économiques et financières entre la France et l'Allemagne de 1898 à 1914*. Paris 1969.

6. PUBLIC OPINION; SOCIAL AND INTELLECTUAL FACTORS

Jean-Jacques Becker, *1914: Comment les Français sont entrés dans la guerre*. Paris 1977.

E. Malcolm Carroll, *French Public Opinion and Foreign Affairs 1870–1914*. New York 1931.

R. Chickering, *Imperial Germany and a World Without War: The*

Peace Movement and German Society 1892–1914. Princeto[n]
1975.

I. F. Clarke, *Voices Prophesying War 1763–1914*. London 1970.

Oron James Hale, *Publicity and Diplomacy with Special Reference [to]
England and Germany 1890–1914*. New York 1940.

Georges Haupt, *Socialism and the Great War*. Oxford 1972.

Paul Kennedy and Anthony Nicholls (eds) *Nationalist and Racial[ist]
Movements in Britain and Germany before 1914*. London 1981.

Arno J. Mayer, *The Persistence of the Old Regime: Europe to the Gre[at]
War*. New York 1981.

G. R. Searle, *The Quest for National Efficiency 1899–1914*. Oxfor[d]
1971.

Bernard Semmel, *Imperialism and Social Reform: English Social an[d]
Imperial Thought 1895–1914*. London 1960.

J. Springhall, *Youth, Empire and Society: British Youth Movemen[ts]
1883–1940*. London 1977.

ERRATUM

The captions have been omitted in error from the map section. The maps should be labelled as follows:

Page 215: **Map 1** Europe in 1914
Page 216: **Map 2** Austria-Hungary
Page 217: **Map 3** The Balkans and the effects of the
Balkan Wars
Page 218: **Map 4** Africa and the Middle East

INDEX

Note: Subentries are listed in chronological order

225

91 028